PLEASE SCREAM INSIDE YOUR HEART

BREAKING NEWS AND NERVOUS BREAKDOWNS IN THE YEAR THAT WOULDN'T END

DAVE PELL

hachette
BOOKS

New York

Hachette Books
Hachette Book Group
1290 Avenue of the Americas
New York, NY 10104
HachetteBooks.com
Twitter.com/HachetteBooks
Instagram.com/HachetteBooks

First Edition: November 2021

Published by Hachette Books, an imprint of Perseus Books, LLC, a subsidiary of Hachette Book Group, Inc. The Hachette Books name and logo is a trademark of the Hachette Book Group.

The Hachette Speakers Bureau provides a wide range of authors for speaking events.

To find out more, go to www.hachettespeakersbureau.com or call (866) 376-6591.

The publisher is not responsible for websites (or their content) that are not owned by the publisher.

Print book interior design by Amy Quinn

Library of Congress Control Number: 2021942059

ISBNs: 978-0-306-84739-4 (hardcover); 978-0-306-84741-7 (ebook)

Printed in the United States of America

LSC-C

Printing 1, 2021

For, and in some ways from, my parents.

Books have a unique way of stopping time in a particular moment and saying: Let's not forget this.

—Dave Eggers

ABOUT THE TITLE

In July of 2020, the Fuji-Q Highland amusement park outside of Tokyo reopened under tight pandemic rules: riders of the park's famed Fujiyama Roller Coaster were required to wear face masks and were advised not to scream to avoid unnecessary germ spread. When park attendees complained that being told not to scream on such a scary ride was an impossible demand, the amusement park released a video of two park executives in suits, and without a hair out of place, who sat completely stone-faced through the entire roller coaster ride. The video, which went viral, ended with the message:

Please Scream Inside Your Heart.

CONTENTS

BEFORE RIDING: THIS IS HOW I ROLL

We are in the same tent as the clowns and the freaks—that's show business.

—Edward R. Murrow

"Can we record it?"

My mom asked the question as she squinted through the screen of my childhood bedroom window. It was May of 2020, and I was standing outside in the bushes holding my laptop open with rubber gloves so my parents could watch Fareed Zakaria deliver a personal birthday message for my dad's ninety-sixth. I had called in a favor from a virtual friend at CNN, and Fareed had generously recorded some very kind words. My dad teared up and said, "I really appreciate it, David. This is something!" My mom reminded me that *she* was actually Fareed Zakaria's biggest fan. When I shared that message with Fareed, he recorded a personal message for her too.

To the average family, this birthday moment would have seemed a bit odd. This wasn't a message from Springsteen, or Obama, or even Vanna White. This was Fareed Zakaria, the anchor of a weekly cable news show. But in my family, a sane newsman, cogently delivering international news is the equivalent of Springsteen, Obama, and Vanna White rolled into a single super mensch. Zakaria's Sunday morning CNN show, *GPS*, had been appointment viewing in my parents' house for years. So even though my parents and I couldn't be in the same room, this was a moment to celebrate.

My dad was happy. My mom was impressed. And, just when everyone least expected it, I had self-actualized as a son.

Looking back, it's clear this is where we'd have to begin: with my parents looking through one screen at another screen with their favorite journalist delivering a personalized message in the midst of the biggest news story of a lifetime (mine, definitely not theirs).

Once they had seen the video, I backed up to where my face-masked wife and kids stood in the driveway. For months, that was as close as we'd get to my parents. Even though they regularly compared their coronavirus-mandated home confinement to being in jail, we managed the physical separation easily. We were never a particularly touchy family. When I confessed to my mom that I was actually hopeful that handshaking, especially among strangers, would never make a comeback as a traditional greeting, she responded, "And all the hugging. Who needs it?"

We didn't hug much. But we talked a lot. Mostly about the three big subjects: news, anti-Semitism, and news. And in the year 2020, there was more to talk about than usual.

"Can we record it?" became a funny line among my siblings. As I explained to my mom in the moment, "This *is* a recording." But, as usual, my mom had tapped into a broader question: Can we record the experience of 2020, the madness of an era when a middle-aged son is separated from his aging parents by facial coverings and window screens, a period that was already crazy before a global pandemic, a ferocious recession, millions of masked protesters taking to the streets, and the hysterical buildup to one of the most important elections in American history? We were all waist-deep in a news deluge, then it turned into a tsunami.

Can we record it? Probably not *all* of it. Hindsight is supposed to be 20/20, but 2020 was a blur. It was the year George Floyd called out, "I can't breathe." When the coronavirus asphyxiated its victims. When Donald Trump continued to blow off norm-defying steam on Twitter. And when we were all smothered by nonstop news coverage that alternated between steady distracting jabs and breathtaking body blows.

Like everyone else, I had to get up off the canvas for my share of standing eight-counts. But I've been news-obsessed since my parents raised me to be a media Jedi, and I've spent a large portion of my adult life digesting and regurgitating the news for an audience that refers to me as the Internet's Managing Editor. So, in a weird way, I'd been training for 2020 all my life.

CLICK

Click. The box is on. That's what my dad called the TV when I was growing up. It's 1978. He's on his chair, dozing in and out behind a wrinkled newspaper. I'm on the couch watching a network television broadcast of a miniseries called *Holocaust*. This was during the period when my dad didn't say much (the '60s, '70s, and '80s), so it was surprising whenever I heard his voice.

Couch. Screens. News. Holocaust. Daddy issues. We're only a few paragraphs in, and you know me already.

On the TV, it's World War II. Several Jewish partisans are on their stomachs, hiding behind bushes, guns drawn, when they spot a group of pro-Nazi Ukrainian militiamen approaching on a dirt path. The partisans fire. Most of the militia members are killed or injured, but one gets away. A young partisan is told to chase after him. He races behind the boyish, blue-eyed, blond-curled adversary, streaking across an open field of tall grass before finally tackling him from behind. He grabs the soldier's dropped machine gun, pins him to the ground, and aims the gun at the face of his target.

He pauses. The drama builds. The viewer can feel the weight of the moment on the shoulders of the young partisan. Should he kill someone who would surely kill him if the roles were reversed, or should he hang on to some shred of humanity in a time and place so devoid of it?

That's when I hear my dad's newspaper rustle, and in a thick accent, he yells, "Shoot him, goddamn it! Vat are you vaiting for? Kill him!"

Click. The partisan shoots. The scene ends. The newspaper is back up. And I realize that might be the first time I've really heard my dad yell. It's also probably the first time I'd seen a Jewish guy catch someone from behind in a footrace.

RING BEARER

There's a ringing sound as I write this. There's a ringing sound when I write anything. It reverberates like tinnitus. Several years ago, I started using an app from Twitter called TweetDeck to track my likes and retweets—they call tools like these *social media dashboards*, but they're better understood as the vital signs for an internet dopamine junkie. One of the options in the app is to hear a shrill, school alarm bell sound anytime anyone interacts with one of your tweets.

Out of curiosity, I enabled the feature. The first ring startled. The second one went down a little easier. The third ring calmed. And after that, I *needed* the fourth ring. When the alarm bells went off in quick succession, it felt good, like a song I wanted stuck in my head. So, that day, I decided to leave the feature on for a little while.

That was about a decade ago. Since then, anytime someone responds to me, mentions me, retweets me, likes one of my tweets, shares anything related to my newsletter, *NextDraft*, or links to any of my other writing online, I hear the ring. And I experience a positive response each time. Ring, response. Ring, response. It's like someone forgot to pick up after Pavlov's dog.

The bell has sounded so often, and has become such a pervasive source of background music in my house, that no one in my family ever even mentions it. It would be more noticeable if my laptop were open and there was *no* ringing. Every now and then, during a quiet, dry spell, one of my kids will hold a finger under my nose to make sure I'm still breathing.

YOU HAD ME AT HELLO

While away at college in the mid-'80s, I dial my parents' house, and a man's voice on the other end of the line says, "Hello," with a standard American accent. I hang up. Aside from me, no male voice in my house sounds like that. I dial again. The same "Hello." I hang up, assuming I dialed a wrong number. It turned out that on the way home from his office that day, my dad was listening to talk radio and the guest was a guy who taught a course to help people drop their accents. To give listeners a sample, he used his appearance on the show to teach one word: *Hello*. On the third dial, I hear the same American "Hello." "Hello . . . ?" I curiously responded.

The voice on the other end of the line:

"Vhat's cooking? Vhat do you make of this Gorbachev guy?"

And just like that, we were beyond the Americanized greeting and back to our comfort zone. Not, *How are you?* Not, *What are you up to?* But, instead, *Let's talk about the news.*

I was used to it. I liked it. These were the topics over which we connected. Some dads played catch with their sons in the backyard. We threw news topics back and forth like section editors at the *New York Times* daily Page One meeting.

Years later, during another call, both of my parents were on the line when I told them I was writing this book. My mom said, "David, please don't use our real names. I'm not at a point in my life when I want to be famous." My dad said, "My ears are ringing already."

Then we went back to talking about that day's news.

VOWEL MOVEMENTS

Dinner was news, issues, debates, interrupted by a nightly half-hour interlude for *Wheel of Fortune*. I learned everything I know about business from my dad's commentary on unnecessary vowel purchases.

Looking back, watching people purchase vowels after they already knew the puzzle should have been a key indicator that our economy would soon be on the ropes.

My dad grew up the son of a kosher butcher in a small Polish town. I was a picky-eating vegetarian who often wondered whether, if you listened closely enough, you could hear lettuce scream when you tore leaves from its head.

Is it any wonder we were both looking to avoid the interpersonal exchanges I always imagined took place around most family tables?

How are you feeling? I'm feeling like Gorbachev is doing a pretty decent job opening things up. You?

News was more than information. It was a topic of discussion that enabled us to avoid other topics. There was some repression going on. There still is. But both of my parents were smart. They'd seen it all. Their predictions were usually right. Their ethics never wavered. And I knew why the news—and reading between the lines to understand what it meant to us and the rest of the world—was so important to them.

GLASS HOUSES

The defining moments of my life happened long before I was born.

As a young girl in Cologne, Germany, my mom, Eda, heard the breaking glass downstairs as the club-wielding horrors of Kristallnacht trampled down her street. Soon thereafter, her mother had to make a Sophie's choice. A relative had two extra passports. My grandmother had three daughters. My mom and her sister Henni, who most closely matched the ages of the girls in the passport photos, took the train to France, where they were shuffled in and out of foster families, until being placed in a children's home run by a heroic guy named Ernst Papanek.

Papanek somehow gave my mom and the other children a semblance of a childhood, even as they constantly moved locations to escape the doom that was never far. The kids and teachers never called the home an *orphanage*, even though they knew that for most of the children, including my mom and her sister, that's what it was.

Eventually, Eda and Henni, by now teens, got on a list to come to America. The boat they were to board was headed for San Francisco. The teachers told them to leave their jackets behind. California was always warm. As the boat cut through the thick fog approaching the Golden Gate Bridge, the sisters quickly realized that America also had some surprises.

My mom didn't spend her life looking back, but she didn't look away either. An autodidact and a voracious reader, she spent much of her time examining the roots of hatred and genocide, was the founding president of an adult education program called Lehrhaus Judaica, and designed courses on anti-Semitism that were taught at several universities.

Aside from a brother who escaped to Palestine and her sister Henni, everyone else in her family perished, including her sister Chana, who was too young to match either of the passports.

My dad wasn't so lucky. Let's start in the barn. That's where teenage Joe Pell (or Yosel Epelbaum, back then) was hiding behind bales of hay in a barn in World War II–ravaged Poland. By then, he had already lost several members of his family, including his dad and two brothers, who were betrayed by a neighbor as they hid in an outhouse during a sweep of their town by

German-led forces. All three were captured and taken out of town where they were stripped, beaten, cursed, and ultimately shot along with hundreds of others.

Shortly thereafter, my dad's older brother received a tip that the Nazis and their Ukrainian henchmen were combining two adjacent Jewish ghettos, since both were underpopulated after thousands had been killed or shipped off to concentration camps.

The plan was for my dad to hide in the barn until the coast was clear, and then knock on a wall. On the other side, his brother would be waiting. An armed soldier entered and searched the barn. My dad held his breath. Somehow, the soldier didn't find him. At the agreed-upon time, my dad knocked on the wall. His brother wasn't there. He knew at that moment that no one else in his family would survive.

In the darkness, my dad crawled on his hands and knees through mud and shit until he reached the edge of the Polish forest. He survived there for months, alone, often getting through the night by stealing some warmth while lying on top of outdoor bread ovens.

Eventually, he got a gun. A gun meant you could join the partisans, an organized group of insurgents, protecting each other and launching attacks from their hideaways in the woods. He spent years fighting the Nazis, specializing in blowing up German trains headed toward the front (a bomb with a button was buried beneath a railroad tie, and when the train approached, the button would be pressed and the engine and the tracks were destroyed).

When the war was over, he returned to his hometown of Biała Podlaska, where he threw a firebomb into the house owned by the family who ratted out his dad and brothers. My theory is that he was addicted to risk when he then went into the postwar European smuggling business, moving leather, coins, and anything else that would sell, from country to country, climbing out the windows of trains and riding on the roof to avoid officials who came through the cars checking papers.

After a successful smuggling career, a friend and fellow partisan convinced him to come to America. By way of New York, he met the friend in Baltimore, where he was working in his American uncle's sweatshop. That wasn't a reasonable landing place for my dad, so he got his friend out of there. At a bus stop, they saw a poster with a picture of the Golden Gate Bridge. A few days later, they were on a bus heading west. On the way, my dad leaned over to his friend, and in Yiddish, asked, "Who is this guy Motel? He seems to own half the country."

He arrived in San Francisco with no family, no English, a few bucks in his pocket, and a Leica camera. Long story short: he met Eda, opened an ice cream store called Moo's with the same friend who had urged him to come to America, got into the building business, and became one of Northern California's most successful real estate developers. Many years later, he'd pair up with a Jewish scholar named Fred Rosenbaum and write *Taking Risks*, a book about his life in Poland and America.

THE SHADOW KNOWS

When the shadow of history shapes one generation's life to this extent, it shapes the next generation too. It dominated my thinking and determined the topic of many conversations, even though, on the surface, I had the same coming-of-age issues as my other Jewish friends: the bed-wetting at overnight camp, the subpar sports career, diarrhea at an outdoor concert, and a never-ending litany of anxiety-induced psychosomatic symptoms that left me reaching for Ativan the way other kids reached for Tic Tacs. I had Hebrew school on Tuesdays and Thursdays, and saw my childhood shrink on Mondays, Wednesdays, and Fridays. When it came to developing Jewish angst, I came to play.

But compared to my parents, my life has been a revolving door of lottery wins. I was the fortunate son of an overwhelmingly generous real estate developer. If someone had thrown in racist tendencies, malignant narcissism with psychotic features, and an obsession with seeing my last name in giant gold letters, things could have gone sideways. Instead, things were relatively normal.

Normal, but dark. History would always be bigger than the present. World events would always be a focus. No one in my family ever questioned what leaders were capable of, or what our fellow citizens, even the ones next door, would go along with. And the connection between headlines, politics, and our individual lives was never lost on me.

BOARDWALK OF SHAME

While world events were front of mind, that wasn't the only topic we talked about. We also talked about business, and because that business was real estate, we often talked about a highly leveraged New York blowhard with a phony book about making deals. His name was Donald Trump.

When I was living in New York City in the early 1990s, I emptied my bank account and bought my dad and myself two tickets on the Trump chopper to the newly opened Trump Taj Mahal in Atlantic City.

In the elevator, my dad sniffed a couple of times and said, "You can smell the kitchen from vay up here. That means this place isn't vell built." (I swear I noticed the same odor in America from 2016 to 2020.)

LIFE INHALE

If news is a drug, I'm the world's foremost user. Unlike Bill Clinton, I inhaled. I took my first hit of news as a curious adolescent, and I haven't stopped using since. I took it any way I could. Newspapers, radio, TV, CompuServe, AOL, Netscape, Twitter. (Not Facebook. What am I, nuts?) News has been coursing through my veins and addling my mind for four decades running. So I productized my disease. I became a functioning news junkie.

And like many people who live and work on the internet, I created a career out of my addiction. Each morning, I open more than fifty browser tabs and look for the day's most fascinating news. I then write up a series of blurbs describing the top ten stories and share links to the full articles. There's no secret technology. There's no team of editors or click farms tapping away in some remote location. There's no high-tech algorithm. I am the algorithm.

WINDBAG

News is the drug. The internet is the syringe. And Donald Trump as president was the hardest drug I ever took.

Even after decades of building up my tolerance, I could barely handle the digital meth of the Trump news cycle at first. But then, like the rest of America, my tolerance went up. And good thing it did. Because we were about to get hit nonstop with the purest-grade stuff, in infinite quantities, and at unprecedented velocity. And it pulverized our sense of reason like grist in a giant windmill. To give you a little taste of the hard stuff, here's Trump on windmills, lightly edited for your safety:

I never understood wind. You know, I know windmills very much. I've studied it better than anybody I know. It's very expensive. They're made in China and Germany mostly, very few made here, almost none. But they're manufactured—tremendous, if you're into this, tremendous fumes, gases are spewing into the atmosphere. You know we have a world, right? So the world is tiny compared to the universe. So tremendous, tremendous amount of fumes and everything—you talk about the "carbon footprint"—fumes are spewing into the air, right? Spewing. Whether it's in China, Germany, it's going into the air. It's our air, their air, everything, right? So they make these things, and then they put them up, and if you own a house within vision of some of these monsters, your house is worth 50 percent of the price. They're noisy, they kill the birds. You want to see a bird graveyard? You just go, take a look, a bird graveyard? Go under a windmill someday. You'll see more birds than you've ever seen ever in your life.

IT'S SHOWTIME, FOLKS

It's no coincidence the Ringling Bros. circus was shut down early in the Trump presidency. We didn't need it anymore. Donald Trump was the Greatest Show on Earth. (I'm writing that because I need a blurb for Fox News. Also because I mean it.)

The show was on every day, and we couldn't turn away. It was a five-year telethon that wanted all your attention. And when your attention was spent, eyes glazed over, frontal lobe battered like a speed bag, the larger-than-life story shrank itself down to the size of microscopic particles. Your pandemic face mask could slow the spread of coronavirus, but it was helpless against the Trump virus. It was everywhere.

BEING THERE

As president, Trump was widely despised (and loved) by millions, but he encroached into our lives more than any public personality, ever. The pandemic, the recession, shelter-in-place, the BLM protests, social media debates, entertainment, news, sports, random chats by the watercooler or around our dinner tables. Wherever the discussion, whatever the topic, Trump was there.

Nobel laureate Herbert A. Simon coined the term *attention economy*. That turned out to be the one economy Trump wouldn't bankrupt.

Love him or hate him, he owned the place.

Some were under his spell. Others, with an agenda to push and power to amass, attached themselves like barnacles to an empty vessel; a purely transactional being who'd trade his support for any policy (all of which, to him, were meaningless anyway) for power, fame, wealth, and the display of admiration from others, admiration that he'd drop like tokens into a coin slot on his *mirror, mirror on the great big beautiful wall*.

Anyone possessed of common sense, ethics, patriotism, or at least a hint of respect for America and her institutions looked at the reflection in that mirror and saw the forty-fifth president for what he really represented. A danger so significant, it could mean the country's undoing.

POTUS OPERANDI

Trump didn't turn our politics into a show. He simply became its most compelling host. He promised we'd get tired of all the winning, and he delivered. He was winning our attention and we were getting tired of it. But never too tired to share one more Trump-related tweet, one more Facebook post, one more snappy aside during a Zoom conversation.

When the pandemic hit, we lost sports, we lost movies, we lost live music; Trump went from the Greatest Show on Earth to the only show.

I covered that show every day, and now I'm re-covering it. I'm part of the problem. You're reading my coverage, so you're implicated too. But you already knew that. You don't get this fucked up this fast as a country unless everyone does their part.

Almost all we ever talked about during the pandemic was Trump and the pandemic. Then someone in your group Zoom or around the dinner table would plead with the others: "Oh no, let's not talk about Trump again." Everyone nodded in agreement . . . and then they started talking about Trump. Especially the guy who suggested the change of subject.

I'm that guy.

Before I type a single letter into my keyboard, my iPhone's predictive text suggests three words: *I, The, Trump.*

In other words, I'm you but a little worse.

THIS IS ENEMY TERRITORY

Throughout his presidency, Donald Trump hammered the media and called the press the "enemy of the American people." In my daily news coverage, I leaned heavily on the reporters who covered the Trump era. Many of them did their work in a manner that informed and saved lives, while struggling under the constant attack from the top and from Trump's online army of corrupted minions. I will lean on many of those reporters in this book as well. Was the media perfect? Far from it. And we'll get into some of those imperfections. But the work of top journalists who worked tirelessly to hammer the truth through a wall of distortions should be celebrated and remembered, and I hope this book will be part of that effort.

THE FAMILY BUSINESS

By the time I started high school, my three sisters had moved out of the house, and my parents and I had four years of dinner small talk to make. My mom found herself across the table from my dad (who said almost nothing) and me (who said almost nothing of interest). There was a lot of silence. When my friends called the house, my mom would answer the phone and ask, "What's new with David? He never tells us anything."

So we filled the void. And since they were interested in current events, and CNN's twenty-four-hour cable news had conveniently just launched, we filled it with talk of news. It eased the tension of silence. And I learned a lot. I understand the news and the world infinitely better because of those conversations.

It also enabled us to avoid plenty of other topics that may have been more sensitive or painful to discuss. Even the worst news story isn't as emotionally formidable as a real feeling related to your own actual experiences.

I guess the coping mechanism worked because I kept using it. When I'd have lunch alone with my dad as a young man, I often hoped to avoid the topic of real estate—a business he always hoped I'd go into—and the broader questions like: "Are you sure this blog writing is what you want to be doing with your life?" So I always came prepared with a few choice news stories to discuss. As an old man in quarantine, my dad was stuck at home feeling his last good years being stripped away in every ache and pain of his homebound, deteriorating body, so he was looking to change the subject too. News and Trump became an almost full-time obsession, leaving me to ask him: "Are you sure talking about news is what you want to be doing with *your* life?"

But by then, it was too late for either one of us. Our socially distanced get-togethers could all have fit, unedited, into a reality series called *Let Me Tell You Something About Donald Trump*. The conversations went on and on, and the topic was locked in. Don't take my word for it; ask my kids who were left to suffer through the same-shit-different-day exchanges that could drag on endlessly. For my dad and me, this was all perfectly normal. We were getting together and tossing stories back and forth like we did when I was growing up. For my kids, it was a form of confusing torture. On one visit, my thirteen-year-old son got an hour or so on the history of America's mistakes dealing with Russia, beginning with Trump's treachery and working all the way back to the 1945 Yalta Conference. I know the whole time my son wanted to interrupt and say, "I know, Grandpa, my dad already told me."

I'm not suggesting these moments weren't fulfilling or valuable. On the contrary, like I did, my kids will grow up having a clearer understanding of current events and how to read between the lines of history because they had access to my dad's wisdom.

When I was a kid, my bookshelf was lined with a series called We Were There, with titles like *We Were There in the Klondike Gold Rush* and *We*

Were There at the First Airplane Flight. This book will be a *We Were There in 2020 Even Though We Would Have Preferred to Be Anywhere Else.*

In addition to reliving what sometimes felt like countless stories hitting us at once, I'll try to wrap some context around the explosion of content. When you're in the thick of the news cycle, stories seem like thousands of strands of hair shooting off in a million different directions. But when you pull back, you realize you're looking at a braid.

I've been in the front row, pulling my own hair out, watching this news cycle drop from the bowels of history, all the while writing about it, thinking about it, and tweeting about it. We were hit with a series of stories that impacted every part of our lives. It was the ultimate year for a news addict like me. It was also the year when the historical trauma of my parents' dangerous past would bleed into the fabric of American society, as the all-too-familiar authoritarian tactics and messaging they thought they left in the old country emerged in their new one.

So we did what we do. We talked about the news. We found ways to connect. Like many families, we hung on to each other any way we could, and though we didn't know it at the time, the year would end with loss and grief as it would for so many. And everywhere, there was an invisible virus that left the most independent people I know waiting for sanitized groceries to be left on their doorstep or for occasional visits when their kids stood in the driveway and they talked to them through window screens.

1

JANUARY— BOARDING THE ROLLER COASTER

January 1, 2020

In the beginning, God created the heavens and the earth. (Okay, so far, so good.) Then God said, "Let there be light"; and there was light. The universe was on a roll. Fast-forward to 2020 when things went Old Testament as we were faced with an honest-to-God biblical plague and a roller-coaster ride of other unexpected plot twists and turns. I'm not a particularly religious guy, but it's hard not to conclude that the pope got a tip about 2020. As the world, in its ignorant bliss, rang in the new year, Pope Francis, who's known for washing the feet of complete strangers, aggressively pulled his hand away from a devotee who gripped it a bit too long and a bit too hard. The pope angrily slapped her hand, creating the year's first—but for the love of God, not last—viral video.

Before the sun had set on the first day of the year, the pontiff had publicly pontificated on the matter, and issued an apology for setting a bad example and almost certainly puncturing the pilgrim's pride. "Sometimes even I lose patience."

The day before the papal slap, Chinese health officials had warned the World Health Organization (WHO) that they'd discovered forty-one cases of a mysterious pneumonia, all of which seemed to be connected to Huanan Seafood Wholesale Market. Soon we'd all learn of the downsides of touching, or even getting near, strangers. And within a few months, patience would be the world's most endangered virtue. The word *pope* is derived from the Latin word *papa*. In this case, Father knew best. The Holy See saw the future.

Dave Pell ✓
@davepell

We're making too much out of the Pope's slap on the wrist. That's the same penalty the Church gives everyone.

4:10 PM · Jan 2, 2020 · 🐦 Twitter

THE FIRE DOWN BELOW

The bottom of the world burning seems about as good a place as any to get warmed up for 2020. As the new year began, a story that closed 2019 was still searing its way across Australia. On January 2, Andrew Constance, the transport minister of New South Wales, told the *Sydney Morning Herald,* "It's going to be a blast furnace."

Given rising global temperatures, that description would soon fit many other parts of the world as bigger and more damaging fires continued to emerge.

Like everything else, even the charred Outback provided fertile ground for falsehoods, attacks on science, and dangerous conspiracy theories. And like in many other places and cases, the seeds for these stories were planted by Rupert Murdoch–owned media outlets.

His standard-bearing national newspaper, *The Australian*, has also repeatedly argued that this year's fires are no worse than those of the past—not true, scientists say, noting that 12 million acres have burned so far, with 2019 alone scorching more of New South Wales than the previous 15 years combined.

And on Wednesday, Mr. Murdoch's News Corp, the largest media company in Australia, was found to be part of another wave of misinformation. An independent study found online bots and trolls exaggerating the role of arson in the fires, at the same time that an article in *The Australian* making similar assertions became the most popular offering on the newspaper's website. (Damien Cave, *New York Times*)

Climate change may have led to the destruction. But the Murdoch empire seemed determined to make it worse. Soon, Murdoch's Fox News would spread misinformation that helped turn America's pandemic response into a raging dumpster fire.

WAG THE DON
January 6, 2020

With the House impeachment in the rearview mirror, and the Senate trial on the way, our January fixation on whether or not President Trump should hold on to that title was briefly interrupted by a reminder that the international tensions weren't going to slow down for American obsessions.

In a story line few saw coming, the administration responded to a breach of the American embassy in Baghdad with a drone strike that killed Iranian major general Qasem Soleimani. Tens of thousands in the region took to the streets to mourn Iran's second-most powerful person, and Iranian leaders vowed "severe revenge."

An errant Iranian retaliatory missile downed a commercial airliner, Iranian protesters took to the streets, this time to protest their own government's mistake and attempted cover-up, and World War III started trending on social media.

Before Trump was elected, people would joke that he'd eventually run a war on Twitter.

> **Donald J. Trump** ✔
> @potus
>
> These Media Posts will serve as notification to the United States Congress that should Iran strike any U.S. person or target, the United States will quickly & fully strike back, & perhaps in a disproportionate manner. Such legal notice is not required, but is given nevertheless!
>
> . 3:25 PM · Jan 5, 2020 · 🐦 Twitter

Americans didn't have enough data to understand the broader meaning of the killing, and matters were further confused by changing explanations from the White House.

But it felt like a fuse had been lit, and since it was also the beginning of an election year, it was hard not to panic that our dog was about to be wagged by Donald Trump.

Soon, Iranians and Americans would be consumed by another topic and a common foe, and news stories that seemed massive in this moment would fade out of memory. We were not about to start a war. A war was about to come to us.

The Middle East did not explode into a state of further destabilization as some had predicted. Iran did not launch a massive attack. Was this because powerful players wanted Soleimani dead? Was it because the Iranian military proved itself too weak to retaliate? Or was the reaction to the drone strike merely interrupted, like everything else on the planet, by a microscopic and common enemy lurking right around the corner? (And for Trump supporters, I mean the pandemic, not Adam Schiff.)

WUHAN SOLO
January 11, 2020

A sixty-one-year-old man in Wuhan, China, dies from a respiratory illness. Doctors there warn that his death seems to have been caused by a new virus.

HARVEY CALLBANGER

The #MeToo movement dominated the news and shifted the culture, and its poster boy, the once powerful producer Harvey Weinstein, was at long last on trial for rape. On the second day of proceedings, Weinstein hobbled along using a walker and surrendered two mobile phones upon entering the courtroom. He also kept two on his person and began fiddling with them in the courtroom. Sadly, the call could not be completed as trialed. If Weinstein hoped Judge James Burke was just going to phone it in, he was wrong.

> Mr. Weinstein, I strongly urge you to exercise your right to remain silent at this point; that is, don't say anything . . . But is this really the way you want

to end up in jail for the rest of your life, in violation of a "do not text in court" rule?

A PRINCESS CRUISES

"We intend to . . . fully support Her Majesty The Queen." And with that, Prince Harry and Meghan Markle telegraphed their intention "to step back as senior members of the Royal Family." In a traditional year, this would have been the perfect story to transfix some and irritate others. Both groups were sorry to see it overwhelmed by other matters.

Dave Pell @davepell

When I heard that someone was giving up their crown, I figured it was Ivanka...

12:12 PM · Jan 8, 2020 · Twitter

My relationship to royal news can best be described as a conscious uncoupling. But there was something remarkably compelling about Harry and Meghan's social media announcement that they planned to work to become financially independent. Members of the American elite are often criticized for being "born on third base and going through life thinking they hit a triple." Harry was born on third base and deliberately moved back to second.

The move was viewed either as a spoiled abdication of duty or a crowning achievement. Or maybe these royals just craved a different kind of buzz. But the story was about more than the royals. It was about the media, celebrity culture, race, an obsession with fame, and ultimately, us. More importantly, it gave us, at least briefly, a topic to discuss other than Trump news (which was also about the media, celebrity culture, race, an obsession with fame, and an abdication of duty).

ID AND NANCY

Historians will one day look back at the deeds of Donald Trump and wonder aloud, "Wait, that's the first thing he got impeached for?"

At issue were two articles of impeachment approved by the House: The first article was for abuse of power: Trump used his power to pressure the Ukrainian government (including President Volodymyr Zelensky, who was on the other end of what Trump repeatedly called a "perfect phone call") to dig up dirt on Joe and Hunter Biden before he'd authorize the release of military aid to Ukraine. The POTUS had blackmailed a foreign government into helping with a domestic election. (Believe it or not, this used to be considered a no-no across the political spectrum.) The second article was for obstruction of Congress, related to Trump's limiting of testimony and withholding of documents.

SNOW JOB
January 13, 2020

A Gizmodo headline: *White House Tweets "First Snow of the Year" On Same Day It Hits 70 Degrees in Washington D.C.*

By now, we were so used to the falsehoods from the White House that fake weather was ignored as easily as fake news.

Also on January 13: Thailand reports the first coronavirus case outside of China.

UNDER NEW MANAGEMENT

On January 15, a story that had been playing out over several months took over the headlines as the Senate prepared for the impeachment trial of Donald Trump. With a two-thirds majority required for a conviction and the GOP holding the Senate majority, the House managers team led by Adam Schiff had a formidable challenge: figuring out a way to get a guilty verdict out of a jury of the defendant's enablers.

In a 1999 interview with the *New York Times*'s Maureen Dowd, Donald Trump said of Ken Starr: "Starr's a freak. I bet he's got something in his closet." Cut to 2020, when Trump tapped that very freak to represent him. Starr would be joined by Alan Dershowitz on an impeachment defense team that looked like a who's who of WTF. The craziness of the Starr selection was perfectly described by a Monica Lewinsky tweet: "This is definitely an 'are you fucking kidding me?' kinda day." (Just wait until she sees the next few hundred.)

The House managers may have sought solace in an adage from America's most famous manager, Yogi Berra: "It ain't over 'til it's over." But the spirit of that quote would be slid into, spikes up, by Senate majority leader Mitch McConnell, who indicated there was "zero chance" of conviction. He said that *before* the trial began. (It was only midway through the first month of 2020, and already, those odds didn't sound half-bad.)

Trump's challenge in the court of public opinion would be to embody one of Berra's other adages: "I never said most of the things I said."

RUDY'S G-MEN

On the same day the articles of impeachment were delivered to the Senate, we got more details about Trump's Rudy Giuliani–led campaign to make the Ukrainian dirt-for-dollars quid pro quo a reality. Those tidbits (yes, there was a pressure campaign; yes, it was led by Rudy; and yes, Rudy indicated he was representing Donald Trump) came by way of a trove of texts, documents, and other evidence provided by Lev Parnas, who, along with his colleague Igor Fruman, served as Rudy's fixers in Ukraine.

Parnas would make the media rounds and explain his role in a blockbuster interview with Rachel Maddow: "President Trump knew exactly what was going on. He was aware of all my movements. I wouldn't do anything without the consent of Rudy Giuliani or the president."

The interview made big news. But while the media had Lev, the Senate GOP had leverage. Rudy was the godfather to Lev Parnas's son. The GOP had its own godfather, Mitch McConnell, who made them an offer they couldn't refuse: you hold on to power as long as you relinquish your ethics.

WHAT TO EXPECT FROM YOUR EXPECTANCY

There's an old joke about a mugger who points a gun at a man and asks, "Your money or your life?" The man pauses and then answers, "My life. I'm saving my money for my old age." Like many jokes, this one has a tie to reality. Your money and your life are inexorably connected. The findings of a decade-long study published in the *Journal of Gerontology* found that in the US and UK, being wealthy added nine years of life expectancy, and not just any life expectancy, healthy life expectancy.

Bottom line: it turns out being broke is the most dangerous medical precondition. The broader inequalities driven by the economic divide were hardly breaking news in 2020. But the pandemic would put a magnifying glass over America's flaws.

STACKED DRECK

Inside the Senate chamber, the majority's bias made sense, as power-hungry party members faced with shifting national demographics had sold their political souls for an inexplicably popular mad king that most of them secretly despised.

But what about outside the chamber? How could an act of corruption so clear have almost no chance of moving public opinion? Part of it was tribalism. Politics had become a sport, and in sports, you root for your team no matter what. Part of it was that after several years of screaming at each other from different media universes, members of each party hated each other more than they loved the truth. Part of it was that Americans from different parties were watching two different impeachment trials: one real, and one through the filter of Fox News and Biden-related conspiracy theories spreading willy-nilly through Facebook.

The goal of Trump's authoritarian style of messaging was never intended to get people to believe in a single truth. It was intended to overwhelm people with so many conflicting realities that they'd exhaustedly shrug, not knowing what to believe. As Steve Bannon once explained, "The real opposition is the media. And the way to deal with them is to flood the zone with shit."

And the shit hit the fan almost immediately. The Trump presidency began with a bizarre lie about a meaningless stat: the inaugural crowd size. Trump fixated on the topic, insisting that the crowd was much bigger than the one we could all see with our own eyes. The inauguration attendance debate was endless. But it was about something much more important than crowd size. It was about reality. Garry Kasparov summed up the strategy: "The point of modern propaganda isn't only to misinform or push an agenda. It is to exhaust your critical thinking, to annihilate truth."

Trump laid out the broader goal of this kind of miscommunication during an address to a Veterans of Foreign Wars convention in Missouri:

> Just remember, what you are seeing and what you are reading is not what's happening. Just stick with us, don't believe the crap you see from these people, the fake news.

MOCK TRIAL

In the early days of the Russia scandal, President Trump famously asked, "Where's my Roy Cohn?"

Joseph McCarthy was an unliked, nearly anonymous politician until he began making unfounded claims about communists working in the State Department. The attacks on communists, real and imagined, in America would be his one and only calling card.

McCarthy's demise was precipitated in part by an Edward R. Murrow television editorial. See if this line sounds applicable to the Trump era: "The actions of the Junior Senator from Wisconsin have caused alarm and dismay amongst our allies abroad, and given considerable comfort to our enemies." (Rachel Maddow basically said that about Team Trump every weeknight for four years.)

Trump is not a student of history, but he heard all about McCarthy's rise and fall in great detail from McCarthy's right-hand man, Roy Cohn. The media helped to kill McCarthyism, so goal number one of the Trump presidency was to attack the media. And it worked.

There were plenty of journalists warning of the dangers of Trumpism and calling for a fair trial in the Senate. But there were no Edward R. Murrows. We were all viewing our own news feeds from the comfort of our shrinking digital silos of homogeneity. And much more importantly, half the country didn't believe journalists and saw the media as the enemy. There were no universally trusted voices.

The senators in Trump's jury pool, free from the threat of the mainstream media and held hostage by Trump's grip on his base, focused their efforts on protecting the defendant.

The House managers could have had phone call transcripts. They could have had testimony from brilliant, eloquent, ethical, apolitical leaders who had made endless sacrifices in the service of their country. They could have had a series of on-camera, public admissions of guilt from the defendant himself. In fact, they did have all that. But the GOP enablers had something more powerful: a majority in the chamber and a political base that believed what they were seeing and what they were reading was not what was happening.

Three years into his presidency, Donald Trump had an answer to his question, "Where's my Roy Cohn?" He had more than fifty of them in the Senate.

WITNESS REJECTION PROGRAM
January 21, 2020

The Senate trial began with marathon sessions during which the GOP majority voted, over and over, against having witnesses during the trial. Day one ran a cool thirteen hours. It was a lot to binge (C-SPAN and chill?), and the content it most resembled? *Groundhog Day.* The House managers offered undisputed evidence of Trump's abuse of power. And the president's lawyers attacked their opponents and littered their arguments with unrestrained distortions. For those who might consider that description an exaggeration, consider that at one point, White House counsel Pat Cipollone said the following, slowly, and with a straight face:

President Trump is a man of his word.

GOING VIRAL
January 22, 2020

The same day the media provided blanket coverage of the opening of the Senate trial, there was another story inching its way into the American public consciousness. This was the headline I saw on NPR's website: *Newly Identified Coronavirus Has Killed 17 People, Chinese Health Officials Say.*

Trump on January 22, talking to CNBC: "We have it totally under control. It's one person coming in from China, and we have it under control. It's going to be just fine."

WHO'S WTF MOMENT
January 23, 2020

The coronavirus outbreak hadn't yet been declared a global health emergency by the WHO, but as the organization's director general explained at the time: "Make no mistake, this is an emergency in China."

THE ARRIVAL

At Providence Regional Medical Center Everett in Washington, a man in his thirties had been admitted to the hospital's special pathogen unit on Monday, January 20. The medical staff used a robot with a microphone and camera to communicate with the patient in order to reduce the risk of viral spread. The patient, an American citizen, had recently returned to the United States after spending time in China.

WHERE THERE'S SMOKE...

Before the Australian fires were done, the flames would burn 72,000 square miles, destroy nearly 6,000 buildings, and kill at least 34 people. The toll on animals was even more dramatic, with an estimated one billion deaths. There would be at least one bush fire in Australia for 240 straight days.

The National Oceanic and Atmospheric Administration's Twitter account shared satellite images with this description: "The smoke is in the process of circumnavigating the planet."

It wouldn't be alone.

SCUM BAGGAGE

While the outcome of the Senate trial was largely determined before it began, Adam Schiff repeatedly reminded Americans what was at stake in a performance that drew near universal praise from legal minds.

He also drew attacks from the president, which was nothing new. In the week just prior to 2020, Trump resuscitated an anti-Semitic trope from the Holocaust era. "Corrupt politician Adam Schiff's lies are growing by the day. Keep fighting tough, Republicans, you are dealing with human scum."

These are the three most infamous politicians to describe opponents as human scum: Hitler. Stalin. Trump.

I'm sure every American politician who exercised their right to remain silent about Trump's trope had their reasons: votes, money, power. But trust me when I tell you that for my parents, a pair of ninetysomething Holocaust survivors sitting at home watching this all unfold, those reasons sounded all too familiar.

I know. Hitler. Stalin. Authoritarianism. I sound like a raving lefty beset by delusional hysteria. So don't take it from me.

If I say, "Trump is using fascist language," people roll their eyes or laugh it off. When my dad says, "You know, Trump's speeches are starting to remind me of Hitler's early speeches," then people stop laughing.

Those who have had a firsthand look at the rise of fascism—who can point it out in a lineup—are slowly dying off. That sad fact is undoubtedly related to the timing of the rise of far-right extremists abroad and at home. There are fewer and fewer people around who can call it out for what it is.

Trump was something different from those whose language he repeated; his authoritarian impulses were motivated more by his own neediness than any broad worldview. But they were authoritarian tendencies nonetheless. And as Adam Schiff explained during the Senate impeachment trial, the increasing level of freedom Americans usually enjoyed couldn't be viewed as a sure thing.

> It turns out, there's nothing immutable about this. Every generation has to fight for it. We're fighting for it right now. There's no guarantee that this democracy that has served us so well will continue to prosper.

My dad, who had been warning of Trump's authoritarian character for years, put it another way:

"We left democracy's door ajar, and Donald Trump walked through."

RIGHT ANGLE

At the close of the first week of the Senate trial, Adam Schiff used the House testimony of United States Army lieutenant colonel Alexander Vindman to sum up what was at stake: "Colonel Vindman said, 'Here, right matters.' . . . Well, let me tell you something, if right doesn't matter, if right doesn't matter, it doesn't matter how good the Constitution is. It doesn't matter how brilliant the framers were. Doesn't matter how good or bad our advocacy in this trial is. Doesn't matter how well written the Oath of Impartiality is. If right doesn't matter, we're lost. If the truth doesn't matter, we're lost."

At the very same time the other cable news channels were broadcasting Adam Schiff, Fox News was busy spreading the same Biden-related misinformation that led to the impeachment in the first place.

The case was playing out in front of two different Americas, each receiving its own version of the trial (or not receiving a version of the trial at all). One side watched the reality play out in real time. The other saw distortions, obfuscations, and conspiracy theories.

That disconnect posed a danger to the Constitution. Soon, it would endanger thousands of American lives.

Did right matter? Did truth matter? I missed the days when those were rhetorical questions.

THE QUID PRO QUO PRO
January 24, 2020

"All of us here today understand an eternal truth—every child is a precious and sacred gift from God. Together, we must protect, cherish and defend the dignity and the sanctity of every human life." So said Donald Trump as he delivered the first ever in-person presidential address to the March for Life.

Trump was a purely transactional politician. No hardened opinions. No steadfast positions. You offer your support for him, and you get his support for what you want. Vice President Mike Pence knew exactly what the religious right segment of the base wanted, and he delivered Trump's speeches, tweets, signatures, and judges.

America fixated on the quid pro quo demanded by Trump in his dealings with Ukraine. But his whole political career was a quid pro quo. You want me to be pro-life? Fine, give me your votes and devotion. Want me to make it easier for your energy company to avoid costly regulations? Double down on your support and I'll set the world aflame. You want judges that believe in an America diametrically opposed to how I've lived my life? Just give me the list and promise to never say anything bad about me. Want me to pretend I despise celebrity culture even though I've spent my whole life obsessed with my own celebrity and trying to be part of the *it* crowd? No problem, just make sure you come to my rallies and sing my praises on Fox News.

When you consider this perspective, is it any wonder Trump welcomed the foreign interference that helped him win an election and shape public opinion during his presidency?

THAT'S WHAT XI SAID

Donald Trump on Twitter on January 24: "China has been working very hard to contain the Coronavirus. The United States greatly appreciates their efforts and transparency. It will all work out well. In particular, on behalf of the American People, I want to thank President Xi!"

DID YOU HEAR ABOUT KOBE?
January 26, 2020

"I'm screaming right now, cursing into the sky, crying into my keyboard, and I don't care who knows it." So wrote *LA Times* columnist Bill Plaschke on the morning we learned that a helicopter carrying Kobe Bryant, his thirteen-year-old daughter, Gianna, and seven other people crashed during a foggy flight from John Wayne Airport to Camarillo Airport.

It turned out Plaschke's scream was joined by millions who didn't have his personal connection with Kobe. Our reaction to Kobe Bryant's death says something about the role of celebrity in American culture. It says something about the value we place on excellence and winning. I think it also says something about our desire to be on the same side of something at the same time, even if that side is built on the slope of a fog-socked mountain of misery.

Kobe Bryant's death also told us something about the pace of news, and how quickly outside events could get onto our screens, and into our psyches. Where does the media's coverage of the outside world end and your own real life begin? As a guy who has wrapped himself in the news for most of my life, I'm in no position to say. But, like many other celebrity deaths, I know Kobe Bryant's death blew past that line at internet speed.

Did you hear about Kobe?

I first heard the news when I was getting out of the shower and my wife, Gina, pulled her phone away from her ear and asked, "Did Kobe Bryant really die?" As I flipped open my laptop to find out what happened, my son came upstairs and asked if I had heard about Kobe. He got the news via an in-game chat on his PS4. The world has become the front stoop, and that front stoop is everywhere.

My family knew Kobe was dead at approximately the same time his family did.

The iPhone news notifications start: buzz, buzz, buzz, because the intersection of sports and celebrity cuts across every chasm, every publication, every post, every tweet. And you start to think about the role of sports in our society and wonder how you're supposed to mourn when someone extremely famous—but who you don't actually know—suffers a tragedy. Then you take your kid to his basketball game, where the gym, like every other court in the world right now, is weighed down by a blanket of grief, like the players are shooting hoops in a mortuary. One of the dads in the next row leans back and says, "Did you hear Gigi was on the helicopter too?"

Now it's not just news, it's human, and so you start to think about the other parents and kids on the helicopter, and their friends and family who find themselves surrounded by the buzz, buzz, buzz of a world of mourners, none of whom is mourning their loss; the loss of the "others on board" who were part of a crash that had no survivors.

And that's when you realize you're lucky to be in the news absorption and regurgitation business, because you don't have time to get emotional about stories. Your job is to make other people feel the appropriate emotion. You get to professionalize the story while the less fortunate have to feel it. It's mourning in America. But there's a story to write.

Meanwhile, there was another story, this one still safely on the other side of that line. More than eighty people had died, thousands were ill, worldwide markets had stumbled, travel had been curtailed, and one of the biggest quarantine efforts ever was underway.

NETFLIX AND PANIC

The virus numbers started to rise in China and a few other countries. There were 4,610 confirmed cases and 106 deaths as of January 28.

During the same week, Netflix released a six-part docuseries called *Pandemic*. Director Isabel Castro explained to the *LA Times*'s Meredith Blake that when she told people what she was working on, they seemed apathetic. "Everyone would be like, 'Oh you're making a show about the flu?' They would talk about it dismissively and I would be like, 'No, this is a big deal.'"

By the time the series was released, many people understood it was a big deal and that a viral pandemic like the one in the series, and in real life, was definitely not the flu. Weeks later, everyone would realize that.

Almost everyone.

By January 30, more than 8,000 cases of the coronavirus had been confirmed across every region of mainland China, with 170 people dead and 60 million people under full or partial lockdown in the country. There were more than 100 confirmed cases in 20 places outside of China, and 7,000 people were being held on a cruise ship in Italy as a couple was tested for the virus. And Italy became the first country in the EU to ban air traffic in or out of China. That was the state of things as the WHO declared the novel coronavirus outbreak a public health emergency of international concern.

LAMAR-A-LAGO

Tennessee senator Lamar Alexander summed up the reasoning behind his vote against having witnesses at the Senate trial of Donald Trump: "There is no need for more evidence to prove that the president asked Ukraine to investigate Joe Biden and his son, Hunter; he said this on television . . . and during his July 25, 2019, telephone call with the president of Ukraine . . . But the Constitution does not give the Senate the power to remove the president from office and ban him from this year's ballot simply for actions that are inappropriate."

In other words, the verdict is that he's guilty and the sentence is nothing. Ultimately, that argument won the day.

> **Dave Pell** ✔
> @davepell
>
> We finally found a type of gun control that the GOP supports.
>
> Smoking Gun Control.
>
> 11:44 AM · Jan 28, 2020 · 🐦 Twitter

Marco Rubio added his own spin on the decision: "Just because actions meet a standard of impeachment does not mean it is in the best interest of the country to remove a President from office." If you were confused, you weren't not alone. If you were surprised, you hadn't been paying attention.

> **Dave Pell** ✔
> @davepell
>
> Finally, a rich, white guy is gonna get a break from the legal system.
>
> 9:31 AM · January 31, 2020 · 🐦 Twitter

ONE GIANT LEAP FOR MANKIND

As our January warm-up drew to a close, American officials announced plans to hold 195 Americans in a fourteen-day quarantine at a base in California. All of them had been evacuated from the Wuhan region of China.

Donald Trump on January 30: "We think we have it very well under control. We have very little problem in this country at this moment—five. And those people are all recuperating successfully. But we're working very closely with China and other countries, and we think it's going to have a very good ending for it. So that I can assure you."

It was a month dominated by the impeachment trial, and like so many of the stories during the preceding three years, the truth didn't seem to matter, the president seemed able to get away with anything, and a sense of hopelessness built among his foes. Even as they fought to amplify the truth, the House managers arguing the case against the president knew their task was impossible. And so did everyone else.

January felt like a confirmation of the notion that nothing could dent Trump's hold on his base and the personal force field of protection engendered by that support.

It also seemed like the longest month of the Trump era, when every day had already felt like a week. To make matters worse, 2020 was a leap year. February would be one day longer than usual.

Because of course it would.

News Divisions
January 2020

Maddow

The New York Times 1
Trump Tied Ukraine Aid to Inquiries
He Sought, Bolton Book Says

ABC News 2
'Take her out': recording appears to
capture Trump at private dinner saying
he wants Ukraine ambassador fired

The New York Times 3
Trump Told Bolton to Help His Ukraine
Pressure Campaign, Book Says

The Washington Post 4
National Archives exhibit blurs images
critical of President Trump

Just Security 5
Exclusive: Unredacted Ukraine Docs
Reveal Pentagon's Legal Concerns

Hannity/Carlson

New York Post 1
How five members of Joe Biden's family
got rich through his connections

Foreign Policy 2
Petraeus Says Trump Helped
'Reestablish Deterrence' by
Killing Suleimani

Politico 3
Schiff may have mischaracterized
Parnas evidence, documents show

RealClearInvestigations 4
Whistleblower Was Overheard
in '17 Discussing With Ally How
to Remove Trump

The Sun 5
Clinton poses with Epstein's 'pimp' &
sex slave on 'Lolita Express'

These are the top news links shared on Twitter
in January by followers of Rachel Maddow versus
followers of Sean Hannity or Tucker Carlson.
Source: MIT Center for Constructive Communication

2

FEBRUARY— KEEP YOUR HANDS AND FEET IN

By the beginning of February, Americans were heading face-first into a gale-force whirlwind of oncoming pandemic news, political activity—including the Iowa caucuses and an upcoming State of the Union address—and the endless days of a Senate impeachment trial that grabbed everyone's attention but changed no one's mind. We needed a break. We needed something else to think about. We needed a distraction.

We needed a Super Bowl halftime show.

Jennifer Lopez and Shakira gave us the entertainment we craved, but the show did not provide a break from politics. By now, any American paying attention had realized that everything was political. Maybe we would have saved ourselves from a lot of national grief if we had learned that lesson earlier.

In addition to the expected hits like J.Lo's "Jenny from the Block" and Shakira's "Hips Don't Lie," the halftime show, featuring Latina headliners for the first time, which itself was a political statement, included plenty of references to the ongoing battle to shape what America saw when it looked in the mirror.

Lopez spread her arms to display a winged version of a flag, American in back, Puerto Rican in front; a reference to her heritage, but also clearly a reference to the Trump administration's failure to support the hurricane-ravaged island. Shakira's wiggling, warbling, meme-ifying tongue set social media on fire when she let out a sound most would only later learn was a *zaghrouta*, a joyful nod to her Arabic roots.

Two women were celebrating their ancestries and cultures. What could possibly be political about that? In 2020, all of it. If there were any doubts about the political nature of the show, they were put to rest when Lopez's daughter, Emme Muñiz, interluded "Let's Get Loud" with the chorus of Bruce Springsteen's "Born in the USA."

The Puerto Rican flag flashed as the iconic Springsteen song played, as if to remind viewers that Puerto Ricans are American citizens. While Muñiz was singing, other children were dancing in cagelike structures—a subtler reference, but a possible nod to the thousands of children, most from Latin American countries, who have been detained at the border. (Erin Vanderhoof, *Vanity Fair*)

Only in the era of Trump could kids in cages be referred to as a subtle reference.

And yes, there was a game too. As a Bay Area native and a San Francisco 49ers fan, I've tried to ignore that aspect of Super Bowl Sunday. Even though my team suffered a 31–20 defeat to the Kansas City Chiefs, it was almost impossible for anyone not to be impressed by the otherworldly Patrick Mahomes. Even his unusually vigorous, almost birdlike walk from the sideline to the huddle gave one a sense of his enthusiasm, a sense that this thrower could take on anything you threw at him.

What was missing from the game and the halftime show was any real sense of the impending doom represented by the rising virus. This would be America's final grand and global sports event before we were forced to shut everything down. Even the unstoppable Patrick Mahomes would be benched along with the rest of us.

Shakira's hips didn't lie, but I wish they had given us some kind of warning of how bad things would get as we departed the frivolity of the Super Bowl.

But before we moved on to other matters, there was a tweet. There was *always* a tweet. This one was quickly deleted after President Trump congratulated the Chiefs of Kansas City, Missouri, for representing "the Great State of Kansas." Oh well, they say Missouri loves company.

HOLLYWOOD AND WHINE

Adam Schiff closed out the House managers' case against Trump with this: "You can't trust this president to do the right thing, not for one minute, not for one election, not for the sake of our country. You just can't. He will not change and you know it . . . Is there one among you who will say enough?"

Not for one minute, not for one election, not for one tweet.

Schiff's congressional district included West Hollywood, home to some of the most famous entertainers in the world. But there was no question which resident gave the best performance during the weeks that encapsulated the House impeachment and Senate trial. By the time the trial ended, liberal parents were buying their toddlers Superman pajamas telling them the *S* stood for Schiff.

But three years into the relentless, unabashed enabling of an anything-goes presidency, the US representative from California's Twenty-Eighth District may have intended as rhetorical the question: "Is there one among you who will say enough?"

But there was an answer: Yes. Exactly one.

In the most famous scene of the 1960 blockbuster *Spartacus*, a group of recaptured slaves led by Kirk Douglas's character are told they could save their own lives "on the single condition that you identify the body or the living person of the slave called Spartacus."

Spartacus courageously stands to announce his identity, but before he can speak, Tony Curtis (playing the part of Antoninus) stands beside him and calls out, "I'm Spartacus." And one by one, other slaves stand and heroically risk their lives and call out the same.

At the conclusion of the Senate trial of Donald Trump, Mitt Romney boldly gave a speech explaining why he would vote to convict the president on the abuse of power charge: "My own view is that there's not much I can think of that would be a more egregious assault on our Constitution than trying to corrupt an election to maintain power. And that's what the president did."

Romney stood and declared, "I'm Spartacus!" And his colleagues nodded in his direction and said, "Yup, that's Spartacus, alright."

In an odd irony, Kirk Douglas died on the day Mitt Romney stood up while the rest of his party remained seated. Something else died a little bit more that day too: the rule of law.

How did so many Americans stand by and not only accept but embrace a clearly wrong, historically absurd verdict in favor of the president of the United States? One answer to that question is that millions of Americans saw a completely different trial, one that took place in their algorithmically driven Facebook feeds.

The *Atlantic*'s McKay Coppins provided many valuable insights into this world that most Americans were missing. In the months leading up to the impeachment trial, Coppins ran an experiment. He created a new Facebook account that he used to follow several pro-Trump groups and pages. He then let Facebook's algorithm work its magic.

> What I was seeing was a strategy that has been deployed by illiberal political leaders around the world. Rather than shutting down dissenting voices, these leaders have learned to harness the democratizing power of social media for their own purposes—jamming the signals, sowing confusion. They no longer need to silence the dissident shouting in the streets; they can use a megaphone to drown him out. Scholars have a name for this: censorship through noise.

Days after the trial, Lindsey Graham would remark: "When I die God isn't going to ask, 'Why didn't you convict Trump?'" (No, he'll just step aside and let John McCain beat the shit out of you.)

HOSPITAL, STAT

Three hundred sixty-two deaths. Seventeen thousand three hundred cases. Those were the latest global COVID-19 numbers on February 3, as the virus had spread to at least twenty-five countries. The Wuhan region of China still represented the vast preponderance of the spread. China's leaders knew this, and from experience with other outbreaks, they knew the numbers would increase dramatically.

The world watched a time-lapse video of the one-thousand-patient Huoshenshan Hospital go from foundation-laying to being partially operational in the course of ten days. (I once waited six times that long for a permit to replace my bathroom tiles.)

The *New York Times*'s Amy Qin: "For Beijing, the facility would also serve as a potent symbol of the government's drive to do what needs to be done."

CAUC BLOCKED
February 4, 2020

Americans expecting to awaken to the results of the Democratic Iowa Caucus and ring in what everyone hoped would be a year of free and fair elections with clear winners instead awoke to another day in 2020. The glitches that delayed the results for three days were ultimately blamed on a software company called Shadow, proving an old Silicon Valley adage: never use newly coded software when an abacus will suffice. It would take days before voters would learn that Pete Buttigieg had won the caucus, and much longer for the Iowasca hangover to wear off.

THIS SOTU SHALL PASS

The State of the Union Address on February 4 had such a WWE vibe to it that I wouldn't have been surprised if Nancy Pelosi had spun the president around on her shoulders before launching him into the turnbuckles. Trump opened by refusing to shake the Speaker's hand—sadly, this wasn't an early sign of reverence for social distancing. Pelosi closed by tearing up the transcript of the president's speech with a vigor reminiscent of the Bionic Woman, Jaime Sommers, ripping a phonebook in half in a scene that marked the first stirrings for a generation of adolescent boys.

COVID-19 would show we had little need for anyone to provide an overview of the union's state; the germ would peel back the layers on that condition. Thus, the evening would be most remembered for the optics, and these words from the president: "In recognition of all you have done for our nation—the millions of people today that you speak to and that you inspire and all of the incredible work you have done for charity—I am proud to announce tonight you will be receiving our country's highest civilian honor, the Presidential Medal of Freedom." To whom did the POTUS deliver this honor? Rush Limbaugh.

At that moment, Rush shared the distinction with Jonas Salk, Helen Keller, Neil Armstrong, and Mr. Rogers (who was likely rolling over in his cardigan that night).

DOCTOR'S ORDERS
February 7, 2020

"He didn't want to become a hero, but for those of us in 2020, he had reached the upper limit of what we can imagine a hero would do." According to the *New York Times*'s Li Yuan, that's what one Chinese social media user wrote about Li Wenliang, the doctor who was the first in China to warn about a mysterious virus that had pandemic potential. Dr. Li's late December warning earned him a visit by police, and he was later compelled to sign a statement admitting illegal behavior.

What prompted many Chinese citizens to take the unusual step of voicing emotional and political support for the doctor on social media?

Li Wenliang, worldwide whistleblower, died of the virus on February 7.

Donald J. Trump ✔
@potus

Just had a long and very good conversation by phone with President Xi of China. He is strong, sharp and powerfully focused on leading the counterattack on the Coronavirus. He feels they are doing very well, even building hospitals in a matter of only days. Nothing is easy, but.......he will be successful, especially as the weather starts to warm & the virus hopefully becomes weaker, and then gone. Great discipline is taking place in China, as President Xi strongly leads what will be a very successful operation. We are working closely with China to help!

5:31 AM · Feb 7, 2020 · 🐦 Twitter

In these still early days of the pandemic, the idea of squelching the admonitions of a health expert trying to save lives seemed like an act unique to authoritarian regimes.

STONEHEDGE

"This is a horrible and very unfair situation. The real crimes were on the other side, as nothing happens to them. Cannot allow this miscarriage of justice!" tweeted the president as his Justice Department announced plans to undercut its own sentencing recommendation for Roger Stone, who had been found guilty of witness tampering and obstruction of justice during the Mueller investigation into the Trump campaign's ties to Russia. The prosecutors handling the case for the Justice Department had recommended a seven- to nine-year sentence for Stone (Trump confidant, friend, advisor, and renowned super freak).

> All four career prosecutors handling the case against Roger Stone withdrew from the legal proceedings Tuesday—and one quit his job entirely—after the Justice Department signaled it planned to undercut their sentencing recommendation for President Trump's longtime friend and confidant.
>
> The sudden and dramatic moves came after prosecutors and their superiors had argued for days over the appropriate penalty for Stone, and exposed what some career Justice Department employees say is a continuing pattern of the historically independent law enforcement institution being bent to Trump's political will. (Matt Zapotosky, Devlin Barrett, Ann E. Marimow, and Spencer S. Hsu, *Washington Post*)

The Justice Department would ultimately argue for a shorter sentence than the one the Justice Department had recommended for a criminal the Justice Department had prosecuted. Sound extreme? It was just a stepping-Stone.

> Officials in the offices of Mr. Barr and Mr. Rosen decided to override the prosecutors' recommendation after they filed it in court on Monday night, officials said. The line prosecutors were even more upset because they were

told that they would be reversed only after Fox News had reported it. (Katie Benner, Sharon LaFraniere, and Adam Goldman, *New York Times*)

So the decision chain went Trump > Barr > Fox News > Prosecutors. If nothing else, it was refreshing that Fox News wasn't at the head of the chain.

Days later, William Barr would appoint an outside prosecutor to review the case of Michael Flynn.

> **Dave Pell** ✓
> @davepell
>
> Trump 2018: "Where's my Roy Cohn?"
>
> Trump 2020: "Why did I ever want a Roy Cohn? I've got a William Barr."
>
> 3:31 PM · Feb 11, 2020 · 🐦 Twitter

APPLE WATCH

On Sunday, February 16, my family and I took a trip to our favorite city, New York. We crowded around a cramped table at a Chinese restaurant with our good friends. We gripped poles as we stood clear of closing doors in a full subway car. In a tiny, airless studio, we watched my nephew in an NYU production of *Romeo and Juliet*. We squeezed into four orchestra seats and enjoyed an amazing production of the musical *Jagged Little Pill*. We ate second dinners. We fought in museums. We argued as we crammed into taxis and Ubers. Everything seemed normal. Like always, when we slept, the city didn't. We had no idea that in a few weeks the city, and the world, would be turned upside down. *Yo!* would soon become *Oy!*

ROGER RABID

February 20, 2020

"Sure, the defense is free to say: So what? Who cares? But, I'll say this: Congress cared. The United States Department of Justice and the United States Attorney's Office for the District of Columbia that prosecuted the case and is still prosecuting the case cared. The jurors who served with integrity under difficult circumstances cared. The American people cared. And I care." So ruled Judge Amy Berman Jackson as she sentenced Roger Stone to three years.

There was at least one person still saying, "Who cares?" The most powerful person in the Western world.

ROLL CREDITS

"Harvey is very strong. Harvey is unbelievably strong. He took it like a man." That was the take from defense attorney Donna Rotunno after her client was convicted of rape and sexual assault on February 24. How did the most notorious producer in Hollywood go from being an all-powerful studio mogul to being led out of a courtroom in handcuffs as the villainous poster child of the #MeToo movement? What forced this plot change?

First, he did what he was accused of, and then some. And second, his years of crimes met the headwinds of a movement that swept the nation. And third, courageous whistleblowers stepped forward and great journalists investigated and shared their stories. Even Harvey Weinstein wasn't powerful enough to survive a combination of factors that would be enough to bring anyone down. Almost anyone.

NANCY DREW THE LINE
February 24, 2020

Nancy Messonnier, director of the National Center for Immunization and Respiratory Diseases at the CDC, upped the warning levels about the novel virus that was infecting people in at least forty countries: "We're going to have community spread here. It's not a question of if this will happen, but when this will happen, and how many people in this country will have severe illnesses. We are asking the American public to prepare for the expectation that this might be bad."

The warning got the attention of the stock market. In its first broad reaction to COVID-19, the Dow plunged one thousand points and gave up its earnings for the year.

It also got the attention of the president. Messonnier stopped appearing at administration press conferences on COVID-19, and, according to several reports, was nearly fired.

The truth hurts. That adage was amended during the Trump reign. The truth hurts those who tell the truth (especially when the truth impacts the Dow).

Most Americans still had no idea what was about to hit them. And none could have imagined that when it did hit, the market would actually soar.

Donald Trump on February 25: "You may ask about the coronavirus, which is very well under control in our country. We have very few people with it, and the people that have it are . . . getting better. They're all getting better. . . . As far as what we're doing with the new virus, I think that we're doing a great job . . . I think that's a problem that's going to go away."

FACE THE FACE
February 26, 2020

With fifty-seven known coronavirus cases in the US, the *Washington Post*'s Reis Thebault published what was the commonly held belief, and the CDC recommendation at the time. "And those surgical masks? If you're not sick, you don't need to wear them—and you certainly don't need to buy every box your local pharmacy has in stock."

We'd soon learn that there were two major fallacies in that summary: We'd need to wear masks. And there weren't nearly enough in stock.

Donald Trump on February 26: "Because of all we've done, the risk to the American people remains very low. . . . When you have 15 people, and the 15 within a couple of days is going to be down to close to zero. That's a pretty good job we've done."

Donald Trump on February 27: "It's going to disappear. One day, it's like a miracle, it will disappear."

Donald Trump on February 28: "We are working on cures and we're getting some very good results . . . Now the Democrats are politicizing the coronavirus. . . . And this is their new hoax."

PETER PANDEMIC

In an indication of community spread, California became home to the United States' first COVID-19 case of unknown origin. Faced with the growing crisis, President Trump got more serious about his misinformation campaign and put VP Mike Pence in charge of the Coronavirus Task Force.

Japan ordered schools closed. Australian prime minister Scott Morrison explained, "We believe the risk of global pandemic is very much upon us and as a result, as a government, we need to take the steps necessary to prepare for such a pandemic." California governor Gavin Newsom said the state was monitoring more than 8,000 people who had recently traveled to Asia. In China, case numbers were growing as the country tallied 327 new cases and 44 deaths in a day. Facebook became one of the first American companies to cancel a major conference. Canada found cases in at least three provinces. The signs were coming from everywhere, except the White House, where the president minimized the virus, compared it to the flu or the common cold, and described it as something that presented little threat and that would just go away.

At this point, Trump still managed to control the story and the news cycle as he had done throughout most of his presidency. But this was no ordinary foe. COVID-19 didn't care what Donald Trump or anyone else had to say.

AMERICA'S FIRST

February 29, 2020

The CDC announces the death of a man in his fifties at a hospital in Kirkland, Washington. We didn't learn many details about him, but we did know that he had not traveled abroad prior to his positive test. The virus was spreading inside the US. We'd later learn that two Santa Clara residents had died of coronavirus earlier in February.

News Divisions
February 2020

Maddow

The New York Times 1
Russia Backs Trump's Re-election, and He Fears Democrats Will Exploit Its Support

The Washington Post 2
Secret Service has paid rates as high as $650 a night for rooms at Trump's properties

The Washington Post 3
Justice Dept. to reduce sentencing recommendation for Trump associate Roger Stone, official says, after president calls it 'unfair'

CNN 4
OMB filing reveals Trump involved in discussions on Ukraine aid as early as June

The New York Times 5
Impeachment Witness Alexander Vindman Will Be Transferred From the White House

Hannity/Carlson

CNN 1
US intelligence briefer appears to have overstated assessment of 2020 Russian interference

The New York Times 2
Russia Backs Trump's Re-election, and He Fears Democrats Will Exploit Its Support

BlazeTV (via Youtube) 3
Glenn Beck Presents: Ukraine: The Final Piece

Daily Mail 4
Ilhan Omar DID marry her brother, reveals Somali community leader

New York Post 5
Nancy Pelosi 'pre-ripped' pages of Trump's SOTU speech, video shows

These are the top news links shared on Twitter in February by followers of Rachel Maddow versus followers of Sean Hannity or Tucker Carlson. Source: MIT Center for Constructive Communication

DO YOU WANNA GO FASTER?

When I was a kid, there was a roller coaster at our annual county fair that rumbled around a short circular track, as songs like Foreigner's "Urgent" blasted through giant speakers. Every few face-distorting laps around the track, the ride's operator would pause the music and, in a heavily reverbed voice, ask:

"Do you wanna go faaaaaster?"

I screamed, "No?" All the other kids screamed, "Yeah!" But it didn't matter how anyone answered. Either way, the roller coaster accelerated.

That ride serves as a decent analogy for our experience of news during the social media era. The internet sped up news delivery, and it just kept getting faster.

Through our behaviors, news consumers kept yelling, "Yeah!" But we didn't stop there. We weren't satisfied merely being riders, so we became drivers of the news cycle, adding our collective weight to the pedal being pushed to the metal.

Yes, I'm mixing metaphors between roller coasters and automobiles, but when information moves fast enough, details like that don't matter.

I could hear that county fair roller coaster voice echoing in my head in January of 2011, when Gabby Giffords, an Arizona congresswoman, was shot in the head outside a Safeway in Tucson. The pace of news had already increased dramatically since the early days of the internet. But there was something about the Giffords shooting that felt like we had hit a new gear.

I remember exactly where I was at the moment of that Arizona shooting that killed six and wounded many others, including Giffords: right behind my laptop. Like thousands of others, I felt an urgent need for data. I opened about six tabs in my web browser and started hitting the refresh button. Most news outlets had a breaking news alert about the shooting, but little else. So I searched Twitter to increase the pace of incoming details.

Within minutes, the tweets shifted away from what happened and leaned into a deeper assessment of what it meant. There were tweets about gun control, tweets about political hate speech, and tweets about the increasingly angry partisan divide between Americans. Seconds later, those opinions were forcefully rebuffed by opposing views. The crime scene had barely been roped off, and the news gathering had already been eclipsed by news analysis.

Do you wanna go faster?

I did. I left my Twitter search window open as I returned to refreshing news sites. Give me something new. I need. Boom. NPR reported that Giffords was dead.

As the news swept through the socials, I headed over to the *New York Times* homepage. Nothing new. It still featured a stale paragraph with conflicting reports on Giffords's health. Below the blurb, the italicized phrase: *Updated 4 minutes ago.*

Do you wanna go faster?

NPR obviously did. But there was a reason the *New York Times* had allowed its updates to lag for an interminable four minutes.

Gabby Giffords wasn't dead.

While surgeons were racing to save her life, the false news of Giffords's death was being spread so feverishly that it made it all the way to her family members in the hospital waiting room, where they were compelled to confirm with doctors that Giffords was still alive.

There was a weird irony that the usually reserved NPR was the source of the mistake. It's hardly a brand one associates with speed. Even news that calls for urgency is delivered with conspicuous slowness. I mean, they have a show called *Wait Wait . . . Don't Tell Me!*

But even NPR felt the urgency. Everyone was on the ride.

Walter Cronkite once complained about the evening news: "Everything was being compressed into tiny tablets. You take a little pill of news every day . . . and that's supposed to be enough." By 2011, we were already swallowing tablets by the truckload.

NPR issued a mea culpa: "Already all of us at NPR News have been reminded of the challenges and professional responsibilities of reporting on fast-breaking news at a time and in an environment where information and misinformation move at light speed."

Light speed? 2011 felt fast then, but it was a tortoise compared to the 2020's hare wired on Red Bull, Adderall, cocaine, and a quad-shot macchiato.

In the past, once the din of theories, hypotheses, and manufactured realities had receded, we could count on getting the real story (or at least part of it) when we heard the thump of the morning paper landing on the foot stoop. But these days, the thumping starts right away.

We expect the news to be the first rough draft of history. But it can't be *this* rough. In an era of accelerating and always-on information moving at the speed of Twitter, where clarity and accuracy are the rare exceptions, we find ourselves counting on news professionals more than ever. The job is critical. But it can't be accomplished unless journalists rise above the din instead of getting sucked into it.

NPR apologized, but they were hardly the only ones to succumb to the sense of urgency. The errant report of Giffords's death didn't make it from their newsroom to the waiting room at Tucson's University Medical Center on its own. The rest of us helped.

While it's not difficult to understand why journalists would race to break a story first, it's harder to explain why news consumers felt the need to become faux reporters and immediately deliver the latest news about a member of Congress whose name most didn't know ten minutes earlier. What drives so many of us to become human breaking-news outlets, providing second-by-second details of a story along with simultaneous analysis? What possessed thousands of my fellow human news hunter-gatherers to breathlessly feed the machine before law enforcement officials on the ground even had a chance to put together a preliminary outline of what exactly happened?

If I had the answer, I would have tweeted it by now.

Do you wanna go faster?

Just like that old county fair roller coaster, it probably doesn't matter what you answer. At least on that ride, there was a moment when the voice asked, "Do you want to go backward?" And the ride did just that. Alas, the internet-driven news machine affords us no such opportunity for reflection. The speed only increases, and the ride only goes forward. The pressure to keep up and immediately chime in grows more urgent. The challenge of maintaining a reasonable level of factual accuracy grows more daunting. And actually taking the time to carefully gather details and reflect on information before adding an opinion to the discussion requires more restraint than society has exhibited so far.

Are you really sure you wanna go faster?

At this point, you've got no choice. We're headed to March.

3

MARCH— PULLING OUT OF THE STATION

In *The Sun Also Rises*, Ernest Hemingway's character Mike Campbell is asked, "How did you go bankrupt?" He answers, "Two ways. Gradually, then suddenly." The full force of COVID-19's arrival in America felt similar. For weeks, we were frozen in our reaction to the oncoming bus, but at the last second, we stepped off the sidewalk and walked right in front of it.

As March began, we thought we knew how to keep ourselves safe. Avoid large gatherings if possible. If you interact with others, be sure to wash your hands. And, the advice that gave us a national case of OCD, try not to touch your own face—which was something none of us had a particularly strong desire to do until we were told we shouldn't. Keeping one's hands away from one's face was made especially difficult by comments from the Oval Office that seemed intended to provoke facepalms; from the questioning of the WHO's numbers based on a presidential hunch, to familiar attacks on presidents past (apparently for not preparing us for something that didn't yet exist), and gems like this: "We have thousands or hundreds of thousands of people that get better, just by, you know, sitting around and even going to work, some of them go to work, but they get better."

Dr. Anthony Fauci, director of the National Institute of Allergy and Infectious Diseases, who guided the nation through the AIDS crisis and would soon become the most famous TV doctor since Leonard "Bones" McCoy, issued warnings, but tried to keep things in perspective: "What is the risk of actually getting infected with the coronavirus? The risk in the United States as a whole is still low. If you're a young otherwise healthy individual, the risk of your requiring any kind of medical intervention is low."

> **Dave Pell** ✓
> @davepell
>
> When Trump put Pence in charge of Coronavirus, God put on a face mask.
>
> 8:57 AM · Mar 1, 2020 · 🐦 Twitter

Hemingway once explained: "There is nothing to writing. All you do is sit down at a typewriter and bleed." He never had to write about March of 2020 (though in fairness, my fingers were bleeding less because of all the typing, and more because of all the vigorous handwashing). In truth the news was becoming as painful to read as it was to write. Consider this warning from the *Atlantic*'s Anne Appelbaum in a piece titled "Epidemics Reveal the Truth About the Societies They Hit."

> Even though we have the highest-tech health-care system in the world, even though we have the best surgeons and the best equipment, we have not created a public-health culture that induces confidence. The hospital system has been pared down to the bone; there is no extra capacity, and everyone knows it. If people have to pay to be tested, then many may refuse. If people have to be quarantined, they may escape. Worse, instead of seeking to halt conspiracy theories, it is possible that our government will create them.

The *Atlantic*'s editors should have titled Applebaum's article "Spoiler Alert."

As we entered the month of March, there were around one hundred thousand coronavirus cases and three thousand deaths worldwide.

Washington Post media reporter Margaret Sullivan issued a warning under the following headline: TRUMP IS PUSHING A DANGEROUS, FALSE SPIN ON CORONAVIRUS—AND THE MEDIA IS HELPING HIM SPREAD IT.

Spring was in the air. But winter is coming. Which brings us to our final Hemingway quote: "Never go on trips with anyone you do not love," which in 2020 jargon translates as, "Never quarantine with anyone you loathe."

OK, BOOMERANG

There was still a presidential race happening in the background. If the pandemic came gradually and then suddenly, Joe Biden's surge in the Democratic primary came suddenly and out of nowhere. The Democratic presidential primary season seemed like a wide-open affair, with the winds blowing in the direction of a newer, more liberal candidate. But things narrowed dramatically when House majority whip Jim Clyburn endorsed the former veep in the South Carolina primary, leading to a sweeping win that swept several other candidates aside.

After Biden's Sweet Carolina win, good times never felt so good. For months, his campaign was on the fritz. Clyburn had unplugged it, waited thirty seconds, and plugged it back in. It worked.

THINGS GO SOUTH (BY SOUTHWEST)
March 2, 2020

In addition to covering the news, I have the benefit of knowing many people who are much smarter about diseases, data, and government than I am. By this point, there was a lot of confusion about what was safe and what wasn't. My wife, Gina, and I were already concerned when we got on a Zoom call that included former Obama officials, several scientists and doctors, and a top Pentagon official. The extreme concern I heard in that update, and the momentum of this story and the virus, led me to email Hugh Forrest, the chief programming officer for SXSW, to let him know I was going to have to cancel my trip to Austin and skip my scheduled presentation. I lived with my eightysomething mother-in-law and hung out a couple of times a week with my ninetysomething parents. So being exposed to a large group just wasn't worth the risk, however remote it seemed at that moment.

I only sent the email after conferring with friends and family and thinking long and hard about the decision. At the moment I pressed Send on that email, I was a little embarrassed, and the move felt a bit extreme.

Within four days, SXSW had been completely canceled. That's how quickly this story was moving and how quickly our lives and expectations were changing. I probably surprised Hugh Forrest with my email. Fewer than one hundred hours later, it felt entirely predictable that the whole event wouldn't happen.

KIRKLAND OF THE LOST
March 3, 2020

Officials in Washington announced that the state's number of known coronavirus cases hit twenty-seven. The number itself may have seemed low, but the growth was not, as it marked a 50 percent increase from the day before.

How big a deal was it? My friend Mordy called to tell me that his son's junior high in Kirkland had just canceled school for the next six weeks. I screamed, "Holy shit! You poor, poor man!" into the phone. Mordy appreciated it. In retrospect, I should have reserved that pity for myself.

By this early point in the pandemic, the UN reported that nearly three hundred million kids across the world were missing school.

MINE SHAFT

Chronic pain. Unhappiness. Drug and alcohol abuse. According to economists Anne Case and Angus Deaton, those are a few of the side effects of being a non–college educated adult in America.

The other side effect: premature death.

If we're to understand what was to come in 2020 America, we have to understand what was already here: massive inequality.

From the opioid pill mills along Interstate 95, to the flattened quality of living, to an exploding economic divide, to the unjustifiable wealth being pumped out by the tech sector, to the way those on one side of the divide looked down on those on the other, to poisoned water supplies, to boarded-up factories, to CEOs making 278 times as much as the average employee; the story was always the same. The America of the twenty-first century was not merely leaving some groups behind, it was quite literally killing them.

I'm lucky enough to live on the right side of the American divide, where tech start-ups can turn the excellent into billionaires and the mediocre into millionaires, where pandemic quarantines mean boredom, not hunger, and where life expectancies go up, not down. I've participated in and benefited from that economy.

While talking a good game about factory workers and coal miners, Donald Trump was actually pushing for policy changes that would only increase the divide, cut my taxes, and hurt those he pretended to care about. But his message to groups like coal miners couldn't have landed with such force without the callous silence from others that preceded it.

Yes, climate change is real. Yes, we need alternative energies to save the planet. Yes, we need to migrate away from fossil fuels. But people on the fortunate side of the economic divide left something out of that message. Put yourself in the boots of a coal miner whose grandfather and father died of black lung, but who were rightly told that their work was noble and put the power into America's superpower. We forgot to say something to those workers: thank you. And we forgot to provide them with alternative energy-based jobs so they could make a better living with fewer health risks. Donald Trump couldn't have filled a void had there not been a void in the first place. And COVID-19 couldn't have ripped the scab off America's faded promise had a scab not been needed to cover the festering wound of American inequality.

THERE WON'T BE A TEST
March 6, 2020

To slow the spread of a deadly virus, you need to know who has the virus. To know who has the virus, you need to test for the virus. To test for the virus, you need to have large numbers of accurate tests. The *Atlantic*'s Robinson Meyer and Alexis C. Madrigal were on America's failures to fulfill the last piece of that puzzle as early and often as any journalists. Mike Pence, who was by now running America's Coronavirus Task Force, promised that 1.5 million tests would be available in the first week of March. America missed that number. And Meyer and Madrigal began their search for an answer to "one of the most urgent questions in the United States right now: How many people have actually been tested for the coronavirus?"

Americans were left to sift through news reports to figure out which symptoms to watch for—fever, dry cough, flu-like symptoms, loss of taste and smell—and figure out how worried to be. Like most middle-aged Jewish men, I was sure I had the virus about four hundred times within a couple weeks of the first US case.

Donald Trump on March 6: "We did an interview on Fox last night, a town hall. I think it was very good. And I said: 'Calm. You have to be calm. It'll go away.'"

ROLLED GOLD

In many places in the world, the panic buying that would define the early weeks of the pandemic was kicking into high gear. No product was in more demand than toilet paper. Manufacturer Kimberly-Clark posted to its Australian Facebook page to assure citizens down under that they had their down under covered. "We are working around the clock at our mill in South Australia to keep the supermarket shelves stocked with Kleenex Complete Clean toilet paper." This post was in response to one customer tasing another over a few rolls.

An Australian newspaper called the *NT News* printed an edition with eight blank pages "complete with handy cut lines, for you to use in an emergency." (I knew newspapers would eventually come up with a new business model . . .)

FLY-BY-NIGHT OUTFIT

No one was particularly surprised that Trump would habitually mislead about the virus risk or that his administration would be ill-prepared to deal with the coming illness. But the White House also actively worked to stifle common-sense, science-based health recommendations.

The White House overruled health officials who wanted to recommend that elderly and physically fragile Americans be advised not to fly on commercial airlines because of the new coronavirus. The Centers for Disease Control and Prevention submitted the plan as a way of trying to control the virus, but White House officials ordered the air travel recommendation be removed. (Mike Stobbe, AP)

While the average citizen was still in the dark, experts were increasing the volume of their warnings. During a March 7 Harvard forum, three of them expressed their concerns.

Harvard epidemiologist Michael Mina: "It's the most daunting virus that we've contended with in half a century or more."

STAT's infectious disease reporter Helen Branswell: "Having written about the possibility of something like this for years, I still find myself really startled that it's happening."

Panel participant Juliette Kayyem, formerly of the Department of Homeland Security, in the next day's edition of the *Atlantic*: "If Americans conclude that life will continue mostly as normal, they may be wrong. The United States is far less prepared than other democratic nations experiencing outbreaks of the novel coronavirus. Low case counts so far may reflect not an absence of the pathogen but a woeful lack of testing."

It's worth noting that, even with the dire warnings, the Harvard forum was held in person in a room with an audience.

Donald Trump on March 7: "We're doing very well and we've done a fantastic job."

WHO COUGHED ON MY PORTFOLIO?
March 9, 2020

Consumers stocking up for potential closures were lining up outside of big-box retailers, making those companies some of the few winners on a day when oil crashed and the Dow dropped more than two thousand points, its biggest point drop ever and its worst single-day percentage drop in more than a decade.

Donald Trump on March 9: "The Fake News Media and their partner, the Democrat Party, is doing everything within its semi-considerable power (it used to be greater!) to inflame the CoronaVirus situation, far beyond what the facts would warrant. Surgeon General, 'The risk is low to the average American.'"

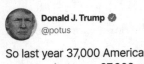

Donald J. Trump ✔
@potus

So last year 37,000 Americans died from the common Flu. It averages between 27,000 and 70,000 per year. Nothing is shut down, life & the economy go on. At this moment there are 546 confirmed cases of CoronaVirus, with 22 deaths. Think about that!

10:47 AM · Mar 9, 2020 · 🐦 Twitter

HOOP DREAMS DEFERRED

On March 9, my family was emailed the schedules for the upcoming weekend's basketball championships for my two kids. On March 10, the games were canceled. Like so many moments in March, you could see decisions coming, and you could agree they should be made, yet when they arrived, there was a feeling of shock. There was definitely some "Why us?" going around my house. Soon it would be going around everywhere. The abrupt end to a season, and for my eighth-grade son, an era shared with several

Dave Pell ✔
@davepell

My dad escaped the Nazis, crawled to the woods, joined the Partisans, and fought heroically for the allies in WWII.

In a race for some hand sanitizer at CVS, I outran an elderly woman and a little kid (who in retrospect may have been heading for the candy aisle).

#neverforget

8:20 PM · Mar 9, 2020 · 🐦 Twitter

teammates for years, was probably worse for me, as I had spent several seasons as *that* dad—the one who isn't a coach but offers nonstop feedback from the bleachers and lives vicariously through his kids (and anyone else's kids who will let him). Soon, roles would reverse as my kids lived vicariously through me and my weekly masked, rubber-gloved escapes to the local grocery store.

RSVP SHOOTER
March 10, 2020

Yascha Mounk's headline in the *Atlantic* was straightforward: *Cancel Everything.* "Anyone in a position of power or authority, instead of downplaying the dangers of the coronavirus, should ask people to stay away from public places, cancel big gatherings, and restrict most forms of nonessential travel."

By now, it was clear that when countries acted quickly, the curve of rising cases could be flattened. In countries where there were delays, the virus spiked. *Cancel Everything* sounded hysterical to most Americans. But not to Italians, whose government put the entire country on lockdown on the same day that Mounk's article was published.

Donald Trump on March 10: "It hit the world. And we're prepared, and we're doing a great job with it. And it will go away. Just stay calm. It will go away." And . . . "I've been briefed on every contingency you could possibly imagine. Many contingencies. A lot of positive. Different numbers, all different numbers, very large numbers, and some small numbers too."

WE TALKIN' ABOUT PRACTICE?
March 11, 2020

There are Facebook families where every shared experience is filled with posed smiles, loving compliments, and perfect moments. My family is a Twitter family.

As the first activities started to get scratched because of COVID concerns, my son texted me to ask if he could attend an after-school volleyball practice. I had a feeling that schools would close and this might be his last chance, so I told him he could do it as long as he had no physical contact with other kids and washed his hands during every break.

His mother had a different plan: no to volleyball but yes to picking up our kids immediately after school and making a family run to the grocery store to stock our freezer for the apocalypse. The change induced a memorable case of teen fury. The Facebook version of this story is that my son was a bit disappointed and wanted to calmly chat about the mixed messages and missing what could be his last athletic experience before such encounters were postponed for an indeterminate period. The Twitter story is that he delivered an expletive toward his mom that was offensive even by Billy Bush–Donald Trump locker room standards. The C-word had been dropped. And soon he would be.

Long story short: Car pulled over. Back door opened. Teen removed. Back door closed. Car back on the road. Teen in rearview mirror beginning what would be a thirty-minute jog through the burbs to meet the rest of his family at the grocery store.

The sad irony (this was still a few weeks before 2020 killed off irony altogether) of my son's rare punishable outburst was that it was made in defense of a practice for a season that would never be played at a school that wouldn't reopen. That reality still felt off in the distance, but it would arrive in just a little more time than it took my son to jog to the store.

Back home, I wrote an open letter explaining why my wife and I would be pulling our kids from their Bay Area school effective now, even though the school remained open.

I laid out the key reasons. Every expert I've read or listened to had shared information suggesting this is the right move, including another parent from our school who is the smartest doctor I know and who was also pulling her kids. The more knowledgeable the person, the more worried they are. My kids lived with one grandparent and regularly interacted with two others. They could miss some class to keep their grandparents safe. And we could afford to do this. We could stay home with our kids and care for them with no real financial impact. Pulling our kids from school made sense for us, but doing so also made sense for the rest of the students and adults at the school. The fewer people gathered, the less chance of transmission. Everyone who could stay home, must. Everyone who could pull their kids from school, should. All these decisions needed to take into account both individual circumstances and the well-being of the community.

On this particular Wednesday, open letters would be as futile as scientific facts in the White House. By the time you finished typing a sentence, the whole world had changed. But even now, even waist deep in the story both as a curator of the news and a civilian experiencing its pace, I still underestimated the speed of this story. Ferris Bueller famously said, "Life moves pretty fast. If you don't stop and look around once in a while, you could miss it."

On March 11, you could have looked around nonstop without blinking a single time and you would've still missed most of it.

NOBODY TOLD ME THERE'D BE DAYS LIKE THESE

There's almost nothing that can make a virus seem more real faster than finding out that someone you know has it. Someone everyone knows got COVID-19. Tom Hanks and his wife, Rita Wilson, announced they had tested positive for the virus and would be getting treatment under quarantine in Australia.

The NCAA announced that its wildly popular March Madness tournament would be played in front of arenas that would be empty, other than essential personnel and limited family members.

We'd learn that this NCAA plan was overly optimistic within hours. Fans at an NBA game in Oklahoma City were waiting inside of their arena for their home team Thunder to face the visiting Utah Jazz. What could be weirder than something from Utah being named after jazz? This. Fans sat in Chesapeake Energy Arena waiting for the game to start. Thirty-five minutes after the scheduled tipoff, the PA announcer told them that game had been postponed: "You are all safe. And take your time leaving the arena tonight and thank you for doing so in an orderly manner." Within twenty minutes of that announcement, we learned that, following a positive test for a Jazz player named Rudy Gobert, the NBA would postpone its entire season. On the same day, the NHL made the same decision. Out of nowhere, we were confronted by a new rule of thumb. Every gathering is a clusterfuck.

Update: it's still March 11.

President Trump, who two days earlier was still blaming the fake news and the Democratic Party for inflaming virus concerns, gave only his second Oval Office address. It was an ineffective presidential address, but by giving it at all, Trump acknowledged a crisis he had heretofore denied. For him, that was a pivot. He didn't, however, pivot when it came to substance, and he certainly didn't pivot when it came to his bedside manner. Viewers of the address learned about a partial European travel ban at the same time European officials learned about it. This was on top of a partial China travel ban already in effect. (Side note: the virus was. already. here.) There was no clear plan, and no soothing, not even for his favorite constituent, the stock market. Market futures began to plummet as he spoke, and the next morning, the Dow suffered its biggest drop since 1987.

Trump canceled trips to Colorado and Nevada, "out of an abundance of caution" (a phrase that would be repeated by everyone in every industry until it became clear that it wasn't an abundance, it was just caution).

New York City canceled the Saint Patrick's Day parade.

Seattle closed its schools for at least fourteen days.

San Francisco banned large-group gatherings.

Disneyland officials decided to close the park later in the week.

Fox News execs prepared an internal email sent out the next day that would announce the implementation of several safety measures, including a directive that any staff member who was able to work from home should begin doing so. (Their viewers received no such warnings. On air, the lies about the virus continued apace. At least in this one way, it was just another Wednesday.)

In Washington State, ten long-term-care facilities reported virus cases.

Late-night shows recorded in front of empty studios.

Twitter announced all employees would be required to work from home.

Twenty-three states declared a state of emergency.

US State Department employees were barred from nonessential travel.

The WHO, for the first time, labeled COVID-19 a global pandemic.

The US had 1,267 COVID-19 cases, and the death toll was at 37.

Donald Trump on March 11: "I think we're going to get through it very well."

There was plenty more, but it was one of those historic days so unforgettable that it's hard to remember everything that happened. For my son, it provided a valuable lesson about the virtue of patience. If he had only waited a few more hours to yell his expletive, it would have been easily drowned out by the rest of America doing the same.

(MIRA)MAX SENTENCE

At his sentencing hearing, Harvey Weinstein addressed the court, saying he was "remorseful." He also listed many of his charitable deeds and made a comparison between his conviction and the Red Scare. "You know, I just—dealing with the thousands of men and women who are losing due process, I'm worried about this country in a sense too. I'm worried there is a repeat of the blacklist there was in the 1950s." On a day when it seemed everything changed, it was somewhat comforting that Weinstein remained pathetic.

The once powerful mogul was ordered to shelter in place in prison for the next twenty-three years. He may have had the worst March 11 of anyone.

STOCK RACING
March 12, 2020

While mass unemployment and nationwide food lines would soon display the impact of the pandemic, it didn't take long for the stock market to demonstrate that it was immune to COVID-19. With an epic collapse barely in the rearview mirror, stocks posted their biggest rally since 2008.

Donald Trump on March 12: "It's going to go away . . . The United States, because of what I did and what the administration did with China, we have 32 deaths at this point . . . when you look at the kind of numbers that you're seeing coming out of other countries, it's pretty amazing when you think of it."

WHICH PART OF *PARTISAN* DON'T YOU UNDERSTAND?

By now, we definitely knew that deadly viruses can be passed from animals to humans. But could concern about the virus be passed across even more distant species, like, say, Republicans and Democrats?

FiveThirtyEight took a look at some early polling on COVID-19 and found that partisanship drove every belief.

> There are some pretty stark differences in how Democrats and Republicans view the threat of coronavirus. Some polls, like a recent Quinnipiac University survey, show just one-third of Republicans expressing concern, compared with 68 percent of Democrats. Other pollsters have found a narrower gap—in a recent Public Policy Polling survey, for instance, 44 percent of Republicans said they were concerned versus 67 percent of Democrats. But . . . a partisan split is emerging.

Donald Trump on March 13 when asked if he takes responsibility for America's dearth of coronavirus testing: "I don't take responsibility at all." (Historians should note this was his first honest response during his presidency.)

HOUSE HOLDUP
March 13, 2020

After midnight in Louisville, Kentucky, three white police officers knocked on a door before using a battering ram to enter the apartment of an ER technician named Breonna Taylor. Believing the men to be intruders, Taylor's boyfriend, Kenneth Walker, fired a warning shot, hitting one of the officers in the leg. The police opened fire, unleashing thirty-two shots. Walker was not hit. Breonna Taylor was hit several times and died at the scene.

Throughout 2020, Breonna Taylor's name and image appeared on social feeds, placards, and T-shirts in the form of protest art as Louisville residents and others around the country demanded to know how a health worker could have been killed by police in her own home.

Initially, no charges were brought against any of the officers involved in the shooting. However, Kenneth Walker was charged with attempted murder. Those charges were eventually dropped, but the topic of Breonna Taylor wasn't. Calls for justice would grow as other acts of police violence against

Black Americans rose to the top of the news—and the broader issue of racism once again battered its way into American consciousness.

BOOTS ON THE GROUND
March 14, 2020

The US military halted domestic nonemergency travel for service personnel and their families. On the same day, Apple announced it would be closing all its retail stores in the US. In other words, the two world superpowers both closed up shop on the same day. Even though the world's strongest military and the world's most valuable company were sending a clear message, most Americans refused to shut things down.

After reading a couple of articles suggesting that information and routines are both salves during a crisis, I decided to publish *NextDraft* seven days a week. This enabled me to look dedicated to my readers while having an excuse to avoid my already Zoom-bored, quarantined kids. At this point, most of our exchanges were about stocking up and wiping down enough food to last what we thought would be a few weeks of sheltering in place. Everyone was tasked with adding to the list of essentials. My son texted me his list: Sprite, Watermelon Red Bull, Coke, Dr Pepper, Mountain Dew, sea salt and vinegar chips, Lucky Charms, Flamin' Hot Funyuns, Red Vines, Gummi Bears, and chocolate. (In fairness, it's hard to imagine that even a novel virus could contend with that chemical combination.) Inspired by his focus on items that provided upbeat comfort, I decided to switch from indica to sativa.

By now, the administration's staggering failures had come clearly into view.

In the United States, the pandemic has devolved into a kind of grotesque caricature of American federalism. The private sector has taken on quasi-state functions at a time when the executive branch of government—drained of scientific expertise, starved of moral vision—has taken on the qualities of a failed state. (Derek Thompson, the *Atlantic*)

And the *New Yorker*'s Masha Gessen explained how the coronavirus pandemic fueled Trump's autocratic instincts (like they needed more fuel).

The Trumpian response to covid-19 has been compared to the Soviet government's response to the accident at the Chernobyl power plant, in 1986. For once, this comparison is not far-fetched.

I read both those articles and doubled my son's shopping list.

WE WERE YOUNG, HEARTACHE TO HEARTACHE

My son and I strapped on rubber gloves and took our two beagles, Pumpernickel and Rye, for our usual walk. The blocks were familiar, but our whole world had changed. My son, thirteen at the time, reflected on his school being shut down, his hangs with friends being halted, and in some ways, his childhood suspended in time. He told me he planned to be extra careful and avoid all social activities and unnecessary interactions, out of concern for his grandparents. It wasn't worth taking risks if it meant risking their health.

Even with the unknowns ahead, for me, the moment introduced the possibility that something positive could come out of this experience. Maybe there was something good about my young son understanding the importance of sacrifice, family, and being part of a community. For those lucky enough not to face immediate financial pressures or health-related challenges, these early days of the pandemic were accompanied by a surge of adrenaline, a sense that our petty national divides might be set aside and replaced by the common goal of protecting each other.

Oddly, my son was teaching me something at the very moment when I felt less like a dad than ever. Usually parents have the answers, or at least pretend they do. In the age of COVID-19, it was immediately clear I didn't. *When will school be back in session? Is Grandma gonna be OK? How do we protect ourselves? What's coming next?* Like every parent, I had no idea.

During one of his occasional interviews with Howard Stern, Maroon 5's Adam Levine was reflecting on the most influential band of his youth and stumbled upon the feeling I'm getting at: "When I was fifteen, all I wanted to do was be Pearl Jam . . . That was my band for my *adolescent, shut-in, fucked-up, angsty, crazy, the world is a crazy place, I don't understand* phase of my life, which seems to have come back now in 2020, which is amazing. [In] that era I was holding on by a thread like every other fifteen-year-old kid . . . and that band kept me going."

That phase of life came back for people of all ages in the early days of the pandemic. We were all fifteen again. We needed Eddie Vedder. We needed a leader of the band. We needed a "Better Man" as president.

THE DIVIDES OF MARCH
March 15, 2020

Some Americans were sheltering in place, working to flatten the curve to protect health workers already running short of personal protective equipment, and washing the skin off their hands to the tune (and for the duration) of Gloria Gaynor's "I Will Survive." Others went on with life as usual, even with the facts of COVID-19's wrath filling up the obituary pages in Italy and elsewhere.

By now, we knew that asymptomatic carriers could spread the disease to others and that the outbreak could spread exponentially. At least those listening to experts knew that. Those who listened to other voices were getting a different picture, like the one provided by GOP California congressman Devin Nunes on Fox News, in what might be remembered as the glass-is-half-full statement of a lifetime: "If you're healthy, you and your family, it's a great time to go out and go to a local restaurant, [it's] likely you can get in easy."

Messages like that were, unfortunately, being heard loud and clear along one side of the partisan divide.

Sixty-eight percent of Democratic voters are worried that an immediate family member might catch the coronavirus, compared with just 40 percent of Republicans who agree.

Fifty-six percent of Democrats believe their day-to-day lives will change in a major way, versus only 26 percent of Republicans.

And 79 percent of Democrats say the worst is yet to come, versus just 40 percent of Republicans who hold the same opinion. (NBC / *Wall Street Journal* poll)

The ides of March are come. And so are the divides of March. And so is one last quote from *Julius Caesar*: "Men in general are quick to believe that which they wish to be true."

There were three thousand cases in the US. And sixty-one people had died of COVID-19.

Donald Trump on March 15: "This is a very contagious virus. It's incredible. But it's something that we have tremendous control over."

GERM WARFARE

The next great world war had arrived. But this time, it wasn't country versus country. It was humanity versus a virus. And in this war, the soldiers on the front lines were health care professionals, grocery store employees, janitors, sanitation workers, delivery drivers, and all the others who keep the gears of society turning. The generals were the governors, mayors, principals, and others making the tough decisions to keep us safe; and who kept working for their constituents and students, even as they were dealing with their own health and safety concerns. And then there were the rest of us, the people on the home front, a term that, in this case, could be taken entirely literally. "Ask not what your country can do for you—ask what you can do for your country." What you could do for your country was: stay home, work from home, learn from home, inform and support your neighbors, drop off stuff for older people who shouldn't be going out, and wash your hands. As a bonus, you could take the lead of some Italians and sing with neighbors from nearby balconies or do like the Spaniards and play apartment complex bingo. Uncle Sam Needed You . . . to just sit on the couch and watch TV. It was a vital role and one many of us were born to do. But *many* wasn't enough.

The CDC advised that gatherings of more than fifty should be canceled, and sixteen national health care leaders laid things out in *USA Today*.

COVID-19 is spreading, and you won't know you're infected until you've already infected others. Right now, you have no immunity to prevent you from getting the disease. It's especially lethal for older people or those with underlying conditions. This will come to communities in waves and will be a marathon, not a sprint, so pay attention to local events. And our hospitals won't have sufficient resources—people, beds, ventilators or protective gear—if cases keep spreading as fast as they are in Italy.

But there's something important you can do.

STAY AT HOME as much as possible. It may be in your community now or it may be soon. Until you hear otherwise from health care officials, even if you have no symptoms. That means avoiding play dates, sleepovers, bars, restaurants, parties or houses of worship. Avoid all crowds.

We knew what to do. It wasn't that complicated. It didn't need to be that hard.

HELTER SHELTER
March 16, 2020

While life continued in some American cities, such was not the case in my neck of the woods. My county of Marin used to be known for hot tubs, peacock feathers, and cocaine. That party ended in the '80s. All the rest of the parties ended on this day in March as we became one of six Bay Area counties to encounter life under America's first shelter-in-place order. The initial order was only intended to last three weeks. The directive: all but essential businesses would close; the exceptions were restaurant deliveries, grocery markets, hardware stores, and pharmacies (or as my friend Mordy calls them, the Jewish man's hardware stores). As individuals, we were tasked with staying home as much as possible, although outdoor activities such as running or hiking were encouraged, as long as people remained more than six feet from one another. My family had by now loaded up on rubber gloves and scored a few containers of medical-grade disinfectant wipes from a friend, and we spent much of our time sanitizing surfaces, our groceries, and even our mail.

It turned out we had a lot more information than the essential workers who were tasked with keeping our society running. I happened to run into my postman, and I noticed he was wearing rubber gloves; but he was wearing them under his usual work gloves. Since I had been schooled by some folks in scientific fields, I explained that this wasn't an ideal method and that if he wanted to reuse his work gloves, he needed to wash them (or put them in the dryer, which also kills the virus) nightly, and avoid touching his face in the meantime. He thanked me and said that he and his fellow deliverers really hadn't been given any health-related rules yet.

On the same day, Amazon announced they would be hiring one hundred thousand new workers in the US to keep up with demand and that, for the time being, essential products would be given priority.

There were few advisories coming from Washington, DC, so local governments and mega tech companies (the new nation-states) had to lead the way.

PATRIOT ACT

As if the nation weren't destabilized enough, Tom Brady announced he'd be leaving the New England Patriots, telling the team's fans on social media that "my football journey will take place elsewhere." By this point in 2020, that's pretty much where everyone wanted to go. And we weren't even out of the first quarter yet.

WIPE OUT

The hoarding of food and hand sanitizer made sense, but why had we wiped the shelves of toilet paper, the suddenly legendary thin sanitary absorbent paper? How did this become our commodus operandi? Our latrine age wasteland? What caused the great Charmin squeeze? How did number two turn into issue number one? Why was there nothing but a stripped cardboard tube at the end of this lavatory story?

The toilet paper shortage had to do with two key factors, both of which were related to people starting to work from home. First, being at home all day meant that you wouldn't be defecating in your office's public restroom (hey, I never said the pandemic didn't have some upsides), so you'd need more rolls at home. Second, many paper factories were tooled to create larger rolls for commercial use, and it would take time to retool them to match the sudden surge in demand for residential toilet paper.

The concern over toilet paper was global. I knew citizens of the world would eventually unite over a common cause. My money was on climate change, but a cause is a cause. Mark Rutte, the prime minister in the Netherlands, reassured his citizens: "There's enough in the whole country for the coming 10 years. We can all poop for 10 years." (Sure, if you go Dutch . . .)

The great battle to secure toilet paper provided one of the rare victories of the year for my family. My wife hadn't remembered signing up for auto delivery of toilet paper from Amazon the month before. But she had. And it wasn't just any toilet paper. It was extra-comfort, triple-ply, ultra-plush Quilted Northern.

The Bay Area has been home to three gold rushes. The original gold rush of the mid-1800s. The internet gold rush of the late 1990s. And the arrival of forty-eight rolls of toilet paper that UPS left in front of my gate in March of 2020.

BROADBANDING TOGETHER

My daughter attended her first Zoom birthday party, and it was actually pretty fun. It was a sign—along with the simultaneous Zoom cocktail party the parents were holding—that we'd be able to quickly adapt and move some of our activities, traditions, and ceremonies online. But there was a caveat: millions of American birthday boys and girls didn't have decent broadband. That would make socializing harder, schooling difficult, and keeping up impossible for those already behind.

While my daughter's friend celebrated her birthday, Joe Biden won the Arizona, Florida, and Illinois primaries, building an insurmountable lead in the race to the top of the Democratic ticket.

NO MORE RHYMES NOW, I MEAN IT.
"ANYBODY WANT A PEANUT?"

This was around the time I decided to publish Famous Lines of Poetry Revised for the Age of Coronavirus in *McSweeney's*. A few outtakes:

Two roads diverged in a wood, and I—I took the one less traveled. Duh.

. . .

He was my North, my South, my East, and West,
My working week and my Sunday rest.
But when I had a fever, he had no test
Just looked at me and said, Be Best.

. . .

I wandered lonely as a cloud, as the CDC advised.

. . .

The caged bird sings
with a fearful trill
of things unknown
but longed for still
Another night of Netflix and Chill.

. . .

We few, we happy few, we band of brothers;
For he to-day that shares his Zoom with me
Shall be my brother.

. . .

Do not go gentle into that good night
without first Purelling.

. . .

Because I could not stop for death / He kindly stopped for me.
Fortunately, I remained more than six feet away.

. . .

O Captain! my Captain! our fearful trip is done,
The ship has weather'd every rack, the prize we sought is won.
Invite me on another cruise, and I swear to God I'll run.

. . .

I am the master of my fate:
I am the captain of my soul.
I am not coming to your luncheon.

. . .

Is all that we see or seem
But a dream within a dream?
Still stocking toilet paper? I'll take a ream.

. . .

What happens to a dream deferred?
Does it dry up
like a raisin in the sun?
We're gonna find out, because you're not acting on it until at least May.

. . .

I have eaten
the plums
that were in
the icebox
Alexa, order more plums.

. . .

April is the cruelest month
Unless you count March, which sucks bigly.

. . .

We wear the mask that grins and lies,
It hides our cheeks and shades our eyes,—
This debt we pay to human guile;
Donate it to your doctor, they did not stockpile.

. . .

Such wilt thou be to me, who must,
Like th' other foot, obliquely run;
Thy firmness makes my circle just,
And makes me end where I begun.
Jog 'round this kitchen island I must
I should have bought a Peloton.

. . .

I celebrate myself, and sing myself,
What the fuck else am I gonna do? I'm by myself!

GREY'S REALITY

Some of the world's most expensive health system's doctors and nurses took to social media to beg for excess personal protection equipment, and others shared images of their colleagues using bandannas, sports goggles, and homemade face shields. A lucky few were treated to hand-me-downs from a source perfectly suited for an era when the country was being run like a television show. I'll let this headline from the Wrap diagnose the situation: *TV Medical Dramas Donate Their Medical Supplies to Hospitals in Need During Coronavirus Pandemic: Fox's "The Resident," ABC's "Grey's Anatomy" and NBC's "New Amsterdam" Are Giving Items to Real Doctors and Nurses Fighting COVID-19.*

A LITTLE ITALY ADVICE

With their country on lockdown and more than two thousand dead, an Italian filmmaking collective called A Thing By created a video to warn Americans to take the virus seriously. These were some of the messages from a country that was a couple of weeks ahead of the US in terms of the viral curve:

"A huge mess is about to happen."

"The worst-case scenario? That's exactly what will happen."

"Hospitals are literally blowing up. Lots of infections, even among young people."

And the video's final message: "We underestimated this. You don't have to do the same."

PLEASE CLAP
March 18, 2020

On social media, French residents joined a trend that would sweep across the globe. They stood at windows and on balconies to applaud health care workers. This was a tribute that began in Wuhan and spread throughout the world. Concern was high, but so was adrenaline. People wanted to do something, anything, to contribute to the cause. When the trend hit my neighborhood, the clapping and cheering had been replaced by an 8:00 p.m. group howling. This nightly ritual marked the first time my beagles could howl freely without ending up in an angry Nextdoor post.

THE SHOW MUST GO ON?

March 20, 2020

"What do you say to Americans who are scared?" NBC's Peter Alexander asked the president.

"I say that you're a terrible reporter," the president answered.

This was just one unsettling scene that took place at what had become daily White House Coronavirus Task Force press conferences. That's what they were called. What they *were* could be better described as campaign rallies being held by a president who could no longer hold them in person because of the virus. Like those campaign rallies, the live press conferences were filled with contempt, false information, and outright lies about the virus and the administration's management of the crisis.

So one had to ask, as many did, why the cable news networks continued to broadcast these mis- and disinformation-riddled political rallies when going live could cost lives.

Since the earliest days of the 2016 election, the cable news networks had fixated on Trump, and once he took office, they went all Trump all the time. Trump wanted to turn the presidency into a show, and a show needs a network, and Trump had several. Even when things started to get dangerous, both in terms of health and democratic norms, the show just went on, for Trump, for the cable nets, and for everyone.

The spigot of Trump propaganda would continue to flow. Our coffee would not. Starbucks announced it was closing its cafés across the US and Canada. Luckily for me, my newsletter readers, and my relationship with my twelve-year-old, iced caramel macchiato–loving daughter, we live near a Starbucks drive-thru.

A couple of days later, the Tokyo Olympics were postponed.

What could be bigger than the shutdown of the world's biggest sports gathering and a pause of the nonstop dealing of America's caffeinated, sugar-infused drug of choice? Vegas shut down its casinos too.

CONTROL, HALT, DELETE
March 23, 2020

The *New York Times's* science and health reporter Donald G. McNeil Jr., who had covered pandemics in the past and had a rolodex of top epidemiologists, delivered their near-universal view: THE VIRUS CAN BE STOPPED, BUT ONLY WITH HARSH STEPS.

> The next priority, experts said, is extreme social distancing. If it were possible to wave a magic wand and make all Americans freeze in place for 14 days while sitting six feet apart, epidemiologists say, the whole epidemic would sputter to a halt.

You don't even need me to say "Spoiler Alert" here. While everyone was not in tune with what needed to be done, some were. And there were many moments of humor and support, such as the one offered by Neil Diamond, who sat in front of his fireplace and sang to America an updated version of "Sweet Caroline":

> *Hands, Washing Hands*
> *Reaching Out, Don't Touch Me.*
> *I Won't Touch You.*

What struck me about the YouTube recording from Diamond, who had been forced from the road by Parkinson's disease, was not so much the song but rather the intro. It was so simple. It was the message we needed from our leaders.

> Hi, everybody. This is Neil Diamond, and I know we're going through a rough time right now. But I love ya, and I think maybe if we'd sing together, well, we'll just feel a little bit better. Give it a try, OK?

Neil, you had me at *Hi.*

FEEDER PROGRAM

Restaurants were struggling to stay alive. Health workers were working overtime and stretched thin. My friend Jeff Berman and virtual friend Andy Sarver both set up programs in California that funded local restaurants to feed hospital workers and others in need. These programs were a win-win-win. They supported shuttered restaurants, saved jobs, and assisted those on the front lines of the crisis. The organization that supported these and many similar efforts across the country (and the world) was José Andrés's World Central Kitchen. Andrés's already heroic efforts achieved legendary status during the pandemic as he traveled from city to city, providing a steady supply of the basic needs that underpin Maslow's hierarchy. It seemed like wherever there was need, World Central Kitchen was there.

We needed to report on the depth of the crisis, and we justifiably critiqued the villains in this story. But we also need to amplify those who did the right thing because it was the right thing to do. When we celebrate the names we've heard of, we also celebrate those whose names we'll never know. The absence of leadership from the top made the grassroots efforts all the more inspiring.

I FOUND MY TRILL

I Found My Trill, on Capitol Hill. Two Trill, actually. How do you know this pandemic was serious? At the end of March, Congress got a bipartisan deal done. The massive stimulus package included money to prop up the airlines, forgivable loans for small business, and $1,200 in cash for many Americans making less than $75,000 a year. The package was good news for almost everybody. But it was especially good for the stock market, which began to party like it was 2019. And unlike the rest of the American economy, which now included a record 3.3 million unemployment claims, it never really looked back.

Meanwhile, while New York City case numbers were doubling every three days, Donald Trump announced that he wanted America back open for business. "I would love to have the country opened up and just raring to go by Easter." For that, empathetic, effective leadership would have had to rise from the dead.

> **Dave Pell** ✔
> @davepell
>
> Trump: We'll be open by Easter.
>
> Jesus: I'm sheltering in place.
>
> 12:10 PM · Mar 24, 2020 · 🐦 Twitter

Donald Trump on March 25: "It's hard not to be happy with the job we're doing, that I can tell you."

COLD HARD NUMBERS
March 27, 2020

My friend DJ Patil, chief data scientist in the Obama administration, went on leave from his private sector job to work as an unpaid volunteer for Gavin Newsom and a team of experts leading California's COVID fight. He told a group of us on a Zoom call that one of his toughest assignments was determining how many bodies you could fit into a refrigerator truck so the state could order the correct number of them to deal with the toll. According to the New York experts tasked with the same grim math problem, the number was around forty-five. With 325 deaths and 33,000 cases in California, they made an initial order of eighty-five refrigerated trucks to house the dead.

HOW THE STORY ENDS

The *Washington Post*'s excellent Eli Saslow collected many first-person, as-told-to stories from ordinary people encountering an unordinary time. These were much-needed reminders of the purely human side of the story. During 2020, we all sometimes cared so much about Trump news that we forgot to care for each other.

Tony Sizemore, on the death of his partner, Birdie Shelton.

She's dead, and I'm quarantined. That's how the story ends. I keep going back over it in loops, trying to find a way to sweeten it, but nothing changes the facts. I wasn't there with her at the end. I didn't get to say goodbye. I don't even know where her body is right now, or if the only thing that's left is her ashes.

From normal life to this hell in a week. That's how long it took. How am I supposed to make any sense of that? It's loops and more loops.

The news cycle moved at a dizzying and relentless pace. But for some, the pain arrived and time stood still.

Donald Trump on March 30: "Stay calm, it will go away. You know it is going away."

AIR 404

We were social distancing, we were wearing rubber gloves, we were sterilizing our homes; but even as the pandemic altered almost every part of modern life, Americans still weren't getting clear direction when it came to wearing masks. It was hard not to wonder if consumers were being directed away from mask purchases because a national shortage made it difficult for health workers to maintain an ample supply to protect themselves.

Suggesting that masks could lead to one touching one's face more often, Anthony Fauci had told *60 Minutes*, "Right now, in the United States, people should not be walking around with masks."

On *Fox & Friends*, Surgeon General Jerome Adams warned, "You can increase your risk of getting it by wearing a mask if you are not a health care provider."

Health and Human Services secretary Alex Azar explained, "If it's not fitted right you're going to fumble with it."

Seriously, have you ever seen a person without a medical degree try to put on one of those complicated face masks?

Whatever the driver behind the *don't wear a mask* message, it was on the brink of changing, which meant that mask wearing would be something new to hate each other over.

So glove up, mask up, and suck it up, because we're heading around the next bend. But if you're worried, don't be.

Donald Trump on March 31: "It's going to go away, hopefully at the end of the month and if not, it hopefully will be soon after that."

News Divisions
March 2020

Maddow

The Washington Post [1]
U.S. intelligence reports from January and February warned about a likely pandemic

The Daily Beast [2]
Sen. Kelly Loeffler Dumped Millions in Stock After Coronavirus Briefing

ProPublica [3]
Senator Dumped Up to $1.7 Million of Stock After Reassuring Public About Coronavirus Preparedness

NPR [4]
Burr Recording Sparks Questions About Private Comments On COVID-19

Politico [5]
DOJ seeks new emergency powers amid coronavirus pandemic

Hannity/Carlson

Gateway Pundit [1]
CBS News Caught Using Footage from an Italian Hospital to Describe Conditions in New York City (VIDEO)

The New York Times [2]
The U.S. Now Leads the World in Confirmed Coronavirus Cases

Judicial Watch [3]
Judicial Watch: House Lawyers for Adam Schiff Assert Privilege over Schiff Subpoenas of Impeachment Phone Records - Judicial Watch

Washington Examiner [4]
Los Angeles Times and Bloomberg News: Federal stockpile of N95 masks was depleted under Obama and never restocked

New York Post [5]
Florida man with coronavirus says drug touted by Trump saved his life

These are the top news links shared on Twitter in March by followers of Rachel Maddow versus followers of Sean Hannity or Tucker Carlson. Source: MIT Center for Constructive Communication

4

APRIL—
THE FIRST DROP

THE FIRST TIME I REALLY WORRIED ABOUT THE SPREAD OF THE VIRUS IN MY own community was when I read about a cruise ship that had docked in San Francisco, where its passengers were allowed to offload—*after* which there was a mad scramble to track, trace, and test them. By that point, cruise ships had been transformed into floating petri dishes of misery, and disembarking passengers represented a threat to communities that suddenly went beyond having to occasionally interact with a guy wearing Bermuda shorts, white shoes, and black socks. Unwanted on shore, there were passengers stranded for weeks at sea, and crews who would be stuck on mostly empty boats for months.

It wasn't particularly surprising that the masters of these floating hotels were left disorganized, defenseless, and feeling like they were rearranging deck chairs on the Love Boat. It *was* surprising when we started hearing April mayday distress signals from a navy ship.

Captain Brett Crozier of the USS *Theodore Roosevelt*, faced with an outbreak of COVID-19 on his vessel, and a slow response to his request to dock and empty the ship in Guam, issued an email to his navy superiors (soon leaked to the *San Francisco Chronicle*) warning that quarantining ill sailors on the nuclear aircraft carrier was proving impossible. The US military chain of command doesn't generally include the media, and those at the top didn't appreciate having their chain yanked. Crozier was relieved of his command by acting US Navy secretary Thomas Modly.

After being cashiered, Crozier addressed his sailors, and the public got a look at several viral videos of the crew cheering and chanting his name as he departed the ship. A few days later, a recording of Acting Secretary Modly addressing the ship's crew was leaked. In the remarks, Modly criticized Crozier as being "too naive or too stupid" to know his email would be leaked. "So think about that when you cheer the man off the ship who exposed you to that . . . I understand you love the guy . . . But you're not required to love him." It wasn't a good look, and shortly after the remarks were made public, Modly was asked to tender his resignation. The person who relieved the captain of his duties for leaked remarks was let go because of his own leaked remarks. For a boat, the USS *Roosevelt* sure had a lot of leaks.

Thus concluded an absolutely brutal week for the military, already facing an enemy they were ill equipped to fight, and further sidelined by the administration's lack of foresight and ongoing management failures. This frustration was shared with me in an email from a friend in high places at the Pentagon.

> For me, the concern is acute. Millions of the citizens I am sworn to protect are about to have the worst weeks of their lives. I am helpless to ameliorate that, presently. So I am miserable.

Every part of this debacle was decidedly unmilitary. Captain Crozier should not have needed to send the letter. The letter should have never been leaked, and Crozier probably should have been more worried it would be. Crozier should not have been immediately relieved of his duties, if for no other reason than it was wildly obvious that such a move would create a media shitstorm. The cheering by Crozier's crew, while understandable and even inspiring, was not a good look in military circles. The navy, like so many other institutions of this era, should not have been led by an "acting" secretary, that acting secretary should not have made his senseless and wholly unprofessional comments about Crozier (especially to a crew that loved him), and those comments should not have been made public. And at a time when Americans needed strength and stability more than ever, we should not have been subjected to watching a branch of our armed forces being sucked, like everything else, into a never-ending reality show.

O captain, my captain, this is what happens when the chain of command begins with a guy who is off the chain. No one put a more accurate spin on the situation than a sailor who, about a minute into the recording of Modly's speech, could be heard yelling, "What the fuck?"

IT'S GO TIME

I was forced to jump on a few grenades of my own in early April. Unsurprisingly, the first call involved parental tech support. My dad needed an audiobook downloaded onto his iPad. Ordinarily, such a mission would be a breeze. But by this point, I hadn't been closer to my parents than their driveway.

I masked, face-shielded, and gloved up. As I pulled into my parents' driveway, my mom placed the iPad on her washing machine, opened the garage door, and quickly shuffled back into the house, where she gave me the signal. It was go time. I raced into the garage, gained access to the device, and with *Hurt Locker*–like speed and precision, downloaded the book, Clorox-wiped the iPad, and retreated to my vehicle where I gave my parents the all-clear sign. It was now safe to listen to Yuval Noah Harari's *Sapiens: A Brief History of Humankind*.

My brush with valor was short-lived. During a subsequent visit, a lifetime of needing to use the restroom in the wrong place at the wrong time caught up with me in my parents' driveway.

"Mom . . . "

"What's wrong, David?"

"Mom, I have to go to the bathroom, it's an emergency."

The exchange was one that had taken place a thousand times during my childhood, but never during a global pandemic, when it wasn't entirely impossible that my having to take a shit could expose my parents to a deadly virus.

Because of my dad's experience serving with the partisans, blowing up trains, and fighting Nazis in World War II, and my mom's experience dealing with five decades of my irritable bowel syndrome, both my parents remained calm. They quickly laid out a plan. They would unlock the front door and then hunker down in my sister's old bedroom at the far end of the house. I would then enter the front door, race downstairs, and use the bathroom at the extreme other end of the house, before using disinfectant wipes on everything as I retraced my steps like a serial killer departing a crime scene.

The mission seemed to work, although it would be another ten to fourteen days before I'd be sure that my bowel movement hadn't killed my parents.

EARTH TO AMERICA
April 2, 2020

The job losses that shook America in March, accelerated in April.

A staggering 6.6 million people applied for unemployment benefits last week as the coronavirus outbreak ravaged nearly every corner of the American economy, the Labor Department reported Thursday.

The speed and scale of the job losses are without precedent. In just two weeks, the pandemic has left nearly 10 million Americans out of work, more than in the worst months of the last recession. Until last month, the worst week for unemployment filings was 695,000 in 1982. (Ben Casselman and Patricia Cohen, *New York Times*)

But the story wasn't just about those who couldn't keep their jobs, it was also about those who couldn't stop working, regardless of the risks. Among them were those we had ignored, shunned, or even attacked as outsiders before the pandemic. Once it hit, they were suddenly called essential. That included Nancy Silva.

Ms. Silva, who has spent much of her life in the United States evading law enforcement, now carries a letter from her employer in her wallet, declaring that the Department of Homeland Security considers her "critical to the food supply chain."

"It's like suddenly they realized we are here contributing," said Ms. Silva, a 43-year-old immigrant from Mexico who has been working in the clementine groves south of Bakersfield, Calif. (Miriam Jordan, *New York Times*)

As an obsessive eater, maybe I'm biased, but I'd argue that food was as essential before the pandemic as it was during it. Nancy Silva was also essential before the pandemic. So when we stick a fork in the fruits of her labor, maybe it's also time to stick a fork in the political myth that she's some kind of threat to America.

KING PINHEADS

While three hundred million or so Americans under various lockdown orders may have felt like the whole country was in lockdown mode, it wasn't. At least not at airports, where people continued to land, including forty thousand Chinese travelers who were exempt from the much-touted China travel ban.

The lucky among us were stuck in our houses with too much time to kill, and apparently not enough decent television to watch. A Netflix show called *Tiger King* roared into our living rooms and sank its claws into the cultural zeitgeist. The show featured Joe Exotic, a freakish, snake oil–selling tiger tamer followed with cultlike allegiance by a group of otherwise unhirable employees who worked under the constant threat of avoidable death to win the favor of a population of wild animals by throwing them raw meat. Sometimes a metaphor just works.

SURGEON GENERALIZED ANXIETY

Roses are red, violets are blue, risk is low for the coronavirus, but high for the flu. That delightfully snappy poem came from the Twitter account of US surgeon general Jerome Adams back in February, at about the time China was building a pair of emergency hospitals in ten days. By the first week in April, Jerome Adams had a different view of things.

"This is going to be our Pearl Harbor moment, our 9/11 moment, only it's not going to be localized. It's going to be happening all over the country. And I want America to understand that . . . This is going to be the hardest and the saddest week of most Americans' lives." The Pearl Harbor analogy was a bit off. COVID-19 was not a surprise attack. We could see the arsenal headed our way for months, and by now, bombs had been blowing up all around us for a while. But it was nice that Adams was finally expressing the opinions of experts, and no longer rhyming.

A LETTER TO THE CITY

By the end of the first week of April, New York City had become the unrivaled epicenter of America's COVID-19 fight. Governor Cuomo delivered long, detailed, nationally televised press conferences. Doctors from UCSF and elsewhere traveled to the city to help with the onslaught. Patients lined hospital hallways, while in alleys, refrigerator truck compressors hummed their deadly tune as they quickly filled with bodies. I wrote this open letter to the city I love.

> I love New York.
>
> The Brooklyn Bridge is my favorite place in the world. When it was completed in 1883, it was the tallest structure in the city.
>
> I taught high school in Crown Heights during the riot years.
>
> My friend Elaine was my supervisor back then, and we once walked from SoHo to Coney Island. She died unexpectedly a couple of years ago, way too young, so my wife and I took the SFO red-eye to JFK, where I told Elaine's friends and family about our walk and that, for me, Elaine was New York City.
>
> I never get bored on the Circle Line.
>
> The subway is my happy place. I love knowing the lower level of the West Fourth Street Station is still going to hold the summer's humidity in October and that at the top of the stairs I'll be sweating more than the dudes playing hoops on Sixth.

My first day as an educator was as a substitute for a physics teacher who had been stabbed with a pencil trying to take away a student's Walkman.

After college, my dad and I were flying to my new life in New York so he could help me find an apartment, and on the way, I said, "You know, when I think about it, during the past few years, when I'd go to visit my friends on the East Coast, it was usually in Boston or Cambridge. Maybe I should live in Boston?"

My dad said, "Vait. You mean you're dragging me across the country and you don't even vant to live in this city?"

"No, New York will work."

The last time I was near the World Trade Center, a guy was selling peelers on the sidewalk. I bought one. I haven't been back to that spot since. Can't do it after 9/11. I know, I know. The memorial is well done. But I can't.

I probably looked at twenty-five apartments. The broker was walking the long way to each. My dad said, "You know he's walking these veird routes so vee only see the nice blocks?" I knew. We didn't mind.

In one building, the elevator was about 104 degrees. The super said it was the boiler in the basement. My dad asked, "Vhat are you doing down there, burning bodies?" The super didn't laugh.

Finally, an apartment found me. The landlady who lived on the main floor picked me for the upstairs unit because she was impressed my dad came for our "interview." She was an NYC lifer. After a half hour of instruction, I knew everything I needed to know.

I lived above an off-Broadway theater on Vandam. When I'd walk into my front door around showtime, I'd get yelled at for cutting the line.

You know that feeling a pigeon is going to fly right into you, but it never does? One's wing hit me in Washington Square Park. I still remembered the feeling a few decades later when my son was getting a chess lesson on a concrete table from a guy who was probably there the day I was winged. He charged me twenty for the lesson. I gave him forty. Bargain.

When I was young, and emotional, I wrote a poem called "Window Seat at Fanelli." Every time I go to New York City, I take a photo of the last original spot in SoHo and send it to my friend Mordy.

During my first weeks in New York City, there was a telephone strike. I didn't know a single person. My best friend was the city, and I'd walk for hours a day. I never asked myself, "Are we there yet?" I knew I was there, so I kept walking.

I was calling my parents from a pay phone on Spring near Sixth when Madonna, along with her entourage, walked over and dialed the phone next to mine. I hung up with my parents and called a friend back home. "Oh, it probably just looks *like her," he said. This was '89. She was arguably the most recognizable artist in the world. I should have stayed on the line with my parents.*

When you walked back then, without a smartphone, you didn't have your entire world in your pocket. It's like Springsteen sang, "When I'm out on the streets, I walk the way I wanna walk."

I was New York Dave. *Aside from the city, no one else but me even knew that guy.*

My friend Daniel and I used to go to Raoul's in SoHo wearing undershirts and baseball caps. We looked so out of place, they figured we must be someone. We'd talk a little too loud, referring to famous actors and directors by their first names, and they seemed to buy it. We'd just order a beer and ask for a basket of bread. And they gave it to us and let us keep the table as long as we wanted. You had to know Raoul's in the early '90s to know what we were pulling off. Right before the pandemic, I was in Soho eating a late-night second dinner at Raoul's with my wife and son. I told the story. By then, Daniel had become a successful television producer. The town is no more his town now than it was our town then. In New York City, there's only one star, only one power player worth a damn: the city itself.

You walk for an hour in New York and you'll hear twenty languages and visit several different countries. There are some people who see that as a problem. They don't know what America is all about.

I saw Bogosian doing his one-man show Sex, Drugs, Rock & Roll *and Anna Deavere Smith re-creating the Crown Heights riots in her one-woman show* Fires in the Mirror. *You'd leave the theater, and those shows would still be going on out in the streets.*

I once had a former student hide a bottle of champagne and some other items in a garbage can on the Brooklyn Heights Promenade so I could surprise my wife (then girlfriend) on Valentine's Day. It was snowing and freezing, but somehow I convinced her to walk the promenade with me. She was surprised. I had a tape recorder in the bag, and we listened to "Rhapsody in Blue" and drank the champagne. When we kissed, a guy passed by on cross-country skis. Like I said, it was pretty cold. A few years later, I proposed in the same spot.

A few years after that, my wife and I went to Brooklyn so I could walk that former student down the aisle.

I saw the play Fences *on Broadway, and when James Earl Jones threw down a bag of dry grass, some of it landed on my lap. Beat that.*

A colleague of mine was once beaten to a pulp jogging in Prospect Park on Halloween (yes, he knew *it was crazy to do that). He showed up to school to teach the next day. Best teacher I've ever seen. Once, when he was frustrated with a student's performance during a mock trial practice, he threw a chair out a window from his fifth-floor classroom. And it worked. Our mock trial team kicked ass, and no one ever told the principal who broke the window.*

Some mornings I'd be hungry for a bagel. So I'd walk a hundred and twenty blocks and get one near Columbia.

I watched a Super Bowl in a guy named Vito's basement in Bay Ridge. I did Jell-O shots out of a disposable tin pan, and on the way back, with a pretty good buzz, I stood at the very front of the subway and looked out the forward-facing window the whole way. It was my team, the 49ers, in the game. But this was my town.

It's a feeling. It's instantaneous and evergreen. Some people say you have to live in New York for ten years to be a New Yorker. Shit, it took me ten seconds.

I once saw Lou Reed play "Dirty Blvd." during a rehearsal in Letterman's studio. When I say New York, I know what the fuck I'm talking about.

In 1990, I got out of the subway on 125th to hear Mandela speak. It was the first time I'd ever really been aware of my skin. I could feel it. I was changed before Mandela took the mic. I felt my skin again the first day of teaching when the kids found out I was the sub, and one of them called me "Snowflake," before he and three-quarters of the class took off.

After fifteen minutes trying to make conversation with that physics class, I scribbled a note to God promising that if I made it through that day, I'd leave teaching, New York City, and the greater tri-state area forever. I made it through the day. But I didn't leave.

God understood. He knows New York too.

On weekends, I used to take a group of students to Manhattan for different outings—a Broadway show, ice-skating, a museum. It all started when I brought a few of them to see the Thanksgiving Day Parade and half of them were scared shitless walking through Central Park. These kids went to a bottom-five high school with metal detectors and security guards, and they were scared in Central Park.

Vesuvio Bakery is one of the most famous photo ops in the world. The bread was never that good. Anywhere else, that would be a disaster. On Prince Street, it sort of made sense.

One of my former students was an immigrant from Haiti who slept on the floor of her family's studio apartment. Today, she's the dean of a law school.

The school where I taught didn't have enough books for some of my English classes, so I'd buy them myself. This was before Amazon, so that meant walking to about six or seven bookstores to get enough copies. Is there a better way to spend a day?

When he seemed too small to do so, my son rowed me in a boat in Central Park. It was amazing. These days, when we're in the city, he and I head to the Lower East Side and eat pickles, knishes, and bialys like I did when I was young and alone. He's never called it the LES.

During my formative years, New York City was the best friend I had. Now it knows my wife and kids, and an older, grayer me who walks a little slower . . . but still pretty fast when I'm on those streets.

I'm across the country, but my arms are virtually locked around the Apple. My old friend is hurting. My friend is running out of air. I want New York to live, to thrive, and I want all those people off the gurneys in hospital hallways, out of their apartments, and back walking the greatest streets in the world.

I love New York.

A lot of current and former New Yorkers emailed to share their stories of the city, and to tell me that my open letter made them cry. But that wasn't true. They'd been crying already.

CHEESE STAKES
April 7, 2020

Wisconsin's primary would serve as a preview of how voters would be badgered throughout the year. The state opened fewer polling places than usual (like *way* fewer: Milwaukee typically has 180 polling sites, this time there were 5), voters were asked to risk their lives by mingling in long lines during the pandemic, and the Supreme Court ruled 5–4 that even though an understandable surge in absentee ballots resulted in delays, any returned after Election Day wouldn't be counted (not even those that weren't received by voters until after Election Day). Writing the dissenting opinion, Ruth Bader Ginsburg argued: "The Court's order, I fear, will result in massive disenfranchisement. A voter cannot deliver for postmarking a ballot she has not received." Long lines, a pandemic, curious court rulings, issues with the mail, and efforts by some to ensure low poll numbers in places where they'd grown displeased with demographic shifts . . . It was all enough for me to come up with my 2020 election rule of thumb: vote for those who want you to vote.

DR. DEMENTO

I will be unable to fully cover all the pseudoscience pushed by the White House due to strict space limitations set by my editor (he said to keep the book shorter than the Torah). But it's worth sharing a few examples to show why so many of the president's prescriptions left Americans feeling like they were getting a prostate exam in which the index finger made it all the way to their frontal lobe; which brings us to the case of hydroxychloroquine, an antimalaria drug pushed by a French doctor known for denying climate change and downplaying COVID-19, explaining, "I don't feel very concerned." The thread was picked up by Dr. Oz, who shared the quackery on Sean Hannity's show, and thus, inevitably, Trump bought in, ultimately pushing hydroxychloroquine more than Oxy was pushed by the Sacklers. So how did an ineffective drug get into American consciousness by way of Dr. Trump and his fellow White House scrubs? Malpractice, malpractice, malpractice.

On April 8, Bernie Sanders suspended his campaign, setting up a Trump-versus-Biden race for November.

JAIL BAIT

With social distancing available only in solitary confinement, jails and prisons quickly became viral hotbeds. Wardens and administrators looked to remove nonviolent prisoners from overcrowded institutions, and district attorneys from Philadelphia to San Francisco urged police departments to cut back on arresting low-level offenders.

Among those prisoners requesting an early release was pharma bro Martin Shkreli (serving seven years for fraud), who requested three months out of the joint to find a cure for COVID-19. "I am one of the few executives experienced in ALL aspects of drug development from molecule creation and hypothesis generation, to preclinical assessments and clinical trial design/target engagement demonstration, and manufacturing/synthesis and global logistics and deployment of medicines."

If for no other reason, they should have let him out because it would have been funny when he discovered hydroxychloroquine.

THIS ONE GOES TO UNLEAVEN

Proving that their administration could get anything wrong, the State Department wished "everyone a happy and healthy Passover! In Jewish tradition, Matzah, a flat unleavened bread eaten during the Passover holiday, is known as both the bread of faith and the bread of healing." According to the Haggadah, Matzah is the bread of *affliction*. According to family lore, it's the bread of *constipation*. The bread of healing? Not so much. In short, these crackers didn't know much about Matzah. (During 2020, I hid the afikomen in the truth, that way Trump would never find it.)

GOING TO THE MATTRESSES
April 10, 2020

During the 2008 financial crisis, I asked my dad how to best manage my finances. In addition to some expected tips, he told me to take a few grand out of the bank each week and hide the cash under my mattress. That week, I told my shrink that I was worried my dad was losing it, and I described the rather extreme advice he gave me. Without pausing, my shrink responded, "I've got thirty grand and a gun in a shoebox in my closet."

I was mindful of these conversations during the early pandemic. In the days after the shutdowns began, I made about twelve trips to various ATMs within easy driving distance and removed the max amount from each. Because I worried about banks failing and markets collapsing, I opened new accounts at various institutions and spread my savings among them. Like many Americans, I assumed the financial pain associated with an unprecedented hit to the economy would be felt, if not evenly, at least by all. But a few weeks into the COVID economy, it was clear that wasn't happening. As unemployment numbers went up, so did my stocks. I quickly recouped early pandemic losses on the way to what would become the best investment streak of my life.

The feds were printing money and pumping it into corporate America. Our communal dependence on the tech companies (where I tended to invest) was greater than ever. Commission-free investment apps like Robinhood became even more popular as work-from-home investors had more time to day-trade. There were other factors, but this is not a financial statement. It's a statement about an American moment when we thought we were all "in this together," but instead we found ourselves watching as the country's already insane wealth divide was exposed and expanded at a pace almost as breathtaking as the virus itself.

> **Dave Pell** ✔
> @davepell
>
> The main thing I miss during the quarantine is being able to visit my parents, 20 minutes away.
>
> Luckily, I can hear their TV from here, so it feels like I'm there.
>
> 10:06 PM · Apr 12, 2020 · 🐦 Twitter

THE LYIN' KING
April 12, 2020

Easter Sunday materialized. Trump's prediction that the virus would be under control didn't. For many in the reality-based world, 2020 was a year when it was hard to avoid the truth. So maybe this was the year that you watched a young child come to the realization that there's no Easter Bunny. (Our kids learned early, the year we ran out of time and forgot to boil the Sharpie-decorated eggs we used for the hunt.) These moments are temporarily bittersweet, but they quickly merge into an exciting rite of passage; a period of intellectual growth when we each peel away layers of childish, magical thinking, and we're gradually initiated into a world of reality, facts, and adulthood. But what if that transition never happened? As the AP reported, you'd get something like this: "Life-saving medical equipment was not stockpiled. Travel largely continued unabated. Vital public health data from China was not provided or was deemed untrustworthy. A White House riven by rivalries and turnover was slow to act. Urgent warnings were ignored by a president consumed by his impeachment trial and intent on protecting a robust economy that he viewed as central to his reelection chances."

In London, Boris Johnson, the first world leader to be hospitalized for COVID-19, was able to leave the hospital, after thanking health workers and explaining: "It could have gone either way."

I originally had a line here that made fun of England for being a wealthy, advanced country that couldn't even prevent its top leader from getting infected with COVID-19. But then later, I deleted it.

JESUS SAVES, GOVERNORS DON'T?

In Kansas, Governor Laura Kelly won a last-minute case in the state Supreme Court that confirmed her power to limit the size of Easter Sunday services in order to protect lives in her state. Her order and the court's decision were contentious, and the heated debate over religious gatherings would continue across the country throughout the pandemic. I never understood why congregation leaders would want to do more to endanger those in their community and beyond.

Jesus may have been resurrected. Your congregants? Probably not.

WHO'S ON FIRST
April 15, 2020

The decision is "a crime against humanity . . . Every scientist, every health worker, every citizen must resist and rebel against this appalling betrayal of global solidarity." So said Richard Horton, the editor in chief of the *Lancet* medical journal, as President Trump froze funding to the WHO.

While Trump looked to pass the buck on managing the health response, he had a different attitude when it came to doling out the $1,200 checks that were being sent out to struggling Americans. In an unprecedented move (let's save you some time reading and save me some time typing by just assuming every Oval Office move from here on out was *unprecedented*), the treasury ordered Trump's name printed on stimulus checks. (Luckily, they didn't bounce.)

Meanwhile, the health toll grew more ominous. The canaries in the toll mine in mid-April were nursing home residents and health care workers. At the Canterbury Rehabilitation & Healthcare Center in Richmond, Virginia, forty people had already died. Across the country, frontline health care workers, still begging for personal protective equipment, represented 10–20 percent of US virus cases.

BETTER DEAD THAN TREAD

While the toll on lives was building, the toll on jobs was here. In four weeks, twenty-two million Americans had filed jobless claims. And with the joblessness came the first stirrings of the anti-lockdown protests that would grow into an increasingly contentious and dangerous movement. In Michigan, Governor Gretchen Whitmer became a target of protesters and the president. The Operation Gridlock protest included honking cars, traffic jams, Trump supporters, small business owners who were calling for the quarantine rules to be relaxed, and of course, plenty of armed militia members. Also familiar were the chants of "Lock her up." It was like a Kid Rock concert, but with better music.

The movement led by militia groups, Proud Boys, anti-vaccinators, QAnon conspiracy theorists, and, of course, right-wing pundits wasn't merely a demand to reopen, it was a war against those with any connection to science. Among the unhinged ideas was the suggestion that Bill Gates, for years one of America's loudest voices warning of the risk of a pandemic, was supposedly part of a plot to use the virus to gain some kind of control over the globe.

In a 2015 speech, Bill Gates warned that the greatest risk to humanity was not nuclear war but an infectious virus that could threaten the lives of millions of people.

That speech has resurfaced in recent weeks with 25 million new views on YouTube—but not in the way that Mr. Gates probably intended. Anti-vaccinators, members of the conspiracy group QAnon and right-wing pundits have instead seized on the video as evidence that one of the world's richest men planned to use a pandemic to wrest control of the global health system. (Daisuke Wakabayashi, Davey Alba, and Marc Tracy, *New York Times*)

I blamed Gates for Word, PowerPoint, IE6, and Clippy, but when he started trying to save the world, I forgave him.

And the president, who should have been bolstering the state leaders who followed the science, was pouring gasoline on the MAGA-red embers with some all-cap tweeting.

LIBERATE MINNESOTA!
LIBERATE MICHIGAN!
LIBERATE VIRGINIA!

In Denver during a car-parade protest against lockdowns, freelance photojournalist Alyson McClaran captured indelible pictures of health workers mounting a silent protest. In one shot, a health worker stood in a crosswalk, dressed in his scrubs, arms behind his back, blocking an SUV with a yelling woman in a USA shirt leaning out of the passenger window holding a sign that read "Land of the Free."

As McClaran recalled in an interview with *Time*'s Maïa Booker: "I saw two nurses in the middle of the street. I took off running towards them and started firing away my camera, because they were blocking the road at a green light and everyone was screaming and honking at them, and those are the images that you see . . . I was at the right place at the right time. One thing I remember is the lady in the truck was yelling at the health worker to 'go back to China.'"

GOING MY WAY?

While those who took the virus seriously found themselves attacked by others who seemed to be goading it on, that wasn't the country's most pressing divide. Just weeks into the pandemic, it was clear that the virus wasn't creating an American story so much as it was uncovering a story that was there all along. In the first month or so of the pandemic, as more than twenty million Americans lost their jobs, American billionaires saw their fortunes increase by about 10 percent.

As the virus further split an already divided nation, President Trump saw an opportunity to further divide America from the rest of the world as he shut down immigration to the US in the name of saving American jobs.

LET THERE BE LIGHT WHERE THE SUN DON'T SHINE

They say that, aside from hydroxychloroquine, laughter is the best medicine. But no one was laughing after getting the *New York Times* notification that popped up on iPhones on April 22, 2020. "At a White House briefing, President Trump theorized—dangerously in the view of some experts—about the power of sunlight, ultraviolet light and household disinfectants to kill the coronavirus."

Chugging disinfectant is viewed as dangerous by *some* experts?

The president was not a doctor, but every afternoon, he played one on TV. And this time Doogie Howitzer went too far. America was strapped to a gurney and being wheeled, sans PPE, into an alternate universe.

See if you can make sense of this from the president of the United States:

> Supposing we hit the body with whether it's ultraviolet or just very powerful light? And [looking at Dr. Deborah Birx] I think you said that hasn't been checked but you're gonna test it . . . Then I see the disinfectant where it knocks it out in a minute, one minute. Is there a way we can do something like that by injection inside? Or almost a cleaning, 'cause you see it gets in the lungs and it does a tremendous number on the lungs. So it'd be interesting to check that. So you're going to have to use medical doctors but it sounds interesting to me, so we'll see, but the whole concept of the light. The way it kills it in one minute, that's pretty powerful.

Right up until the November election, Trump would insist that he was joking. So it's fair to ask, in the words of Led Zeppelin's Robert Plant: Does anyone remember laughter? Because no one among the viewing public, or in the room, was laughing; least of all Deborah Birx, whose expression looked how America felt. You could almost see the Stockholm syndrome drain from her face.

Executives at Reckitt Benckiser, which owns brands including Lysol, weren't laughing either. The company felt compelled to issue a statement: "As a global leader in health and hygiene products, we must be clear that under no circumstance should our disinfectant products be administered into the human body (through injection, ingestion or any other route)."

CNN ran with the headline: *Lysol Maker: Please Don't Drink Our Cleaning Products.*

Maybe something about this moment could have been almost funny if this make-believe doctor wasn't *also* the president of a country that had redefined American carnage with what was by now nearly sixty thousand COVID deaths. These daily press conferences were a bad show, and a dangerous show. Again, one had to wonder why cable news networks and other outlets continued to endanger lives by playing them live. It was an unforgivable case of media malpractice.

> **Dave Pell** ✔
> @davepell
>
> This all would have been a lot easier if he told us to drink the Lysol three and a half years ago.
>
> 2:04 PM · Apr 26, 2020 · 🐦 Twitter

ONE

With a population of over 8 million residents, New York City is America's most densely packed city. It sits in a state of over 20 million people who had suffered more than 282,000 COVID-19 cases and 16,000 deaths by this point in the pandemic. The state has 214 hospitals and a health sector that employs well over a million people. With numbers like these, can a single N95 mask possibly make a difference? It turns out the answer is yes. Dennis Ruhnke, a retired farmer from Kansas, had five masks in storage, and he sent one to Governor Cuomo's office, along with a handwritten letter: "I am a retired farmer hunkered down in N.E. Kansas with my wife who has but one lung and occasional problems with her remaining lung. We are in our 70s now and frankly I am afraid for her . . . Enclosed find a solitary N-95 mask left over from my farming days. It has never been used . . . If you could, could you please give this mask to a nurse or a doctor in your city." Cuomo read the letter and held up the mask during his daily press briefing: "You want to talk about a snapshot of humanity. You have five masks, what do you do? Do you keep all five? Do you hide the five masks, do you keep them for yourself or others? No, you send one mask. You send one mask to New York for a doctor or nurse. How beautiful is that? How selfless is that? How giving is that? It's that love, that courage, that generosity of spirit that makes this country so beautiful. And it's that generosity for me makes up for all the ugliness that you see. Take one mask, I'll keep four."

QUARANTINE 101
April 26, 2020

In the first week under the Bay Area's shutdown order, at a time of the evening that used to be rush hour, my beagles and I walked up the street from my house and onto a Highway 101 overpass that stretches across the top of the Waldo Grade, just up the road from the Golden Gate Bridge. I snapped a photo that was so rare that a version of it printed on metal is hanging across from me as I write this. What made the photo so unusual? I managed to capture a shot in which a long stretch of one of the Bay Area's busiest highways had no cars traveling in either direction.

Weeks later, as shelter-in-place exhaustion had set in, that same stretch of road looked almost normal. And this fatigue was more pronounced in some places than others, especially those where state and local leaders refused to take the virus seriously.

One group of people who had no problem understanding the gravity of what we faced was coroners. Michael Fowler, Dougherty County coroner, talked to the *Washington Post*'s Eli Saslow about the reopening of Georgia.

> I'm always driving, going back-and-forth between nursing homes, the hospital, and the morgue. All these roads should be empty if you ask me. But now I see people out running errands, rushing back into their lives, and it's like: "Why? What reason could possibly be good enough?" Sometimes, I think about stopping and showing them one of the empty body bags I have in the trunk. "You might end up here. Is that worth it for a haircut or a hamburger?" . . . I don't believe in getting hysterical. It doesn't do any good. This is a numbers-and-facts job. But we have numbers and facts that are screaming out by themselves.

Donald Trump on April 28: "This is going to go away. And whether it comes back in a modified form in the fall, we'll be able to handle it."

MEAT BY-PRODUCTS

Nowhere was the way we treated so-called essential workers more troubling than along the disassembly lines of America's meatpacking plants. In South

Dakota, Smithfield, one of the nation's largest pork processors, was forced to shut down one of its facilities for two weeks after its workers accounted for half the state's total number of coronavirus cases. Meanwhile, Reuters reported that "at a Wayne Farms chicken processing plant in Alabama, workers recently had to pay the company 10 cents a day to buy masks to protect themselves from the new coronavirus."

After being notably hesitant in his use of the Defense of Production Act, Trump now used it to classify meat plants as essential infrastructure that must remain open. The federal government and the meat plant owners were playing a game of chicken, one that was turning meat-processing plants into slaughterhouses. By the end of April, twenty meat-processing plants had closed, seventeen workers had died of COVID-19.

It's worth noting that the president's most applicable experience was bankrupting Trump Steaks. How do you succeed at protecting workers from a complex challenge when you failed at selling red meat to Americans?

The meat industry lobbied for and got waivers to keep plants open even as people were dying. They also took advantage of the lobbying efforts to enable more plants to speed things up. We'd later learn that the faster the lines, the faster the viral spread. In the final weeks of the Trump administration, the meat industry was in the process of lobbying to make the pandemic speed increases permanent, and by early 2021, speed caps at pork plants had been removed.

Trump also issued an executive order that prevented plants from being held liable for employee deaths. At a Tyson Foods plant in Iowa, the balance between meat and treating humans as meat by-products was clear.

The county health department had recorded 1,031 coronavirus infections among Tyson employees—more than a third of the workforce. Some are on ventilators. Three have died, according to Tyson.

Sheriff Tony Thompson, who is based in Waterloo, asked: "Which is more important? Your pork chops, or the people that are contracting Covid, the people that are dying from it?" (Ana Swanson, David Yaffe-Bellany, and Michael Corkery, *New York Times*)

The answer came quickly. The pork plant reopened days after shutting down. What was more important, pork or people? This was Donald Trump's America. Bet on the white meat.

Donald Trump on April 29: "It's going to go. It's going to leave. It's going to be gone. It's going to be eradicated."

News Divisions
April 2020

Maddow

The New York Times 1
He Could Have Seen What Was Coming: Behind Trump's Failure on the Virus

Politico 2
Trump owed tens of millions to Bank of China

The Washington Post 3
White House rejects bailout for Postal Service battered by coronavirus

The Washington Post 4
The U.S. was beset by denial and dysfunction as the coronavirus raged

NPR 5
Federal Support For Coronavirus Testing Sites End As Peak Nears

Hannity/Carlson

The Detroit News 1
Democrats plan to censure lawmaker who credited Trump for COVID-19 recovery

The Washington Times 2
Hydroxychloroquine rated 'most effective therapy' by doctors for coronavirus: Global survey

The Epoch Times 3
Spygate: No Chance Obama Did Not Know—Tom Fitton

Judicial Watch (via Youtube) 4
Judicial Watch: How Comey Ambushed/Spied On Trump at His Infamous Trump Tower Meeting! | Tom Fitton

The Wall Street Journal 5
Opinion | Schiff's Secret Transcripts

These are the top news links shared on Twitter in April by followers of Rachel Maddow versus followers of Sean Hannity or Tucker Carlson.
Source: MIT Center for Constructive Communication

5

MAY— THE DOUBLE HELIX

The first thing you see in the vertical cell phone video filmed through the windshield of a moving car is a black mailbox posted on one of several well-groomed lawns that frame a tree-lined street in the Satilla Shores area of Brunswick, Georgia. Six seconds later, a jogger named Ahmaud Arbery, wearing a white shirt, comes into view as he runs along the left side of the street. At around ten seconds in, you can see Arbery approaching a white pickup truck parked in the middle of the road. The video bounces around showing the vehicle's dashboard and the side of the road as you hear some yelling in the background. At twenty-one seconds, Arbery can be seen running around the front of the truck. The driver's door is open, and there's one man on the street and another standing in the bed of the pickup. A shot. Arbery struggles with the driver of the truck. At the twenty-five-second mark, a second shot.

Later, a wooden cross covered with red, white, and blue flowers would be driven into the dirt beneath one of those lawns along that tree-lined street in Georgia. It was placed there by Ahmaud Arbery's mother, at the spot her twenty-five-year-old son died after suffering three gunshot wounds while out on his daily jog.

The video that showed what looked like the hunting of an innocent Black man shocked Americans into an awareness of a crime that had actually taken place several months before. Before the video, no charges had been brought in the case. After the video, and the public outcry that ensued (including comments from President Trump: "My heart goes out to the parents and to the loved ones of the young gentleman. It's a very sad thing." And Joe Biden: "The video is clear: Ahmaud Arbery was killed in cold blood."), three arrests were made, and Ahmaud Arbery's name, the grainy video, the white pickup truck, the shots, and that tree-lined street had been etched into our communal memory of 2020.

Arbery took his last steps on February 23. But in May, whether we knew it or not, Americans were stepping toward another historic moment—when millions of people locked down in their homes would pour into the streets of big cities and small towns. For months, our lives and news feeds had been dominated by the novelty of an all-consuming novel virus. A new chapter in America's oldest story was coming around the corner.

OPEN WOUND

A large group of Black and Latino men stormed city hall—many armed with long guns and other weapons, wearing military-style clothing, and hiding behind face masks—where they screamed at law enforcement officers, waved guns in the air, and demanded to speak with public officials. The media took the event in stride, and the president lauded the demonstrators as very good people, and urged government officials to try to make a deal with them.

That scenario is, of course, unthinkable. But if you take out the racial and ethnic profiles of the gun-wielders, it's exactly what happened in Michigan. Meanwhile, at the Reopen Illinois gathering, a woman held up a sign that read: *Arbeit macht frei*. That's the slogan displayed above the entrance of Auschwitz, and translates as "Work will set you free."

Despite the protests, a huge percentage of Americans (93 percent according to one survey from Harvard Kennedy School, Northeastern University, and Rutgers University) did not think the economy should be reopened and supported social distancing measures. But they weren't riding through the streets with machine guns. And they didn't have an American president on their side.

GUIDANCE SUGGESTED

The confusion at the top led to confusion all the way down, all compounded by the fact that we still weren't quite sure of best practices. Dave Eggers lampooned the Trump administration's chaotic messaging in a *New York Times* op-ed, with an imagined dialogue between an average American and the powers that be.

> **People**: No one's giving us this information.
>
> **Answer**: *"Well, you know how we're stretching out the cases over a longer period of time? Flattening the curve? We're also flattening the truth. So just stay inside, and you'll be fine. Order stuff online. Support your local restaurant."*
>
> **P**: Whew. OK. We can do that.
>
> **A**: *"But do so knowing that you are putting the lives of everyone at risk— the cooks, the clerks, the delivery people. I'm actually a bit shocked by your selfishness and the cavalier way you're sacrificing the lives of people who have no choice but to expose themselves to grave danger during a pandemic."*
>
> **P**: It sounds like you're saying we shouldn't order stuff to be delivered.
>
> **A**: *"You shouldn't. Unless you want local businesses to die."*

In other countries, people seemed to have a clearer perception of the steps to take to manage the virus. But why was this the case when America's CDC was known as a world leader?

The AP gave us a clue: "The Trump administration shelved a document created by the nation's top disease investigators with step-by-step advice to local authorities on how and when to reopen restaurants and other public places during the still-raging coronavirus outbreak. The 17-page report by a Centers for Disease Control and Prevention team, titled *Guidance for Implementing the Opening Up America Again Framework*, was researched and written to help faith leaders, business owners, educators and state and local officials as they begin to reopen."

THE BIRTHDAY OY
May 5, 2020

"I don't understand vhy people aren't out protesting in the streets. Vhy are they letting this guy get away with it?" That was my dad's constant refrain. But today was his birthday, and the truth was, he probably wished he could be the one out on the streets himself, or at least out of the house, which was the last place he wanted to spend his ninety-sixth. Up until 2020, my dad never missed a day of exercise (whatever his body would allow, from soccer as a kid, to tennis when I was growing up, to golf when tennis was too hard on the joints, to a daily walk when carrying a golf bag for nine holes became too much), and he rarely missed a day at the office. Like it did for many older Americans, the pandemic changed all that. What could feel like home arrest for younger Americans felt like it could become a life sentence for older ones. My dad's usual walking route had taken him along a flat, manageable, bay-front path near his house. But that path, because it was only six feet wide and didn't allow for proper distancing, had been closed. So like many of us on our 2020 birthdays, he had to settle for a family video conference. (Forty minutes of phone support to set up my parents' Zoom, ten minutes of Zooming.)

In Israel, the Jewish Agency facilitated a unique way for loved ones to visit their older relatives who were sheltering in place in a high-rise and unable to receive visitors as usual. They lifted family members to their windows using a crane. If my sisters and I had tried this with my parents, they would have said it was a sweet gesture but they were about to have dinner and watch *The 11th Hour with Brian Williams*, so it wasn't an ideal time for a visit.

MASK ME ANYTHING
May 6, 2020

President Trump visited a Honeywell plant wearing goggles. But he wasn't wearing a mask. Why did this moment stick out? Because the Phoenix plant he was visiting was making N95 medical-grade masks. It was part of an effort to make up for lost time, since many hospitals were begging for personal protective equipment. As the president and his chief of staff Mark Meadows toured the plant maskless, a song blared in the background. It was Guns N' Roses' cover of "Live and Let Die."

When it came to mask advice, it wouldn't be until October that many of us would see the headline we'd been waiting for.

October of 1918:

WEAR A MASK AND SAVE YOUR LIFE.

That directive, originally issued by the Red Cross, and featured in the *San Francisco Chronicle*, is just one clue that experts have understood the value of mask wearing to prevent the spread of airborne illnesses for quite some time. The fact that doctors tend to wear masks provides another piece of evidence, and the *Chronicle* mentioned that aspect as well: "Doctors wear them. Those who do not wear them get sick. The man or woman or child who will not wear a mask now is a dangerous slacker."

But then, as now, there was resistance to mask wearing. Some of that resistance was organized, including a group known as the Anti-Mask League of San Francisco (Trump was born just a century too late to find some support in SF). The objections to masks during the Spanish flu pandemic will sound all too familiar to those who suffered through the coronavirus: the masks were uncomfortable, the masks didn't work, the mask ordinances were an infringement upon freedoms and civil liberties.

But then, as now, experts made the argument that wearing a mask was not only a benefit to the wearer, they also could lower the risk posed to those with whom the wearer came into contact. Then, as now, not wearing a mask didn't make you a slacker. It made you an asshole.

It's worth noting that the leader of the 2020 American anti-mask league was the president of the United States. He was at least somewhat aware of the Spanish flu era, because he referred to it often, though he continually got the year wrong, calling the 1918 flu the *1917* flu. Maybe it's because the film *1917* had recently won a best picture Oscar. But this error was especially notable since Trump's own grandfather died of the flu. In 1918.

While the resistance wouldn't go away (and often came from the top), there were plenty of Americans who got the memo on masks as soon as the scientists told them it was a good idea to wear one. By early April, Etsy CEO Josh Silverman reported that consumers were searching the site for masks an average of nine times per second and there were already more than twenty thousand sellers on that one platform who were ready to oblige them. Soon, it seemed like every brand, large and small, was making masks. Yet those who resisted, persisted.

I can fully understand those who felt an economic urgency to get back to work. But I'll never fully understand how wearing a mask when in public was seen as some unholy liberty infringement. When I wore a mask and saw others around me doing the same, I felt a sense of patriotic unity. That feeling, like every other feeling in 2020, pissed off half the country. Maybe I'm a bit biased on this topic since I look better in a mask. During the peak of COVID, for the first time in my adult life, I was getting second looks by women at my local grocery store. They say some people have a face for radio. I guess I have a face for pandemic.

Chiming in on the mask debate, Fox News's Laura Ingraham argued: "Control over large populations is achieved through fear and intimidation and suppression of free thought." It's amazing that Ingraham could spew this nonsense and suppress her own laughter. By now, we all knew that control over large populations could only be achieved when a lie machine masking itself as a news network aligned with a criminal administration to so warp reality that its viewers would happily inhale death.

The most fantastically bizarre mask trend from 1918 was that, either as protest, or as an act of addiction, some people would cut holes in their mask to smoke. If I've said it once I've said it a thousand times. The day my lungs aren't strong enough to smoke through my mask, I'm switching to edibles.

At one point during the pandemic, my son asked me if I thought there'd be a World War III. I answered that in some ways I thought the fight of humanity versus the coronavirus was a sort of world war. But I couldn't explain why some humans seemed to be on the side of the germ.

THE PHONY EXPRESS

"Postal workers are the heart and soul of this institution, and I will be honored to work alongside them and their unions." So claimed Louis DeJoy, a businessman, Republican donor, and fundraiser from North Carolina, as he was tapped by President Trump to be the new postmaster general.

At the time, even the cynics assumed this move mostly had to do with raising stamp prices or taking the postal service private.

MIKE DROP

May 7, 2020

The Justice Department had charged former national security advisor Michael Flynn with lying to investigators during the Mueller Russia investigation. Flynn pled guilty to the crime.

So it was unusual to say the least when the Justice Department, now headed by Bill Barr, petitioned the court to drop the charges the Justice Department had brought.

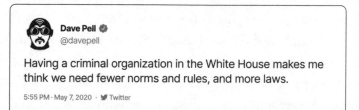

> **Dave Pell** ✓
> @davepell
>
> Having a criminal organization in the White House makes me think we need fewer norms and rules, and more laws.
>
> 5:55 PM · May 7, 2020 · 🐦 Twitter

When asked during a televised interview by Catherine Herridge of CBS: "How will history look back on your decision to drop charges against Flynn?" Barr responded: "Well, history is written by the winners. So it largely depends on who's writing the history."

While we can debate whether that comment sounded fascist, it was definitely at least authoritarian-curious.

Barr's comments to CBS reminded me of another quote about history.

If you win, you need not have to explain.

—Adolf Hitler

Even if the quotes are similar, we shouldn't associate the two men. Besides, Napoleon Bonaparte's quote on history is much more apt. "History is a set of lies agreed upon."

Days after Barr's move to free Flynn of charges, more than 1,900 former Justice Department employees called on Barr to resign as attorney general.

THE MOUTH THAT ROARED

It took three and a half years for anyone to find the perfect way to parody Donald Trump. In the end, it was longtime comedian and creative Sarah Cooper, who, with one of her first TikTok videos, went crazy viral with fifteen million views, leading to internet fame, countless articles, invitations to top talk shows, and eventually a popular Netflix special.

What was her strategy?

She lip-synched Trump. We saw her mouth and expressions. We heard his commentary, word for word. Cooper had shown that the hard part about parodying Trump was that he was a parody of himself in real time. When someone suggests hitting the body with UV light or using disinfectant inside of your body, the best parody is to simply play it back.

As Cooper explained to the *Atlantic*'s Shirley Li: "This is the emperor without his clothes, because when you see Trump, and he's behind that podium with the presidential seal, and he has people nodding behind him, you might think that what he's saying makes sense. But you take all of that away, and you have those words coming out of my mouth? It just brings to light even more how ridiculous it is."

That's what Cooper did, and it worked. And worked and worked. It was funny. But it was also a perfect illustration of the political divide. Half of America was laughing their ass off at the exact same words the other half was willing to bet their life on.

DIVIDED SOME FALL

Over the course of a few weeks, schools closed across the country and the world. According to the UN, schools had shut down in-person learning for 90 percent of the world's students. I'm a board member of a San Francisco nonprofit called 826 Valencia. Like many nonprofit organizations, 826 had to pivot in 2020. In our case, it was from providing writing instruction, tutoring, and general inspiration via in- and after-school programs to being an organization that helped get kids set up for extra help over the internet. What the staff learned right away was that our students, mostly economically challenged Latino and Black kids, almost instantly fell behind, many of them having to share laptops or connectivity with friends or neighbors. These stories were a stark contrast to my own kids' experience in a house with high-speed broadband and enough laptops that we could use old ones as doorstops. My daughter's school actually required kids to use the school-issued Chromebooks. It was a metaphor for the whole education system. One district has so many laptops that they can decide which ones should be used by students, while another district has no laptops and often no high-speed connectivity.

In the *New York Daily News*, Stephanie Sun, who teaches at a charter high school in Bushwick, Brooklyn, shared the story of one of her students.

> Of the thousands of students I've taught in my 10-year career, Natalie is the brightest, sweetest and purest. She shines in my Advanced Placement English class, pushing the thinking of her peers while deftly articulating her own ideas. A relentless hard worker, she juggles two other AP classes, honors math and extracurriculars. Outside of school, she finds time to help her mom, an immigrant from Ecuador, sell Icees from a cart in downtown Brooklyn, while at home she translates bills and documents for her . . . Natalie's family doesn't have reliable internet access at home . . . A few days ago, I called the College Board, which administers AP exams, desperate to find a solution. Their suggestion: She should try to take the test sitting outside a McDonald's.

The broadband divide was something that should have brought people together. If people without decent access in rural America got together with the people without decent access in urban areas, you'd have a political force that could demand change.

That's why it was so vital for those who didn't want such a political force to exist to keep those two groups hating on each other. And without political power, a student like Natalie would have to get her Wi-Fi with a side of fries.

While broadband access could have long-lasting impacts on the kids holding the short end of the Ethernet cable, there was another divide in May that was as urgent as life and death. By now, it was clear that the pandemic was taking a deadlier toll on those we referred to as essential, and a whole lot of those essential workers were people of color.

When it came to calls to reopen (or LIBERATE!) America, it was worth paying attention to who was doing the dying.

The divide between the haves and the used-to-haves also expanded. During April, more than twenty million Americans lost their jobs. And the makers of the $2,200 Peloton home exercise bike couldn't make them fast enough to satisfy demand.

AMERICA FIRST IN BEING WORST?

I'm no expert on international relations, but those who are have told me that America has taken three devastating hits to its superpowerdom in the twenty-first century. First, George W. Bush's disastrous Iraq War that was based on false pretenses and was mismanaged so dramatically that it destabilized the region and triggered the rise of ISIS. Second, the self-imposed financial crash of 2008. Third, the election of Donald Trump.

Perhaps none of those would do as much damage to America's leadership role in the world as the administration's response to COVID-19. Forget trying to lead the world, we couldn't even help ourselves.

MILLER CROSSING

The first somewhat well-known member of the administration to get COVID-19 was Pence spokesperson and Stephen Miller wife Katie Miller. Miller was with the vice president, delivering personal protective equipment to a nursing home in Arlington, Virginia, where *Las Vegas Review-Journal* reporter Debra Saunders noticed her cough, and her subsequent joke that she didn't have the coronavirus. The next day, Miller was removed from Air Force Two after a positive test.

With someone this close to the top getting the virus, the administration immediately got religion, took the pandemic seriously, and began to advise the rest of the country to do the same. Psych! Here's what really happened.

Mere hours after Vice President Mike Pence's press secretary tested positive for COVID-19, he was set to meet with a group of food industry executives who had gathered for a roundtable discussion in West Des Moines, Iowa. But before Pence joined them on the stage, someone came in and asked all five guests to remove their masks. (Daniel Politi, *Slate*)

MOTHER CAN BE A MOFO
May 11, 2020

The pressure to open the economy was coming on strong, and coming from the top. Logic suggested that to reopen the economy, a country first had to flatten the viral curve. In America, opening the economy and flattening the curve were pitted against one another, all without a clear national plan.

Dr. Frieden, the former C.D.C. director: "Every day, I look at the two models for approaching this," he said. "The China model, which is to use the world's most authoritarian regime and best digital tracking system to hunt down and stop every case and then wait for a vaccine. So far, it's working."

By contrast, he said, Sweden is trying to achieve "herd immunity" by letting young, healthy people become infected at what they hope will be slow, steady rates. Primary schools are open, higher ones are closed, everyone is asked to be careful in public and older adults are asked to stay home.

Israel is roughly following Sweden's model, Dr. Frieden said, just as Asian countries are roughly following China's.

"And then," he added, "there's the American approach, which is: 'What the hell—I heard something on Fox News. Let's try it!'" . . .

Having 50 states and more territories do competing and uncoordinated experiments in reopening is "daring Mother Nature to kill you or someone you love," Dr. Frieden said. "Mother Nature bats last, and she bats a thousand." (Donald G. McNeil Jr., *New York Times*)

LET'S AGREE TO AGREE

At this point, you might have the idea that social distancing and mask wearing were ideas that split the country down the middle. Not so. According to a *Washington Post* poll, America's state of mind was remarkably united across geographies and income levels. *WaPo*'s Greg Sargent shared some of the surprising results: "By 78 percent to 22 percent, Americans believe it is 'necessary' for people in their communities to stay at home as much as possible . . . Fifty-eight percent of Americans overall say current restrictions on businesses are 'appropriate,' vs. only 21 percent who say they are 'too restrictive.' What about wearing masks, which is supposed to be prompting the latest culture war? This war doesn't really exist, either. By 80 percent to 20 percent, Americans overall say it's 'necessary' for people in their communities to wear a mask when coming close to others."

It's true that, in the case of a viral disease, 20 percent of people not wearing masks can cause a lot of problems for the 80 percent who are, but, compared to what it felt like, we weren't particularly divided. It wouldn't have taken much to pull us closer together on the issue of staying farther apart.

Instead, the White House worked to deepen the divide, with the assistance of the reopen drumbeat now being pounded nonstop by Fox News. This was happening even as Fox Corporation chief operating officer John Nallen issued a memo extending the stay-at-home order for their own offices.

Of course, Fox News wasn't alone in spreading misinformation. The more outlandish material (made more urgently dangerous by the pandemic) was being spread through social media by relatively unorganized groups under the umbrella of QAnon.

The power of the internet was understood early on, but the full nature of that power—its ability to shatter any semblance of shared reality, undermining civil society and democratic governance in the process—was not. The internet also enabled unknown individuals to reach masses of people, at a scale Marshall McLuhan never dreamed of. The warping of shared reality leads a man with an AR-15 rifle to invade a pizza shop. It brings online forums into being where people colorfully imagine the assassination of a former secretary of state. It offers the promise of a Great Awakening, in which the elites will be routed and the truth will be revealed. It causes chat sites to come alive with commentary speculating that the coronavirus pandemic may be the moment QAnon has been waiting for. (Adrienne La-France, the *Atlantic*)

Conspiracy theories were nothing new. But the internet removed the guardrails, and the Trump election in 2016 proved there was something to gain and apparently little to lose from sparking new falsehoods or pouring gasoline on those that already smoldered.

Dave Pell ✓
@davepell

Who to believe?

The experts who have spent a lifetime studying infectious diseases or a reality show star who lies every time he speaks?

7:25 AM · May 3, 2020 · 🐦 Twitter

If, in the middle of May, someone had a magic fire extinguisher that could quell the flames of disinformation and give Americans a clear view of what was being said by the scientific experts and broadcast through mainstream news outlets, we would have seen that they were getting the story right. The novel coronavirus wasn't all that novel anymore. Distancing was necessary. Masks were necessary. A state-by-state or county-by-county piecemeal plan wouldn't be enough. We needed a national plan. There was near-universal agreement on what this national plan needed to look like. There were near-universal warnings about what would happen if we didn't nationalize the solution. And we were told, quite clearly, about the devastating downside of letting our guard down too early.

Scientists were doing their jobs. Journalists interested in covering the truth were remarkably consistent.

But there was another force at work. Science, truth, and reality had been politicized at the very moment when they pointed toward the only way off of this miserable ride.

SHOTS AND PRAYERS

It was an early result. It hadn't yet been peer reviewed. And the sample size was only eight people. But very first results from a company called Moderna that was using genetic material called mRNA (never before used in an approved vaccine) provided some promising results, as it caused an immune response in all eight volunteers.

In another vaccine trial, Oxford and AstraZeneca started recruiting up to ten thousand volunteers to begin trials.

Speaking of untested remedies, President Trump announced that he was taking his favorite one (no, thankfully not disinfectant, hydroxychloroquine) as a preventative measure. "I started taking it, because I think it's good. I've heard a lot of good stories." My first guess was that he had a stake in the drug. The only other two options were that: He was lying. Or he was taking something he shouldn't be taking because he didn't understand any of this. Maybe it was both: he was lying about something he knew nothing about.

Donald Trump on the US leading the world in COVID-19 cases: "I view it as a badge of honor . . . Really, it's a badge of honor. When we have a lot of cases. I don't look at that as a bad thing. I look at that as, in a certain respect, as being a good thing because it means our testing is much better."

Donald Trump, May 14: "When you test, you have a case. When you test, you find something is wrong with people. If we didn't do any testing we would have very few cases."

CHALLAH BACK, Y'ALL

Historians will note that during the first two decades of the twenty-first century, no biomolecule consisting of carbon, hydrogen, and oxygen atoms was more relentlessly maligned than the once-mighty carbohydrate. From Paleo, to Keto, to the Whole30, the carbohydrate was under near constant attack; and taking the brunt of the war on carbs was anything loaf-like, from biscuits to baguettes to buns.

But then, faced with a pandemic we could barely process, humans returned to their pantries in search of processed grains. Almost overnight,

America's carb footprint expanded dramatically, and nowhere was that rise more evident than on the lightly dusted customer service phone at King Arthur Flour, where sales increased by as much as 600 percent seemingly overnight.

I never made bread. We're more of a GrubHub family. In fact, because of my concerns about the lung-attacking virus making the rounds, I had even quit my decades-long habit of getting baked. But I never stopped believing in carbs, and I never stopped eating them either. It was nice to no longer be going against the grain.

After asking her employees to check their math on King Arthur's growing demand, CEO Karen Colberg answered her company's calling: "During a crisis there are a lot of problems to solve, and you won't be able to solve them all. We decided the one we had to solve was how to get more all-purpose flour to consumers."

It was the yeast they could do.

STRIP TEASE

After a short break, Vegas was set to reopen with sanitized dice, disinfected chips, hand sanitizer, touchless check-ins, and at the Venetian, masked gondoliers serenading passengers from an appropriate distance. What wouldn't visitors find? Buffets, poker, and a mask requirement for guests. So the question was: Were you willing to bet your life? Las Vegas sure hoped so, because the city's economy was one of the hardest hit in the country. Yet the risk of opening too early and taunting a virus that never bluffs was not theirs alone, because what happens in Vegas gets on a plane and goes home to communities around the world.

JACINDA VINCI CODE

If Vegas was looking for a pit boss to reopen safely, they should have tried to hire Jacinda Ardern. As a thirty-nine-year-old mother (and prime minister of New Zealand), Ardern had already garnered international attention for the combination of strength and empathy she'd displayed in response to the 2019 Christchurch terrorist attacks. When the pandemic hit, she used a similar combination of qualities to explain the logic of shutting down now in order to be able to reopen safely later.

There will be plenty of books, courses, and *Frontline* episodes about the leaders who got the pandemic wrong. But it's just as important—both for lessons learned and our sanity—to focus on leaders who got it right. That's what we saw in New Zealand (by this point in the pandemic, I would have settled for a slightly used Zealand).

COOPER UNION

May 25, 2020

Of all the things I expected to go viral during 2020, bird-watching was not high on the list. But on May 25, in a section of Central Park known as the Ramble, Amy Cooper (a Caucasian dog owner) was asked by Christian Cooper (a Black bird-watcher) to leash her dog. When she refused, Christian Cooper called the dog over for a treat. And that's when things went full 2020.

Amy told Christian not to touch her dog. Christian pulled out his phone and started to record. As he explained: "That's when I started video recording with my iPhone, and when her inner Karen fully emerged and took a dark turn."

Amy responded by threatening to call the police. "I'm calling the cops . . . I'm gonna tell them there's an African American man threatening my life." After dialing 911, she said, "There is an African American man—I am in Central Park—he is recording me and threatening myself and my dog. Please send the cops immediately!"

Christian Cooper's video was shared on Twitter by his sister, and thus the most infamous bird-watching dispute of all time fowled the internet.

Amy Cooper was instantly infamous, widely ridiculed, and fired from her job at Franklin Templeton; and she was later charged and arraigned for filing a false police report. She temporarily became the personification of how racists treat Black people with suspicion, and how police react differently depending on which race is placing the call.

Christian Cooper opted not to participate in the misdemeanor case against Amy Cooper, explaining, "On the one hand, she's already paid a steep price. That's not enough of a deterrent to others? Bringing her more misery just seems like piling on."

The Cooper exchange also gave rise to the tagging of certain white women with the label *Karen*. The term had been around for a while, but in 2020, it came to represent middle-aged white women abusing their privilege, usually in racist ways.

The video provided a public service to anyone who thought Black men exaggerated when describing the ways they are often treated in public. The stereotyping of Karens was less productive. From their days providing rides during the Montgomery bus boycott, white women have often been partners in the civil rights movement. With a president who was cheered by White supremacists while doing his best Bull Connor impersonation, we had more important matters to concern ourselves with than caricaturing Karens.

Those matters would become all the more apparent when another much more revolting video, shot on the exact same day, made its way into American consciousness, and altered the history playing out in an already historic year.

I CAN'T BREATHE
May 25, 2020

For months, America had been a one-story town. All that changed in a matter of nine minutes.

A teenage clerk at Cup Foods on the corner of Chicago Avenue and Thirty-Eighth Street in South Minneapolis called police to report that a man had used a counterfeit twenty-dollar bill to purchase cigarettes and then left the store.

Within twenty minutes, another employee called store owner Mahmoud Abumayyaleh and said, "They're killing him." Abumayyaleh suggested that the employee record the scene and call the police on the police.

As the world would soon learn from a video recorded and uploaded to Facebook by seventeen-year-old Darnella Frazier, outside the store, Officer Derek Chauvin was restraining George Floyd by placing his knee on Floyd's neck near the back of a police SUV, while other officers looked on.

Floyd could be heard saying, "Please, please, I can't breathe."

The knee was pressed on the neck for nine minutes and twenty-nine seconds, until long after George Floyd was unresponsive. We'd later learn that Floyd's respiratory system had survived a bout with COVID-19, but it did not survive the encounter with Chauvin. The same video that captured the wanton act of police brutality also showed first responders lifting Floyd's lifeless body onto a gurney.

By the time Americans saw what amounted to a horrific and seemingly endless snuff video, Minneapolis mayor Jacob Frey had fired Chauvin and the other three officers at the scene. During a press conference, Frey explained: "Being black in America should not be a death sentence. For five minutes, we watched as a white officer pressed his knee into the neck of a black man. For five minutes. When you hear someone calling for help, you are supposed to help. This officer failed in the most basic human sense."

The firing and ultimately the arrest of the offending officers wasn't nearly enough to stave off the mournful and angry protests that started with thousands in Minneapolis, and then millions in cities across America and the world; all unified by a common chant: "I can't breathe."

After months sheltering in place, America's newest story, the pandemic, was about to smash into the latest chapter in its longest-running story line.

Donald Trump, who had always chosen the same side when it came to matters of law enforcement and race, remained consistent when it came to the Floyd protests. Echoing Miami police chief Walter Headley's 1967 crackdown on what he called "slum hoodlums," Trump tweeted: "When the looting starts, the shooting starts."

Trump's tweet, labeled by Twitter as *glorifying violence*, was emblematic of a fight he wanted to have: an electoral race about race. For Trump, the moment was less about injustice and more about the response to that injustice. It was about opening a new front—and with demographics shifting, what some saw as a last front—in America's forever war. Trump ran on birtherism and walls, and led with Muslim bans, kids in cages, very fine people on both sides, shithole countries, and political enemies described as *human scum*. "When the looting starts, the shooting starts" was the exact message he was waiting for; a way to turn dog whistles into directives. Exacerbating divisions, fueling racism, and glorifying violence was the brand.

> **Dave Pell** ✔
> @davepell
>
> Trump's been looting America every day for three and a half years.
>
> 12:48 AM · May 29, 2020 · 🐦 Twitter

And for a president doing an unthinkably poor job responding to the pandemic and facing a nearly unprecedented hit to the economy, the protests offered a way to change the subject.

When the protests began in DC, Trump tweeted his enthusiastic support for those who were protecting . . . him.

> Great job last night at the White House by the U.S. Secret Service. They were not only totally professional, but very cool. I was inside, watched every move, and couldn't have felt more safe. They let the "protesters" scream & rant as much as they wanted, but whenever someone got too frisky or out of line, they would quickly come down on them, hard—didn't know what hit them. The front line was replaced with fresh agents, like magic. Big crowd, professionally organized, but nobody came close to breaching the fence. If they had they would have been greeted with the most vicious dogs, and most ominous weapons.

The message was clear: When protesters are expressing anguish over their brothers, sons, and fathers being killed, they're ranting lunatics. When protestors are raging about their right to get a haircut without a mask during a pandemic, they're liberators.

By now, one hundred thousand Americans had died from COVID-19. A pent-up America, which barely took time to mourn the dead, took to the streets to do what George Floyd couldn't do. Scream.

In a call with governors, the president went full Trumptosterone: "Most of you are weak. You have to arrest people . . . You have to dominate, if you don't dominate, you're wasting your time—they're going to run over you, you're going to look like a bunch of jerks . . . It is a war in a certain sense. And we are going to end it fast."

The tough talk was in stark contrast with the mood inside the White House when protesters marched down the streets near the White House. The president was whisked to a downstairs bunker, and the external lighting at the White House went dark.

Trump blamed the violence on the radical left and announced he was naming antifa a terrorist organization. Three big problems with that. That's not what was causing the outrage and violence in the streets. Only foreign groups can be labeled terrorist organizations. And antifa is not really an organization at all. Trump may as well have signed an executive order to label the Oompa Loompas a terrorist group.

Of course, the looting, violence, and burning of property were inexcusable. But among millions of marchers, it represented a tiny percentage of what was taking place in America's streets.

In the ultimate contrast, Joe Biden met with protesters and addressed a group of African American leaders at a church in Wilmington.

> Hate just hides. It doesn't go away, and when you have somebody in power who breathes oxygen into the hate under the rocks, it comes out from under the rocks.

The morning after Donald Trump was elected, *New Yorker* editor David Remnick wrote: "All along, Trump seemed like a twisted caricature of every rotten reflex of the radical right. That he has prevailed, that he has won this election, is a crushing blow to the spirit; it is an event that will likely cast the country into a period of economic, political, and social uncertainty that we cannot yet imagine."

By the end of May, it didn't take much imagination. Anyone who wondered why everything had become so political merely had to look outside. What many saw coming had arrived.

The pandemic failures, the economic collapse, the polarization, the attacks on the press, the destruction of norms and institutions, the moral and ethical degradation that enabled us to look away from kids in cages, the poisoning of the party of Lincoln, America's free-falling world leadership role, the increasingly overt racism, the dictator love, the fleecing of the nation, the firing of people for doing their jobs, the acceptance of treacherous behavior, the climate denial, the treaty torching, the unearthing of the nation's darkest impulses, the lie after lie after lie; all of this and more was leading us into a bleak new reality.

And it was only May. Like the weather, things were just warming up.

News Divisions
May 2020

Maddow

CBS News 1
Trump administration cuts funding for coronavirus researcher, jeopardizing possible COVID-19 cure

Los Angeles Times 2
FBI serves warrant on senator in stock investigation

NBC News 3
Pompeo's elite taxpayer-funded dinners raise new concerns

The New York Times 4
Trump Moves to Replace Watchdog Who Identified Critical Medical Shortages

Politico 5
DOJ seeks new emergency powers amid coronavirus pandemic

Hannity/Carlson

The Wall Street Journal 1
Opinion | All the Adam Schiff Transcripts

The Federalist 2
Obama, Biden Oval Office Meeting On January 5 Was Key To Entire Anti-Trump Operation

Breitbart 3
DOJ: Democrats Paid Pennsylvania Election Officials to Stuff Ballot Box

ABC News 4
Nearly 2000 former DOJ officials call for AG Barr to resign over Flynn case

The Federalist 5
Under Oath, Evelyn Farkas Admitted She Never Had Collusion Evidence

These are the top news links shared on Twitter in May by followers of Rachel Maddow versus followers of Sean Hannity or Tucker Carlson. Source: MIT Center for Constructive Communication

BIGGER NOT BETTER

A group of about twenty English teachers were quietly grading state exams at Prospect Heights High School in Brooklyn when one of them held up a student's essay and asked:

Did someone in this school teach Bruce Springsteen?

In the early '90s, I taught African American literature at a high school in the Crown Heights section of Brooklyn during two years that bookended the summer riots that divided that neighborhood, the city, and at times, the nation. And yes, I taught Bruce Springsteen.

We had just finished studying August Wilson's Pulitzer Prize–winning play *Fences*, when I handed out what I described as a poem titled "Adam Raised a Cain." The students read the "poem" and we discussed the similarities between the two works—namely, the pain and anger a father can pass down to his son.

Cory from *Fences*: "The whole time I was growing up . . . living in his house . . . Papa was like a shadow that followed you everywhere. It weighed on you and sunk into your flesh. It would wrap around you and lay there until you couldn't tell which one was you anymore."

Springsteen in "Adam Raised a Cain": "Daddy worked his whole life for nothing but the pain / Now he walks these empty rooms looking for something to blame / But you inherit the sins, you inherit the flames."

After we analyzed the poem, I asked the students to try to guess its author. They threw out some names of the Black writers we'd studied before I told them it was actually not a poem, but a song by a white singer named Bruce Springsteen. Then I put a boom box on my desk, inserted a cassette, and we rocked.

On a day when the class was discussing *Native Son* by Richard Wright, we were joined by a guest student (the niece of a colleague) who was visiting from Los Angeles.

This was the only time during my New York City teaching career when I wasn't the only white person in the class.

We had reached the point in the novel where its main character, Bigger Thomas, had committed his second killing and was hiding from police in Chicago's tenements. I began that day's class with a simple question: If you lived in the neighborhood where Bigger Thomas was hiding and you knew his location, would you tell the police?

A third of the students said that they wouldn't turn Bigger in because the justice system was too biased and Bigger would never get a fair trial. Another third of the class said that they'd feel compelled to turn him in, regardless of the failings of the justice system, because murder is morally wrong. The remaining students explained that they too would turn Bigger Thomas over to the police—but for a more concrete reason: they didn't want to be the next victim.

I then asked the students how many of them had either been victims of a gunshot or knew someone who had been murdered. Every hand in the class went up.

At the end of the class, our guest from LA approached my desk to let me know that her advanced placement high school English class had just completed the same novel. During the two weeks they spent on the book, not a single issue she had just heard being debated ever came up. She said that if I had asked the same opening question to her class, every student would have said that they'd turn Bigger over to the police. They might have even assumed the question was a joke.

Of course, we didn't need to travel across the country to find a classroom of students who would have been shocked by our discussion. The same disconnect would have existed if our classroom guest had been from a high school on the other side of Brooklyn's Prospect Park.

On that day, I realized that much of what was then billed as *multicultural education* was based on a fallacy. If we wanted to share diverse ideas, we needed more than works by diverse authors, we needed a diversity of people in the same room discussing those works.

I was convinced that the internet could be that room, where people from different backgrounds could calmly and effectively share personal reflections on different topics, fostering a new era of deeper mutual understanding. (It wouldn't be wrong if you just laughed out loud. But I was young. And so was the internet.)

After a year of ed school, I returned home to the Bay Area and set about building a site called the Learning Bridge. The idea was to use the World Wide Web to connect students and teachers who could share lesson plans and ideas. I'd use the modems and phone cords of the internet to solve the problem that was so evident in my classroom on the day we discussed *Native Son*. We didn't need government approval. We didn't need bureaucratic clearance. It would be busing without the buses.

The site did pretty well, but ultimately I shelved the program because it was too early in the development of the internet and ed tech for it to thrive. But the spirit of that project was definitely the spirit of the early web. Many of us working on the first social networks were convinced that those tools would change the world for the better. The internet would open a universe of diverse ideas, and we'd no longer be separated by parks or walls or oceans. And the unbridled sharing of information would shed light on evildoers. It was about to be the worst time in history to be a despot or a genocidal maniac because the whole world would be watching.

In retrospect, uh, maybe not.

Looking back, I should have known that seeing, and even believing, wouldn't make much difference. In 1993, during a trip back to the town where my dad grew up and ultimately lost his family in the Holocaust, my parents and I detoured to visit the Majdanek concentration/extermination camp. The camp itself evoked all the emotions you'd expect, but the part of the visit that really stood out was that the camp was in a shallow valley surrounded by homes and businesses. Up until that point, I'd always thought the camps were hidden and the murders were committed in the shadows. In this case, an entire town had a clear view (and undoubtedly inhaled the sick smell) of mass murder. My dad, as usual, took only a couple of words to get across what takes me a paragraph: "Everybody knew."

So we probably shouldn't be surprised that digitally enabled awareness of atrocities didn't make much difference in 2020 for the million or so Uighur Muslims in China, or the migrants who were both victims of the pandemic and a fire that burned the world's largest refugee camp in Lesbos, Greece, or victims of starvation and torture at the hand of Donald Trump's North Korean pen pal Kim Jong-un, or to the occasional victims of Putin's tendency to poison his opponents.

Not only did despots survive the internet, they thrived while using it as a tool to surveil the opposition and misinform their followers.

So yes, part of the dot-com panacea we envisioned can be written off as naïve exuberance. But even decades later, I'm still surprised that with infinite access to information, we somehow get less diversity of information and ideas than we did before we went online.

Decades later, sitting in front of this screen that's connected to everything, I find myself swimming in a pool of ideas that is even more homogenous than the one I found thumbing through the pages of a New York tabloid—which at least reflected the communities beneath which the 3 train traveled on my commute to Prospect Heights High School.

I've been investing in start-ups, advising companies, and building sites since the earliest days of the first internet boom. And I'm sad to report that in many ways, we built the opposite of what we set out to build. If I were trying to use Springsteen songs as a teaching tool, I'd say we had a "Hungry Heart" for "The Ties That Bind," but we ended up being "Blinded by the Light," "Dancing in the Dark," and hankering for our "Glory Days."

The early-promise internet gave birth to a problem child. Adam really did raise a Cain.

What the hell happened? Part of it is due to cognitive bias. We gravitate toward ideas that confirm what we already think. Part of it is that the internet became a much more centralized place than we imagined, with a few massive companies hosting the ideas of millions (and even billions) of us. Part of it is the algorithms designed by those companies that feed us more of what we've consumed in the past—which for some means a narrow view of reality, and for way too many others means a total disconnect from it. And part of it was that we repeatedly underestimated that there was another side of the equation: people who would see tools we saw as a means to liberate, inform, empower, and unify as a means to stifle, distort, control, and divide.

And that, as it turns out, provides a reasonably good segue into June.

6

JUNE—
THE HEARTLINE ROLL

THE SEPARATION OF CHURCH AND STATE HAS RARELY BEEN AS NARROW AS IT
was during a short walk between the White House and Saint John's Episcopal Church. Even during a year in which the news came in buckets and
events were viewed and quickly forgotten, some moments stood out and remain etched in our minds. One of those moments included the tear-gassing
of peaceful protesters in Lafayette Park.

On the evening of June 1, the White House press corps was given short
notice that the president would be delivering remarks from the Rose Garden. While the speaking venue was being prepared, and during the president's seven-minute speech in which he chicken-hawked directives that law
enforcement had to "dominate the streets," or he would "deploy the United
States military and quickly solve the problem," Lafayette Park was being
dominated by officials in riot gear. The peaceful protesters were hit with
airborne chemicals and subjected to other aggressive tactics for exercising
their First Amendment rights in the city where those rights are supposed to
be held sacred.

With smoke still in the air, President Trump began a stroll through the area that had been forcefully cleared of protesters. The group that followed close behind included Attorney General William Barr (who had been seen observing the protesters shortly before the riot police took action), Defense Secretary Mark Esper (who had earlier urged governors to "occupy the battlespace" where protests were taking place), press secretary Kayleigh McEnany, advisor Hope Hicks, Jared Kushner, Ivanka Trump, chief of staff Mark Meadows, senior advisor Stephen Miller, national security advisor Robert O'Brien, and Mark Milley, chairman of the Joint Chiefs of Staff, who was dressed in combat fatigues.

The five-minute walk took the group from the Rose Garden to Saint John's, a church Trump had rarely, if ever, visited since the day of his inauguration.

Once at the church, where the basement had been damaged by arsonists the night before, Trump stood for a photo op, with a faux–tough guy grimace, holding up a Bible in his hand.

A reporter called out, "Is that your Bible?" Trump responded, "It's *a* Bible."

To Trump's detractors, the photo op represented all that was wrong with his presidency, as he simultaneously desecrated the Bible, a church, religion, the First Amendment, the military, and more broadly, America. And while the speech, the photo op, and the reprehensible use of unnecessary force were all serious business, like Trump moments past, this one had elements of farce that made for instant comic fodder on the internet. The idea of a guy like Donald Trump holding a Bible in front of a church made about as much sense as Cheech & Chong holding a No Smoking sign in front of a rehab clinic.

Mariann Edgar Budde, the bishop of the Episcopal Diocese of Washington, immediately criticized the use of the Bible as a prop and the church as the set for Trump's twisted reality programming:

> He did not pray. He did not mention George Floyd, he did not mention the agony of people who have been subjected to this kind of horrific expression of

racism and white supremacy for hundreds of years. We need a president who can unify and heal. He has done the opposite of that, and we are left to pick up the pieces.

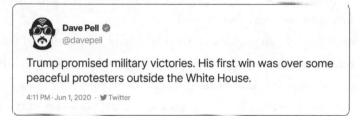

Dave Pell ✓
@davepell

Trump promised military victories. His first win was over some peaceful protesters outside the White House.

4:11 PM · Jun 1, 2020 · 🐦 Twitter

To many, the church scene was the moment Trump finally went too far, and marked a key inflection point for his presidency. But Trump was nothing if not a marketing savant. And tens of millions of his supporters didn't see an evil clown cornered by poor poll numbers and his own disastrous managing of the pandemic. They saw a flawed ally carrying a Bible to the center of the ring where radical secularists, socialists, and violent Black and brown protesters were threatening the role of white religion in America.

READY, WILLING, ENABLE

Not only did plenty of folks in Trump's base appreciate his June 1 abomination, Republican senators, as was their wont, either remained silent about the move or cheered it on.

Florida senator Marco Rubio called the protesters "professional agitators" and supported Trump's tactics, "given what we've seen the last few nights in front of the White House—incredibly dangerous and violent situations . . . They know the police have to move forward on them, that will trigger the use of tear gas and it plays right into the imagery that they want. . . . That wasn't even a protest. It was a provocation that was created deliberately for national television."

This essentially echoed the megachurch and evangelical view of the event, summarized by Ralph Reed: "His presence sent the twin message that our streets and cities do not belong to rioters and domestic terrorists, and that the ultimate answer to what ails our country can be found in the repentance, redemption, and forgiveness of the Christian faith." (Jesus, Ralph, I just ralphed.)

The real message was that, no matter how low he sank, Trump would maintain the support of evangelicals and the Republican leaders who would enable him until the bitter end.

At the 2016 GOP convention, Trump famously proclaimed, "I alone can fix it." But he wasn't working alone. And if a deadly pandemic, a horrific economy, and America's diminishing role in the world wasn't enough to dissuade Trump's enablers, a little tear gas and a Bible photo op sure wouldn't change anything.

My dad, who had a front-row seat to the rise of evil and the ethical weakness of enablers during the Holocaust, remained as concerned about Trump as he had been during the previous three and a half years, and the president's poor polling numbers offered him no relief.

"He vill cheat in the election. And if he can't get away with that, he vill just say he von. And even if he loses, he's not going to concede. How vill they get him out of the Vhite House?"

People who had seen this show before knew exactly what they were looking at.

INSURRECTILE DYSFUNCTION

Less than forty-eight hours after appearing as part of Trump's Rose Garden parade through Lafayette Park, Defense Secretary Mark Esper distanced himself from the event, saying he didn't know about plans for the Bible-holding photo op, and also wasn't aware of the plans to forcefully remove the protesters. In remarks to reporters at the Pentagon, Esper also publicly shot down Trump's threats to use the Insurrection Act of 1807 to control protesters if governors were unwilling to use the required force: "The option to use active duty forces in a law enforcement role should only be used as a matter of last resort, and only in the most urgent and dire of situations. We are not in one of those situations now."

In a highly unusual public policy statement, Mike Mullen, former chairman of the Joint Chiefs of Staff, sharply decried Trump's actions in an op-ed in the *Atlantic*.

It sickened me yesterday to see security personnel—including members of the National Guard—forcibly and violently clear a path through Lafayette Square to accommodate the president's visit outside St. John's Church . . .

As a white man, I cannot claim perfect understanding of the fear and anger that African Americans feel today. But as someone who has been around for a while, I know enough—and I've seen enough—to understand that those feelings are real and that they are all too painfully founded . . .

Even in the midst of the carnage we are witnessing, we must endeavor to see American cities and towns as our homes and our neighborhoods. They are not "battle spaces" to be dominated, and must never become so . . . Our fellow citizens are not the enemy, and must never become so.

This was a detour from the mostly silent treatment from the top brass when it came to Trump. Something cracked. The religious right wouldn't leave Trump's side. But the military might.

MAD DOG DAY AFTERNOON

After the Lafayette Park debacle, James Mattis, Trump's first secretary of defense, finally broke his own silence on his former boss. Many wish he had done this a lot sooner, but that only made the fact that he did it now an indication of how dire the situation had become. And when Mattis's pen did hit paper, it did so with the force of a bunker buster.

When I joined the military, some 50 years ago, I swore an oath to support and defend the Constitution. Never did I dream that troops taking that same oath would be ordered under any circumstance to violate the Constitutional rights of their fellow citizens—much less to provide a bizarre photo op for the elected commander-in-chief, with military leadership standing alongside . . . Donald Trump is the first president in my lifetime who does not try to unite the American people—does not even pretend to try. Instead he tries to divide us. We are witnessing the consequences of three years of this deliberate effort. We are witnessing the consequences of three years without mature leadership. (James Mattis, the *Atlantic*)

John Allen, a retired US Marine Corps four-star general and former commander of the NATO International Security Assistance Force and US forces in Afghanistan, added his voice to the strong chorus of military critiques of the events of June 1 with a piece in *Foreign Affairs*, headlined: *A Moment of National Shame and Peril—and Hope.*

Remember the date. It may well signal the beginning of the end of the American experiment. The president of the United States stood in the Rose Garden of the White House on Monday, railed against weak governors and mayors who were not doing enough, in his mind, to control the unrest and the rioters in their cities, and threatened to deploy the U.S. military against American citizens. It was a stunning moment.

> **Dave Pell** ✔
> @davepell
>
> Colin Powell says Trump has "drifted away from the Constitution."
>
> Yeah, like a missile drifts away from its silo.
>
> 10:36 AM · June 7, 2020 · 🐦 Twitter

Trump's base may not have been moved by stark and dark statements coming from current and former officials in the chain of command, but the sitting Joint Chiefs chairman most definitely was. Shortly after this series of op-eds appeared, Milley himself admitted regret.

I should not have been there. My presence in that moment and in that environment created a perception of the military involved in domestic politics.

PAUL REVERED
June 2, 2020

I attended my first Black Lives Matter rally in Marin City, California. I was worried about the potential for virus spread, but the rally was being hosted by my friend Paul Austin, who ran a program called Play Marin that brought kids together to play sports and participate in other positive activities. When the pandemic hit, Paul did a tireless and steady job getting the word out about the importance of social distancing and worked with Marin County restaurants to provide a consistent supply of food to those who had lost their jobs during the pandemic. The food was good. The information was great. Marin City maintained a low virus rate despite being a lower-economic neighborhood where people lived in closer proximity to one another. Paul is proof that during times of crisis, there is nothing more valuable than a local leader with credibility. While local beat reporters and columnists once helped to play this role, regional news had been on the ropes for years, and in many places across the country, the pandemic brought the knockout punch. The trend enabled local corruption to run amok, and the absence of trusted, local voices left an information vacuum that was often filled by national "news" sources, some of which were dominated by lies and conspiracy theories. By the time the pandemic hit, many communities needed a trusted truth-teller like Paul Austin.

The moment I joined the large, masked crowd, I was glad I had. After months of absorbing bad news from the safety of my shelter-in-place existence, I needed the energy of a crowd. The event confirmed my hunch about the marches around the country. While the primary focus was George Floyd, police violence, and Black Lives Matter, there were two other elements that I could feel. First, after months sheltering in place, the pull to be among a large community of people was strong. Second, there was a direct association between the calls for justice and the desire to make Trump a one-term president. I heard chants of "No Justice, No Peace," but I also heard chants of "Vote Him Out."

For me, the gathering was unique; for Paul Austin, it was just another day in a long struggle. A few months after the rally, Paul Austin and his wife, Tenisha Tate Austin, a middle school principal, had their recently remodeled home appraised. The number came in much lower than the amount of money they had put into the house, and they were convinced that race was a factor. They requested a reappraisal. For that one, they had a white friend fill the house with pictures of her family and greet the second appraiser as if she were Tenisha. This time the house was appraised as being about 50 percent more valuable.

Austin was no stranger to racism, and he was no stranger to highly stressful environments. He spent the months leading up to the pandemic coaching my daughter's fifth-grade basketball team. By comparison, dealing with 2020 was a breeze.

ANTIFA(CTS)

June 4, 2020

In Buffalo, New York, police officers acting in their role as members of the city's riot squad were approached by seventy-five-year-old Martin Gugino during a protest in Niagara Square. Gugino was pushed to the ground, where his head hit the pavement, and he started to bleed from his ear. Gugino, a longtime peace activist, suffered a fractured skull and injuries to his brain, and would spend about four weeks in the hospital.

The Buffalo police department initially claimed that during a "skirmish involving protestors, one person was injured when he tripped and fell." But once again, there was video, and once again, that video went almost immediately viral. It was clear that Gugino was pushed to the ground without cause and that several members of the police unit walked by without coming to his aid. Ultimately, two police officers were suspended and charged with felony assault.

In response to the suspensions, fifty-seven Buffalo police officers resigned from the riot control unit.

President Trump described Gugino, who was in intensive care, as a possible antifa provocateur. The absurdities once limited to the fringes of social media were now being amplified by the world's most powerful leader.

Donald J. Trump ✔
@potus

Buffalo protester shoved by Police could be an ANTIFA provocateur. 75 year old Martin Gugino was pushed away after appearing to scan police communications in order to black out the equipment. @OANN I watched, he fell harder than was pushed. Was aiming scanner. Could be a set up?

8:34 AM · Jun 9, 2020 · 🐦 Twitter

By now, it was clear how far the lies had spread and how deeply the rot had embedded when it came to the nonsensical conspiracy theories driving false realities for an increasingly large—and disturbingly well-armed group of Americans. Decked out in camouflage, they migrated from the internet to the streets, locked, loaded, and ready to fight an invisible, imaginary enemy, when the real enemy was the combination of lies and paranoid fantasies being drilled into their heads in social media groups and amplified from the Oval Office, where dog whistles had morphed into full symphonies. The enemy wasn't antifa, it was antifacts.

That was all too clear in small towns like Klamath Falls, Oregon, where armed groups declared victory over a group of antifa members and outside agitators who never showed up, and never really existed as a threat.

I began to wonder if my ninety-six-year-old dad might be part of antifa. Think about it. In Holocaust-ravaged Poland, as the Nazi front approached, instead of simply allowing himself to be absorbed into the fascist lifestyle and embracing the convincing messaging put together by Joseph Goebbels and his copywriters, my dad's family actually moved *away* from the incursion. After escaping to the woods, my dad finally managed to get a gun, which made him eligible to join a group of partisans who lived in the woods and ran operations *against* the fascists. My dad found himself put in charge of blowing up Nazi trains that were bringing weapons and supplies to the front. I mean, I sure as hell wouldn't call that *protifa*.

REBOUND

The day Adam Silver shut down the NBA marked a turning point in the public's understanding of the virus threat, so getting the league back in action, even in a different form, was a welcome step toward normalcy. The league was set to approve the plan for a twenty-two-team return with eight regular-season games, followed by the playoffs. The twist? The participating teams, the refs, the media, and anyone else involved would spend the entire shortened season living inside a bubble at Walt Disney World Resort. All the teams at one resort the whole time? It made sense. They never call traveling in the NBA anyway.

The NBA's planned return offered a glimmer of hoops and hope. More hope came out of New York, where the city hit a milestone: its first day without a coronavirus death since March.

If that wasn't enough normalcy for people, in Florida, a plastic surgeon known as Dr. Miami began offering drive-thru Botox. After reading about that service, I facepalmed my forehead so hard, my wrinkles flattened.

THE STATUE OF LIBERTY PLAY
June 6, 2020

The eminently quotable John Madden once explained, "Some yards is better than none yards." The NFL, an organization that fumbled most of its chances to do the right thing when it came to player protests related to race, had been gaining none yards for a long time. After punting on the issue, passing the buck, and kicking players like Colin Kaepernick to the curb, it's worth taking a look at a slow-motion replay of the moment when the league managed to move the line of scrimmage a few inches forward. After holding a Zoom town hall with several players and league employees, NFL commissioner Roger Goodell sat in front of his basement camera and recorded a message. "We, the National Football League, admit we were wrong for not listening to N.F.L. players earlier and encourage all to speak out and peacefully protest. We, the National Football League, believe Black lives matter . . . I personally protest with you and want to be a part of the much-needed change in this country. Without Black players, there would be no National Football League."

The combination of the protests in the streets and Trump's response to them was forcing people and organizations to pick a side. The military brass picked theirs. And with this announcement from Goodell, America's most American corporate brand had chosen theirs.

Another perhaps less likely American brand joined the race discussion, when NASCAR stopped driving around in circles on race. Racing legend Jeff Gordon spoke out in honor of his fellow competitor Bubba Wallace, one of the most successful Black NASCAR drivers: "I'll never know what it's like to walk in Bubba's shoes or the shoes of anyone that's experienced racism. I do know I can be better; we can do better to create positive change,"

Gordon said. "We need to step up now more than we ever have in the past. We are listening. We are learning. We are ready for change."

A few days after Gordon and other drivers took a stand, it was announced that the display of the Confederate flag would be prohibited from all NASCAR events and properties. When I heard that announcement, this progressive, Jewish, Volvo-driving liberal decided that I was going to start watching some NASCAR. That's how it's supposed to work. People take small steps toward one another, and before you know it, you have a country.

Later in the month, an entire field of drivers took a side after a noose was found in Bubba Wallace's garage. They all took to the track and made a public display of support for Wallace.

We'd later find out that noose Wallace found was used to open and close a garage door, and that it had been there long before Wallace and NASCAR threw the brand's racial history into reverse. For some on the right, this was evidence that the Black Lives Matter movement had spun out of control. To me, it just seemed like evidence that the racism people were marching against didn't start with a knee on George Floyd's neck; that was just the moment it reentered the consciousness of millions of white Americans.

The side-picking wasn't limited to sports or even by American borders. Not only were the George Floyd protests unprecedented in terms of their size and multicultural scope, they were global, with people taking it to the streets in France, Japan, Sweden, Zimbabwe, England, Brazil, Spain, Senegal, Denmark, Scotland, South Korea, Belgium, Hungary, Italy, Australia, Poland, Turkey, Switzerland, Portugal, Canada, Germany, and beyond.

Among those who attended a march was Senator Mitt Romney. He explained to a reporter: "We need to stand up and say that Black lives matter."

WHAT DEFUND ARE YOU TALKING ABOUT?

After kneeling in Emancipation Hall for several minutes to honor George Floyd and other Black victims of police violence, House and Senate Democrats introduced the Justice in Policing Act, a bill cosponsored by Senators Cory Booker and Kamala Harris, that included calls to create a national database of incidents involving excessive force, ban police choke holds, and remove some legal protections for police.

One word that was not in the proposed bill was *defund*. But the phrase *defund the police* had become a rallying cry at marches across the country. In most cases, even those using the phrase weren't suggesting a complete abolition of police but rather a redistribution of some funds and responsibilities away from law enforcement and toward other local organizations.

Trump would spend months trying to pin the phrase on Joe Biden, arguing that he had a radical plot to remove police from the streets. While Biden never suggested anything of the sort, the slogan always struck me as counterproductive and an example of the poor political message framing that had long hampered Democrats.

Right about this time, I tweeted a critique of the slogan.

The responses, especially from liberal whites, were fast and furious, as I was attacked for being some white guy who hadn't thought about any of these issues for my whole life and then sat on my couch and issued directives about how Black organizers should frame their rallying cries.

While it was true that I am some white guy who generally tweets from a couch, I had in fact been thinking about these twin issues (political messaging and civil rights) for a long time.

More important, I only published my opinion on the matter after having a conversation with my brother-in-law Douglass Fitch, a Black pastor who was an active participant in the civil rights movement. He agreed with my critique of the slogan, thought it was vulnerable to opposition attacks, and added, "I sure wouldn't want to live in a city without police."

Later in the year, Barack Obama chimed in on what he called the "snappy" slogan during an interview with Peter Hamby on a Snapchat political show: "You lost a big audience the minute you say it, which makes it a lot less likely that you're actually going to get the changes you want done. The key is deciding, do you want to actually get something done, or do you want to feel good among the people you already agree with?"

I share this story for two reasons. First, while I zinged my critics on Twitter, it didn't quite satisfy my thirst for revenge, so I decided to include the anecdote here to also zing them in book form. Second, the exchange felt representative of a moment when many progressive Americans seemed like they were competing in the Woke-Olympics. No opinion was pure enough, every exchange was somehow triggering, and even having a budding authoritarian in the White House didn't stop people on the other side of the political divide from attacking one another over petty differences when there was a monumental, unifying, and maybe even existential challenge staring us in the face.

At the Harvard ed school, I wrote my thesis on urban school violence and the use of metal detectors. To conduct a survey for the paper, I returned to my teaching alma mater, Prospect Heights High School in the Crown Heights section of Brooklyn, which at the time was one of the few schools to be part of the city's metal detector program. The metal detectors would be deployed once a week, and on that day, you could see five marked vans parked in front of the school—making it quite clear that if you wanted to attend school armed, one of the other four weekdays would be a better option.

Everyone associated with the school knew that the metal detector program was ineffective. Everyone in the school knew that the metal detector program was racist. As a white teacher, I was free to bypass the metal detectors on my first day at the school, while the students (all of whom were Black or brown) had to go through the detection process anytime it was in place. Yet my survey showed that a huge majority of students and parents wanted the metal detection program to remain in place. Even a weak protection system was better than no protection. While the anger with police and the justice system were similar to what was being vented on the streets of America in the summer of 2020, there was, among the kids and parents who lived in what was one of the rougher neighborhoods in Brooklyn, a general desire for more police on the street, not fewer. For me, the survey results were a wakeup call. And in some cases, it's better to be awake than woke.

CIVIL WARTS

Around the country, statues and monuments associated with Confederate generals were being taken down (with and without official approval). The debate over the commemoration of those who fought for the losing side in the Civil War extended to the naming of military bases. President Trump was in favor of keeping the names. Many in the military, however, were not. Among those were Defense Secretary Esper and US Army general and former CIA director David Petraeus, who penned an op-ed in the *Atlantic*.

> While on active duty, in fact, I never thought much about these men—about the nature of their service during the Civil War, their postwar activities (which in John Brown Gordon's case likely included a leadership role in the first Ku Klux Klan), the reasons they were honored, or the timing of the various forts' dedications. Nor did I think about the messages those names sent to the many African Americans serving on these installations—messages that should have been noted by all of us.

Maybe it wasn't that we were refighting the Civil War, but that, in some ways, the Civil War never completely ended.

THE TORTOISE AND THE HAIR

In Missouri, a hairstylist with COVID-19 infected one of her coworkers. After both had been infected, they gave haircuts to 140 customers. Both the cutters and clients were wearing face masks. After the period of incubation had passed, Missouri health officials reported that none of the customers tested positive. The power of masks could not have been more obvious.

THE GRADUATE

Graduates of Kennett High School in North Conway, New Hampshire, received their diplomas wearing masks and riding chairlifts on the mountain the area is known for. This was one of the cooler work-arounds during a year when almost everything either stopped or had to be dramatically changed.

My son, who hadn't been back to campus in months, ended his eighth-grade year waving to teachers as he and his classmates leaned out of car windows or stood with their upper halves poking through sunroofs during a makeshift graduation car parade. This was a couple of days after he spent his birthday taking his diploma-receiving photo a hundred yards away from the nearest classmate, and he never really got to properly say goodbye to any of them. The school has an annual step-up day that celebrates each class, particularly the kindergartners and the graduates. Along with his closest friends, my son had waited nine years for his turn to take this final step, and instead, he was handed a diploma as he heard his name announced to an empty courtyard.

On one hand, it was a little depressing and a lot weird. The old normal was gone and what replaced it didn't quite feel like the new normal yet, and that was especially evident during life transitions like weddings, birthdays, and funerals.

On the other hand, some of these moments may end up being more memorable. I don't remember a thing about my eighth-grade graduation. Not the venue. Not who gave a speech. Nothing. Yes, that may have something to do with the fact that between then and now I've smoked enough joints to keep San Francisco's foghorns blaring for a decade. But it's also because many of these events are so similar that they blur into one another.

During the era when my friends and I had our bar mitzvahs, almost all the kids in my Hebrew school class arrived at the same temple, wearing roughly the same suit purchased from a store called Young Man's Fancy, gave roughly the same performance, and then had a reception at the same Jewish club on Van Ness Avenue in San Francisco. I have a general recollection of some of the moments with my friends (particularly our tactic of sneaking downstairs to pour the contents of all the nearly empty bottles of alcohol into one glass). But it's impossible for me to differentiate my own bar mitzvah from anyone else's. I'm guessing my son will remember his car-bound eighth-grade graduation forever, unless the trauma of the era is something his brain chooses to repress (or at some point, he gets into my weed stash).

THE ZOOM WHERE IT HAPPENED

We began to see the first excerpts from John Bolton's controversial and much-awaited book on Trump. Bolton hadn't testified during Trump's impeachment, but he was apparently more willing to dish if that meant making it to the best-seller list. As expected, the details provided by Trump's former national security advisor were shocking but not surprising. Trump serially committed impeachable offenses, was mocked, even by those in the White House, and knew almost nothing about the world he oversaw ("Mr. Trump did not seem to know, for example, that Britain is a nuclear power and asked if Finland is part of Russia").

We already knew this. We'd seen it and much worse for years. Bolton's book is titled *The Room Where It Happened*. But the room where it happened was the room where the impeachment trial took place and Bolton was nowhere in sight. He meant the other room where things happened, the Oval Office, where self-serving, power-hungry enablers like Bolton sat back and let a madman humiliate America, destroy norms, and endanger democracy—saving the urgent truth for a moment when it could impact book sales. I always hoped one person would buy one copy of Bolton's book and crush sales by reading the whole thing to America over Zoom.

> **Dave Pell** ✔
> @davepell
>
> Paul Revere: The British are Coming!
>
> John Bolton: My book is Coming!
>
> 4:51 AM · Jun 18, 2020 · 🐦 Twitter

Donald Trump on June 15–18:

"You know, at some point this stuff goes away and it's going away. Our numbers are much lower now."

"If we stopped testing right now, we'd have very few cases, if any."

"I always say, even without it [a vaccine], it goes away."

"The numbers are very minuscule compared to what it was. It's dying
   out."

"It's going to fade away. But having a vaccine would be really nice.
   And that's going to happen."

"America is better supplied and more prepared to [reopen] than, I
   would say, just about any other place."

"It is dying out. The numbers are starting to get very good."

> **Donald J. Trump** ✔
> @potus
>
> Our Coronavirus testing is so much greater (25 million tests)
> and so much more advanced, that it makes us look like we
> have more cases, especially proportionally, than other
> countries. My message on that is very clear!
>
> 12:48 AM · Jun 22, 2020 · 🐦 Twitter

THE SODFATHER

The Constitution, the rule of law, and a liberal democracy walk into a
Barr . . . the question is what will be left of each when they walk back out.

By now, Friday-night assaults on justice via firings were commonplace
in a White House that had fallen into a familiar weekend routine—Friday,
fire truth-tellers; Saturday, golf; Sunday, golf. On Friday, June 19, Attorney General William Barr got into the act when he falsely indicated
(that's media-speak for *lied*) that Geoffrey Berman, the US attorney for
the Southern District of New York, had resigned and would be replaced by
SEC chair Jay Clayton, a person with no prosecutorial experience. The announcement came following a lunch between Barr and Berman, who had
replaced Preet Bharara, a straight shooter, respected prosecutor, and ardent
Springsteen fan who had been unceremoniously canned by the POTUS
shortly after being told he'd be kept on. Like many of those who were
forced from the virtual building, Bharara went on to media, podcasting,
and Twitter fame.

But there was something that wasn't quite par for the course in the case of
Geoff Berman. The administration, now often being run like a crime family,

made Berman an offer he *could* refuse. Berman, whose SDNY included New York City, scene of many of Trump's crimes both alleged and confirmed, refused to be strong-armed by Barr: "I will step down when a presidentially appointed nominee is confirmed by the Senate. Until then, our investigations will move forward without delay or interruption."

It was a solid stand made by a man Trump himself had appointed. In the end, Berman would step down from his position, but Barr and Trump were unable to shift the unqualified Jay Clayton into the position. Instead, Berman negotiated an exit that included being replaced by his deputy, Audrey Strauss, who was familiar with cases involving Trump and who could be counted on to do the job of the people.

A key question that arose in the Berman scandal was which investigation or investigations Trump and Barr were trying to obstruct. Was this about the SDNY investigation into Giuliani? Trump's taxes? Jeffrey Epstein? Money laundering? Deutsche Bank to whom Trump still owed millions? (Did I mention that Jay Clayton used to represent Deutsche Bank before representing Chris Christie in his Bridgegate case?)

Paul Rosenzweig, who once served as a senior counsel in the investigation of President Bill Clinton, explained the move in a piece in the *Atlantic*.

Why replace Berman now, just five months before the election?

. . . This is how an authoritarian works to subvert justice. He purports to uphold the forms of justice (in this case, the formal rule that the attorney general and the president exercise hierarchical control over the U.S. attorneys) while undermining the substance of justice. In the Flynn case, for example, Barr has asserted an absolute, unreviewable authority to bring and dismiss cases at will—a power that, even if legally well founded, is a subversion of justice when misused.

That may be the game plan for New York as well. Barr may want Berman out so that he can use his newly enhanced control to dismiss or short-circuit all of the pending cases in Manhattan that implicate Trump or his associates.

We know those are many. We know that Trump's various organizations, including his inauguration committee, are under investigation. We know that Trump attorney Rudy Giuliani is under investigation. We know that Trump's bank, Deutsche Bank, is under investigation.

Throughout the pandemic, four of my lifelong friends and I had been holding weekly Zoom sessions in which we'd discuss politics, personal issues, and health (the nation's, of course, but as aging Jews, also our own). During the entirety of the year, we only invited one outside guest to appear in these Zoom sessions: a mutual friend named Dan Berman, the equally accomplished (and significantly funnier) brother of Geoffrey.

This was the day after the firing, and we wanted to get the inside scoop from Dan about Geoffrey's strong stand. It turned out that we learned very little new, inside information during the exchange. It was a reminder of just how quickly every detail of every story during the Trump era was leaked to the media. What we were learning in real time was actually pretty close to what happened, and even as book after book came out from administration insiders, we hardly learned anything that didn't seem obvious when stories played out before our eyes. Oddly, this may have been part of what made Trump's dominance of the airwaves (clearly his chief political and personal goal) so complete. What Geoffrey Berman's brother knew, Rachel Maddow already had known the night before. Sadly, we couldn't get Rachel as a guest on our weekly Zoom.

OKLAHOMA IS NOT OK

Any protesters, anarchists, agitators, looters or lowlifes who are going to Oklahoma please understand, you will not be treated like you have been in New York, Seattle, or Minneapolis. It will be a much different scene!

That was the threat issued by President Trump ahead of his first indoor rally planned for Tulsa on June 20, an event that would fly in the face of every COVID-19 prevention recommendation.

The threat sort of worked. There were very few protesters, anarchists, agitators, looters, or lowlifes at the event. There were very few people at all.

Shortly before showtime, when it became clear that risking one's life in an indoor arena in a middle of a pandemic wasn't quite the selling point the Trump campaign imagined it would be, an outdoor overflow staging area was removed because of a lack of need.

TulSAD!

Rumors suggested that young organizers on TikTok had purchased tickets to boost what would be Trump campaign manager Brad Parscale's claims of unprecedented demand. While there was some schadenfreude associated with the event, for Oklahomans, the big news was that the maskless crowd was small. With nearly 120,000 Americans dead, COVID-19 cases were starting to surge in states across the country, including Oklahoma. Seven states had just broken new records for number of cases, while the country suffered 30,000 new cases for two straight days. Included among the new cases were several members of the president's campaign staff who worked the Tulsa rally, including at least two Secret Service agents.

During the rally, Trump again blamed America's coronavirus numbers on testing. "Slow the testing down, please."

ARCTIC TOCK

Aside from the return of political rally season, Saturday, June 20, was notable for two reasons. First, it was my wedding anniversary, and thanks to the quarantine, I was under no pressure to arrange a night out. And second, it hit 100.4 degrees in Verkhoyansk. That's a temperature Miami has only hit once on record. For those not familiar with Verkhoyansk, it's in Siberia.

MURDOCH, SHE WROTE

June 26, 2020

On the pandemic front, America's split-screen experience was coming into clear view. On one screen, we saw COVID-19 cases and deaths beginning to surge from California to Texas to Florida, and Anthony Fauci was warning Congress about the new surge: "A couple of days ago, there were 30,000 new infections. That's very disturbing to me." On the other screen, there was a smokescreen. The administration continued to be a driver of the problem. On June 16, as the latest surge was picking up steam, VP Pence wrote an editorial in the *Wall Street Journal* titled "There Isn't a Coronavirus 'Second Wave.'" The only way that headline could have been true is if you just viewed the whole pandemic as one nonstop, building tsunami. Pence explained that the country was making "great progress" against the disease, and included his usual flair for nauseating, bootlicking sycophancy.

> Thanks to the leadership of President Trump and the courage and compassion of the American people, our public health system is far stronger than it was four months ago, and we are winning the fight against the invisible enemy.

The administration had help spreading this dangerous misinformation. And no one was aiding the invisible enemy more than Fox News.

> In recent weeks, three studies have focused on conservative media's role in fostering confusion about the seriousness of the coronavirus. Taken together, they paint a picture of a media ecosystem that amplifies misinformation, entertains conspiracy theories and discourages audiences from taking concrete steps to protect themselves and others. The end result, according to one of the studies, is that infection and mortality rates are higher in places where one pundit who initially downplayed the severity of the pandemic—Fox News's Sean Hannity—reaches the largest audiences. (Christopher Ingraham, *Washington Post*)

We already knew Fox News could be damaging to the brain. In 2020, they went after the whole body.

BOUNTY PUNTER
June 27, 2020

With all the news about the pandemic and Black Lives Matter, we almost forgot about President Trump's consistently weird behavior when it came to Vladimir Putin. We got a reminder, courtesy of a blockbuster report from the *New York Times,* that indicated Russia had been putting bounties on the lives of US soldiers serving in Afghanistan.

> The intelligence finding was briefed to President Trump, and the White House's National Security Council discussed the problem at an interagency

meeting in late March, the officials said. Officials developed a menu of potential options—starting with making a diplomatic complaint to Moscow and a demand that it stop, along with an escalating series of sanctions and other possible responses, but the White House has yet to authorize any step, the officials said. (Charlie Savage, Eric Schmitt, and Michael Schwirtz, *New York Times*)

In fairness, it's not like Trump did nothing. A few weeks before, he indicated that he wanted to invite Putin back into the G-7.

Meanwhile, a day after retweeting (and later deleting) a video from a random user that featured a guy yelling, "White power!" from a golf cart in the Villages in Florida, Trump retweeted a video of a white St. Louis couple waving guns at protesters. That couple would be made fun of endlessly in memes, would be hit with felony gun charges, and would be lauded enough by those in the administration that they ultimately got a speaking role at the GOP convention. In short, they got quite famous in certain circles. They won't in this book.

FLAG WAIVED

In Mississippi, lawmakers voted to furl the state's flag that featured the Confederate battle emblem. After flying for 126 years, it was the nation's last state flag to feature the symbol. Mississippi Speaker of the House Philip Gunn explained: "We are better today than we were yesterday . . . We are not betraying our heritage. We are fulfilling it."

Anything better than the day before in 2020 America sounded good to me, in part because when it came to pandemic numbers, each day was starting to be worse than the last. But for some, these days were better than you might have expected. At this point in the pandemic, forty-five million Americans had lost their jobs and US billionaires had added $584 billion to their fortunes.

Donald Trump on July 1: "I think we are going to be very good with the coronavirus. I think that, at some point, that's going to sort of just disappear, I hope."

News Divisions
June 2020

Maddow

The New York Times 1
Russia Secretly Offered Afghan Militants Bounties to Kill Troops, U.S. Intelligence Says

The Atlantic 2
James Mattis Denounces President Trump, Describes Him as a Threat to the Constitution

CNN 3
From pandering to Putin to abusing allies and ignoring his own advisers, Trump's phone calls alarm US officials

The New York Times 4
Major Problems With Voting in Atlanta as 5 States Hold Primaries

The Washington Post 5
The May jobs report had 'misclassification error' that made the unemployment rate look lower than it is. Here's what happened

Hannity/Carlson

LifeSiteNews.com 1
Archbishop Viganò's powerful letter to President Trump: Eternal struggle between good and evil playing out right now

The Federalist 2
Media Falsely Claimed Violent Riots Were Peaceful And That Tear Gas Was Used Against Rioters

True Pundit 3
EXCLUSIVE: Bill Gates Negotiated $100 Billion Contact Tracing Deal With Democratic Congressman Sponsor of Bill Six Months BEFORE Coronavirus...

New York Post 4
Mayor Bill de Blasio's daughter, Chiara, arrested at Manhattan protest

The Western Journal 5
Exclusive from Gen. Flynn: If We Don't Act, 2% of the People Are About To Control the Other 98%

These are the top news links shared on Twitter in June by followers of Rachel Maddow versus followers of Sean Hannity or Tucker Carlson.
Source: MIT Center for Constructive Communication

NEWSBREAK

FAKE IT 'TIL YOU MAKE IT

In *Oh, God! Book II*, God—played by George Burns—explains to his co-star why there's pain and suffering in the world. "I know this sounds like a cop-out . . . but there's nothing I can do about pain and suffering. It's built into the system . . . my problem was I could never figure out how to build anything with just one side to it. You ever see a front without a back? A top without a bottom? An up without a down? OK. Then there can't be good without bad, life without death, pleasure without pain. That's the way it is. If I take sad away, happy has to go with it."

Which brings us to the internet. We thought we were building one thing, but we ended up building the opposite thing at the same time.

George Burns as God explained that for there to be good, there also has to be bad. But why was this internet thing we built with the best of intentions so much better at bad than it was at good? Why do lies spread so much more freely than the truth?

Every weekday, I send out a newsletter filled with links to media sources that produce honest reporting around a shared set of actual facts. Every day, I get emails from people who complain that they want to read a story I've shared, but the story is behind a paywall. Trump may have never built his big, beautiful wall. But news sites built theirs. (And

Mexico is not going to pay for your subscription.) This trend toward paid online subscriptions started with the big players, especially those with a financially motivated readership, like the *Wall Street Journal*. It spread to the *New York Times* and the *Washington Post*, and eventually, even regional papers had placed a credit card form between you and their news.

The paywalls make financial sense for the publications, and I'm all in favor of news orgs coming up with a viable business model for the internet age; far too many failed to cross that chasm. But it does bring up a bit of a conundrum in our Misinformation Age.

Real news can be costly. Fake news is free.

In addition to being priced to move, fake news also moves a lot faster.

In 2018, MIT's Sinan Aral, Soroush Vosoughi, and Deb Roy crunched the tweets and delivered research that "found that falsehood diffuses significantly farther, faster, deeper, and more broadly than the truth, in all categories of information, and in many cases by an order of magnitude."

So fake news is more accessible and travels more freely. That seems bad. But let's stay on 2020 brand and make matters a bit worse.

You pay to get real news. But sharing fake news pays you.

It doesn't pay you money. It pays you with a currency that may be even more addictive.

It pays you in likes.

Following the Capitol insurrection, Stuart A. Thompson and Charlie Warzel wrote an excellent piece in the *New York Times* that explained the appeal and rewards associated with falsehood spreading.

[Dominick] McGee is 26, a soft-spoken college student and an Army veteran from Augusta, Ga. Look at his Facebook activity today, and you'll find a stream of pro-Trump fanfare and conspiracy theories.

But for years, his feed was unremarkable—a place to post photos of family and friends, musings about love and motivational advice.

Most of his posts received just a handful of likes and comments.

That changed after the presidential election, when he began posting about what he believed was suspicious activity around the vote . . .

We reviewed the public post histories for dozens of active Facebook users in these spaces. Many, like Mr. McGee, transformed seemingly overnight. A decade ago, their online personas looked nothing like their presences today.

A journey through their feeds offers a glimpse of how Facebook rewards exaggerations and lies . . .

"People are engaging me, encouraging me to share what I think, but these are the inner workings of my mind," he said. "I've been feeling this way for years. That's why it's so easy for me to make posts, because I've been suppressing this stuff forever."

And yet when he talks about Facebook, he focuses on algorithms and optimization, not community or ideology. It's worth considering: Would he be attempting to influence others so forcefully without Facebook's incentives?

As a person who has been trying to go viral since I first used a Global Village modem to dial into CompuServe, let me toss out a possible answer to that question.

No.

Lies are more rewarding to the sharer and they're also more satisfying for the sharee, because the sharer can hone the message based on what works, without worrying about what's real. This was core to Trump's success, but the tactic was explained five decades before he deployed it.

> Lies are often much more plausible, more appealing to reason, than reality, since the liar has the great advantage of knowing beforehand what the audience wishes or expects to hear. He has prepared his story for public consumption with a careful eye to making it credible, whereas reality has the disconcerting habit of confronting us with the unexpected, for which we were not prepared. (Hannah Arendt, *Lying in Politics*)

So let's review. Fake news is cheaper than real news. Fake news spreads faster than real news. Sharing fake news is more immediately gratifying than sharing real news. And fake news is more satisfying to those who receive it.

That combination of factors is pretty hard to digest. No wonder people avoid reality.

7

JULY— INVERSION

"Like an odorless gas, economic inequality pervades every corner of the United States and saps the strength of its democracy." That's how George Packer once described America's ever-widening income gap. In 2020, the pandemic made the noxious fumes more visible, and the odor was stinking up the place.

Jeff Bezos's Amazon ownership had been cut in 2019, as MacKenzie Scott, his former wife, maintained 25 percent of the couple's Amazon stock after their divorce. Yet, less than a year after the divorce was finalized, Jeff Bezos's wealth had already eclipsed the couple's pre-divorce combined wealth. By July 2, Jeff had set a new record for personal net worth, coming in at just under $172 billion. (That's not a bad attribute to have on one's post-divorce Tinder profile.) MacKenzie wasn't doing too badly. She was worth $57 billion, making her the twelfth-richest person in the world. To her credit, Mackenzie gave money away at a feverish pace in 2020, donating nearly $6 billion. But with the market behaving like it was, she earned a lot of it right back and still ended the year as the second-wealthiest woman in the world.

Of course, Jeff Bezos is an extreme example. He was the richest person in the world running what may have been the most vital brand in America. Millions of others made a lot of money just buying Amazon's stock, which would pay for all their pandemic Amazon purchases, and then some. It didn't take a genius to invest in companies that would clearly benefit from the stay-at-home economy. But it did take capital. And that was something plenty of now-jobless Americans were running out of.

Like most of the bad stuff during the pandemic, the jobs crisis hit Blacks and Latinos harder than most. And the virus wasn't playing fair either, nor was the health care afforded to those most in need. In the *New York Times*, Brian M. Rosenthal, Joseph Goldstein, Sharon Otterman, and Sheri Fink explained WHY SURVIVING THE VIRUS MIGHT COME DOWN TO WHICH HOSPITAL ADMITS YOU.

> The likelihood of survival may depend in part on where a patient is treated. At the peak of the pandemic in April, the data suggests, patients at some community hospitals were three times more likely to die as patients at medical centers in the wealthiest parts of the city. Underfunded hospitals in the neighborhoods hit the hardest often had lower staffing, worse equipment and less access to drug trials and advanced treatments at the height of the crisis.

While this hospital review focused on New York, similar scenarios would play out across rural America, where income inequality was also a preexisting condition. Like retail, your odds of surviving COVID-19 often came down to location, location, location. And if you were broke, you were in the wrong place.

The flame stokers of the culture wars had deviously convinced Americans from different regions, and from rural and urban America, that they were on opposing sides. The truth is that they were on the same side, and that side was getting screwed by the widening economic divide.

By midyear, the mirror held up to America was more of a fun house mirror. Looking from the angle of the investor class, the reflection was so fat as to be bursting at the seams. From the less fortunate angle shared by America's working class, millions of whom were now unemployed, the reflection was of a narrowing body being gradually whittled away to nothing. Those at the top were learning to bake bread. The rest of America was lining up for it.

MOUNT RUSHLIMBAUGH

The president delivered an Independence Day speech in which the racial dog whistles became a bullhorn.

> Our nation is witnessing a merciless campaign to wipe out our history, defame our heroes, erase our values, and indoctrinate our children. Angry mobs are trying to tear down statues of our Founders, deface our most sacred memorials, and unleash a wave of violent crime in our cities. Many of these people have no idea why they are doing this, but some know exactly what they are doing. They think the American people are weak and soft and submissive. But no, the American people are strong and proud, and they will not allow our country, and all of its values, history, and culture, to be taken from them . . . In our schools, our newsrooms, even our corporate boardrooms, there is a new far-left fascism that demands absolute allegiance. If you do not speak its language, perform its rituals, recite its mantras, and follow its commandments, then you will be censored, banished, blacklisted, persecuted, and punished. It's not going to happen to us. Make no mistake: this left-wing cultural revolution is designed to overthrow the American Revolution. In so doing, they would destroy the very civilization that rescued billions from poverty, disease, violence, and hunger, and that lifted humanity to new heights of achievement, discovery, and progress.

Happy Fourth of July, everybody!

In other news, Kanye West announced he was running for president. And 2020 was like, "Whatever . . . "

PRISON OUTBREAK

In a year marked by bad decision-making, it was hard to have a single bad decision stand out: which brings us to the case of San Quentin.

In addition to ICUs, nursing homes, and meat plants, jails and prisons were some of the places most susceptible to COVID-19 outbreaks, where the virus could turn short stints into death sentences. City and state leaders had gone to great efforts to reduce prisoner populations, foreseeing the danger of overcrowding in places that were designed to make social distancing nearly impossible.

For the first several months of the pandemic, officials at San Quentin had done a good job keeping the virus out of the facility. But then, following an outbreak at the California Institution for Men in Chino, the California Department of Corrections and Rehabilitation (CDCR) decided to transfer nearly two hundred prisoners to other facilities without testing them first. Predictably, the San Quentin numbers started to climb.

DJ Patil, the former US chief data scientist, was still acting as an unpaid volunteer supporting California's efforts on COVID-19. When I asked DJ about the San Quentin issue, he said that folks at the state level immediately knew that the decision to transfer prisoners from a site with a coronavirus outbreak to a site without one was a terrible mistake. Not long after buses unloaded the prisoners (and the infections) at San Quentin, people on the state's task force began drawing up a series of strategies to minimize the ramifications of the bad decision. When they tried to push the strategies out to the CDCR and affected prisons, what they found was a system too exhausted to react in a timely and effective manner. Most of our institutions were simply unprepared to deal with this unprecedented challenge, and prisons were no exception. The response was basically, "It's taking everything we've got just to keep our heads above water. We can't start implementing new strategies."

My childhood friend Dr. Michael Levin is a psychoanalyst working in San Francisco and acted as my personal advisor on the many psychological impacts of this crazy year that turned our communal unconscious into a boxing speed bag. Very early in the pandemic, he and Dr. Elizabeth Rawson knew that the impact would be particularly striking among frontline health workers who were facing combat-like trauma at work and then returning home, where family members and the community at large were having an entirely different experience of the pandemic. In just weeks, Levin and Rawson developed the Frontline Workers Counseling Project. Through the program, Bay Area therapists provided free psychological support services to hundreds of the doctors, nurses, and first responders providing health care in thankless, and often impossible, situations.

What they found was that many of the doctors-turned-patients were developing the sort of emotional numbness one often sees in war vets who have served multiple tours.

This dissociation happens at the individual level, but it can also be collective. Organizations can go numb, just like the structures of an individual mind and social formations. Sometimes, entire societies can dissociate. With little guidance from the top and an unprecedented challenge on the ground, those tasked with managing the day-to-day operations of frontline orgs often went numb. This was what DJ Patil found when he contacted folks in California's prison system. They could see the problem. They were unable to react. We saw this group psychological exhaustion at many levels in many organizations, large and small, throughout the pandemic.

And exhausted systems make deadly decisions. As *Mother Jones* reported, "On May 30, the prison of about 3,500 people on the edge of San Francisco Bay had zero coronavirus cases . . . By June 30, about 1 in 3 San Quentin prisoners had tested positive, along with 106 prison staff. San Quentin now [accounted] for more than half the coronavirus cases in the state's prisons." By the third week of July, thirteen men were dead.

THE PLOT QUICKENS
July 9, 2020

"PROSECUTORIAL MISCONDUCT! . . . This is all a political prosecution. I won the Mueller Witch Hunt, and others, and now I have to keep fighting in a politically corrupt New York. Not fair to this Presidency or Administration! . . . Courts in the past have given 'broad deference'. BUT NOT ME! . . . This is about PROSECUTORIAL MISCONDUCT. We catch the other side SPYING on my campaign, the biggest political crime and scandal in U.S. history, and NOTHING HAPPENS. But despite this, I have done more than any President in history in first 3 1/2 years! . . . POLITICAL WITCH HUNT!" Those are a few choice outtakes from the president's reaction to a pair of Supreme Court rulings related to his tax returns and financial information. All that being said (whatever it meant), the rulings weren't particularly bad for the president. Yes, by a 7–2 margin, the Supreme Court upheld the Manhattan district attorney's demand for Trump's tax return. But no, we wouldn't see them before the election. Like so many of the Trump-era rulings, they would ultimately have a greater impact on future presidents who, one hopes, WOULDN'T BREAK ALL THE RULES AND SHIT ON ALL THE NORMS. (Just trying out the all-caps thing. It doesn't read any better, but I'll admit it was sort of fun to type.)

Donald Trump on July 9: "We have cases all over the place. Most of those cases immediately get better. They get—people—they're young people. They have sniffles, and two days later, they are fine."

SHAWSHANK EXEMPTION

"You learned the two greatest things in life . . . never rat on your friends and always keep your mouth shut." That was the advice Jimmy Conway gives Henry Hill after his first arrest in *Goodfellas*. It turns out that when it comes to the extended Trump crime family, you only had to heed the first half of that feedback. Roger Stone didn't rat. But he never really kept his mouth shut. That was enough for President Trump to commute Stone's forty-month sentence in a heartbreaking work of staggering corruption. On July 11, the two luckiest people in America were Roger Stone and whoever was going to get stuck being his cellmate.

Stone's commutation was entirely unsurprising, especially to Stone, who a day before it was granted told NBC news analyst Howard Fineman: "He knows I was under enormous pressure to turn on him. It would have eased my situation considerably. But I didn't."

Having lied about his role as a liaison between WikiLeaks and the Trump campaign, Stone was in a perfect position to hurt the president where it counted, by telling all about the president's willingness to accept foreign interference in a domestic election—providing more evidence that the Mueller investigation was no hoax.

But Stone wouldn't roll.

Trump's cover-ups, like his misdeeds, were performed right out in the open. The real version of events was simultaneously the movie version of events. Nothing was left to the imagination, and there was no point in fictionalizing the plot—it was already more than entertaining enough and almost too outlandish to believe.

> Aldrich Ames, Robert Hanssen: They had tradecraft. They didn't troll people on Instagram or blab to reporters. They behaved in the way you would expect of people betraying their country: conscious of the magnitude of their acts, determined to avoid the limelight.
>
> Stone could not have been more different. He clowned, he cavorted, he demanded limelight—which made it in some ways impossible to imagine that he could have done anything seriously amiss. Bank robbers don't go on Twitter to announce, "Hey, I'm going to rob a bank, sorry, not sorry." Or so you'd expect. Yet Stone is a central figure in one of the greatest scandals in U.S. history. (David Frum, the *Atlantic*)

STORM CHASER
July 10, 2020

"I have a reputation, as you probably have figured out, of speaking the truth at all times and not sugar-coating things. And that may be one of the reasons why I haven't been on television very much lately." So said Anthony Fauci in an interview with *Financial Times*. Fauci was in his thirty-sixth year at the National Institute of Allergy and Infectious Diseases, where he was serving his sixth president and facing his most formidable foe. During the interview, Fauci expressed his increasing concern about the exponential slope of the curve and described America as "living in the perfect storm right now."

Fauci also said he hadn't met with the president in more than a month and hadn't briefed him on COVID-19 in more than two months.

With Fauci partially sidelined and the administration spreading misinformation (and germs), health care workers were forced to pick up the reality slack. John Clarke, an emeritus professor of surgery at Drexel University, wrote an op-ed in the *Washington Post* titled: *Your Mask Feels Uncomfortable? Get Over It. As a Surgeon, I Know How Vital They Are.*

> If your child is in the operating room, you want the surgeons, anesthesia providers, nurses and technicians to wear their masks—masks that cover their

noses—and follow the rules. Those in the operating room want to as well. They want to because the constraints are inconsequential to them compared to the risks of contamination to the patient.

We had reached the point where we were being talked to like we were toddlers, because so many Americans were acting like one. However, few of those in the target market for this message were reading opinion pieces from doctors in *WaPo*. So this op-ed didn't do the trick. Neither did this piece of news: For the first time, America recorded more than seventy thousand new cases in a day.

SKINS FLICKED

July 13, 2020

After fifty years of criticism, and in the face of owner Daniel Snyder's steadfast insistence that the name was permanent, the Washington Redskins announced that the team would come up with another name and mascot. The controversy over this team name had been around so long that it had already been seven years since *The Onion* published the best joke on the topic: *Washington Redskins Change Their Name to the D.C. Redskins*.

What changed? Some of America's biggest brands decided to put some skin in the game, or more accurately, they threatened to pull skin out of it.

FedEx urged the team to drop the Redskins moniker and indicated they wouldn't be renewing their stadium naming rights deal unless that urging was met with acquiescence. In addition, both Pepsi and Bank of America supported a name change, and Nike went so far as to remove Redskins-branded merchandise from its online store.

The money talked, and Daniel Snyder listened. He once famously told *USA Today*'s Erik Brady, "We'll never change the name. It's that simple. NEVER—you can use caps." But 2020 was a year when you could never say never (it was also a year when people were pretty sick of all caps).

Around the same time as the 'Skins dropped their name, Disney signed Colin Kaepernick to a deal that would include the production of "scripted and unscripted stories that explore race, social injustice and the quest for equity." FedEx, Pepsi, and Nike used back channels to make their voices heard. And now the Mouse had roared.

With the NFL season approaching, the former Redskins adopted the temporary name *Washington Football Team*, and in doing so, inadvertently found themselves rumbling, bumbling, stumbling to the greatest team name ever. I can't say this about much in 2020, but I hope it sticks.

Donald Trump on July 14: "No other country tests like us. In fact, I could say it's working too much. It's working too well. We're doing testing and we're finding thousands and thousands of cases. If it's a young guy who's got sniffles, who's you know 10 years old, gets tested, all of a sudden he's a case and he's gonna be better tomorrow."

FROM BRAD TO WORSE

By this point in the summer, I wasn't the only one suffering a bit of a breakdown.

A few weeks after the sparsely attended Tulsa rally, President Trump announced that he was replacing campaign manager Brad Parscale with Bill Stepien. The plan was for Parscale to stay on as a campaign advisor, but an incident took place at his Florida home in late September.

> According to a statement she gave to police, Candice Parscale fled their Fort Lauderdale waterfront home after watching her husband cock a handgun. Police reports and video footage depicted a chaotic situation, with Candice Parscale telling law enforcement that her husband was "ranting and raving" . . .
>
> In the police reports and on the call, Candice Parscale said her husband had been making suicidal comments and was suffering from post-traumatic stress disorder. Police also said they spotted large sized contusions on Candice Parscale's arms, cheek, and forehead.
>
> Police eventually coaxed Parscale out of his house. Body camera footage released by the Fort Lauderdale police department showed the 6-foot-8-inch Parscale—shirtless and holding a beer can—being tackled by law enforcement. After officers placed handcuffs on him, Parscale told them repeatedly, "I didn't do anything." (Alex Isenstadt and Gary Fineout, *Politico*)

Law enforcement showing up at the residence of someone who insists he didn't do anything. It was almost a rite of passage for Trump insiders. Soon, getting COVID-19 would be too.

WHO WAS THAT UNMASKED MAN?

The raging debate over mask wearing was happening across the country, and often within individual states. I thought I may have stumbled onto a parody site when I read the AP headline: *Georgia's Gov. Brian Kemp Is Explicitly Banning Georgia's Cities and Counties from Ordering People to Wear Masks in Public Places.*

But Kemp was dead serious in the deadliest of ways, and the next day, he sued Atlanta Mayor Keisha Lance Bottoms over her city's mask ordinance. Kemp explained his thinking on Twitter: "This lawsuit is on behalf of the Atlanta business owners and their hardworking employees who are struggling to survive during these difficult times."

Of course, the whole point of the mask-wearing ordinances was to make it more likely that hardworking employees would survive these difficult times.

Savannah mayor Van Johnson tweeted, "It is officially official. Governor Kemp does not give a damn about us. Every man and woman for himself/herself. Ignore the science and survive the best you can." Yes, the phrase officially official was a bit redundant, but Kemp's ordering of local leaders not to order mask wearing was recklessly reckless, or to paraphrase James Carville: it's the stupidity, stupid.

And this was a stupid fight. The mask-wearing ordinances weren't about keeping people home. They were about letting people get out safely. Limits on one's freedoms when those freedoms endanger others were nothing new. You can smoke, but you can't smoke inside a restaurant because the smoke can impact someone else's health. You can drink, but you can't drink and drive. You can yell, "You're fired!" on an overrated reality show, but you can't yell, "Fire!" in a crowded theater.

It makes perfect sense that, in a time of pandemic, you'd be able to be maskless in your own home but would be required to wear a mask in public when the germs coming out of your nose and mouth could endanger others.

Let me put this another way that freedom-loving 'mericans can relate to. It's not the guns that kill people. It's your breath.

CLEANUP IN AISLE WTF
July 21, 2020

It took a while, but by now, most big retailers were on board with requiring masks inside their establishments. The list included Walmart, Target, CVS, and Walgreens. (Amazingly, it took this long for pharmacies to require masks in places people tend to go when they're sick.) There were still some outliers, including Winn-Dixie, one of the largest grocery chains in the Deep South, where ownership took a stand: no masks required. The chain's parent company, Southeastern Grocers, explained that "stores would not be requiring masks from customers because it did not want to cause undue friction between customers and employees."

That may not have been the real reason, but it described a real and growing tension for store employees who found themselves being verbally (and even occasionally, physically) attacked when informing nonconforming shoppers that they weren't welcome in a store.

Of course, Winn-Dixie's reason for defying the mask rule trend had less to do with friction between shoppers and employees and more to do with avoiding friction between themselves and Trump's political base. How do we know this? Because Winn-Dixie reversed its policy and began requiring masks just days after making the stand, and just hours after Trump tweeted: "We are United in our effort to defeat the Invisible China Virus, and many people say that it is Patriotic to wear a face mask when you can't socially distance. There is nobody more Patriotic than me, your favorite President."

Donald Trump on July 21:

"It will disappear."

"You will never hear this on the Fake News concerning the China Virus, but by comparison to most other countries, who are suffering greatly, we are doing very well—and we have done things that few other countries could have done!"

LAP POOL

"This is such a high award and to get it from Her Majesty as well—what more can anyone wish for? This has been an absolutely magnificent day for me." That was the one-hundred-year-old captain Sir Tom Moore after he was knighted by the Queen during an outdoor, socially distanced ceremony. Moore was rewarded for raising the spirits of his country and raising a ton of money with a walkathon heard round the world. He had pledged to raise money for the National Health Service by completing one hundred laps around his garden by the time he turned one hundred, hoping to raise a few bucks a lap. News of his efforts spread quickly throughout a kingdom looking to be united around something positive. By the time he was done, he had walked his way to a cool $44,285,964.

DEAR JOHN

"When Lewis was a few months old, the manager of a chicken farm named Jesse Thornton was lynched about twenty miles down the road, in the town of Luverne. His offense was referring to a police officer by his first name, not as 'Mister.' A mob pursued Thornton, stoned and shot him, then dumped his body in a swamp; it was found, a week later, surrounded by vultures." So wrote *New Yorker* editor David Remnick in an effort to explain the scope of the life of civil rights hero, congressional representative from Georgia's Fifth District, and lifelong proponent of "good trouble," John Lewis, who died on July 17, 2020.

Barack Obama shared some memories of the man who inspired him: "When I was elected President of the United States, I hugged him on the inauguration stand before I was sworn in and told him I was only there because of the sacrifices he made."

It was sad to lose John Lewis during a particularly sad and sick American era, but it was comforting that he was uplifted toward the end of his life by the massive protests he saw unfolding on America's streets. Obama: "He could not have been prouder of their efforts—of a new generation standing up for freedom and equality, a new generation intent on voting and protecting the right to vote, a new generation running for political office."

OREGON REIGN
July 16, 2020

Run for your life! The scary urban people wearing Powell's Books T-shirts
and hopped up on artisanal ice cream infused with hand-ground, fair-trade
coffee beans are rioting in the streets. No one is safe! Board up your windows, pull your children close, and whatever you do, don't change the channel from Fox News.

That was the imaginary America Donald Trump was looking to create,
and unlike many of his other threats, which amounted to little more than
one-off tweets, the politicizing of America's protests was backed up by the
federal government's uninvited incursion into Portland.

On the day acting secretary of Homeland Security Chad Wolf landed
in Portland and described a city under siege, Oregon governor Kate Brown
described something else. A political stunt.

> This political theater from President Trump has nothing to do with public
> safety. The president is failing to lead this nation. Now he is deploying federal
> officers to patrol the streets of Portland in a blatant abuse of power by the
> federal government.

Portland has always been a city of contrasts. It has the most hipsters per
capita of any city in America, and it also has the most strip clubs per capita.
It's an old, tough, hard-drinking port town. It's also world headquarters for
microbrews and a city where it's always wine o'clock. The tension between
old and new, right and left, and rugged and hipster is part what makes Portland such an interesting town. But in a year when everything was redirected
toward the most negative outcome, the city known for light rain was suddenly known for tyrannical reign. Stumptown had become Trumptown. A
city long celebrated for its most excellent bookstore and airport carpet that
was so ugly it had its own Twitter account was suddenly known for cam-
ouflaged federal agents who were roaming the streets and tossing peaceful
protesters into the backs of unmarked vehicles.

The federal presence increased the determination of the protesters. Yes,
there were some clashes and some vandalism, but like Trump, the protesters

had political strategies of their own, including the Wall of Moms, women locked arm in arm, forming a human barricade between the protesters and agents, and the Leaf Blower Dads, who deployed their gardening-grade weapons to blow tear gas back to where it came from.

For Trump, the politics of the pandemic and the politics of Portland were both about the politics of division. Division is exactly what Trump got, both in terms of how things were playing politically and what things were being covered in the two Americas. The followers of mainstream media got a pretty accurate picture of mostly peaceful protests with occasional outbursts of arson and vandalism. The viewers of the increasing alt-right world of Fox News and even more extreme broadcasts saw a rabid war zone that, if not put down with force by armed federal riot police, would soon be coming to an exurb near you.

To one side, it was a story about moms and dads wearing slogan-covered T-shirts and grabbing leaf blowers from the garage to support police reform and youthful protesters. To the other side, it was a threat to our very way of life. You either saw a war theater or a theatrical version of an imagined war. Or, if you were Yale professor Timothy Snyder, who literally wrote the book *On Tyranny: Twenty Lessons for the Twentieth Century*, you saw familiar tactics from the last century's darkest chapters.

It is a basic feature of a state under the rule of law that a citizen can recognize legal authority and tell the police from the thugs. It is the nightmare moment of repression to be seized by unknown men. When the government itself elides the distinction between those who protect the law and those who break it, when it makes itself into a paramilitary wearing the wrong kind of camouflage, it invites others to do the same. It is not so hard, after all, to rent a van, play dress up, and start hurting people. When citizens do not know whether they are being intimidated by governmental or nongovernmental forces, the situation is rife for the kind of escalation that fascists liked. Fascists thrived in crises and indeed sought them out. (Timothy Snyder, *Foreign Policy*)

Donald Trump on July 22: "I say, 'It's going to disappear.' And they say, 'Oh, that's terrible.' . . . Well, it's true. I mean, it's going to disappear."

WALLACE AND VOMIT

On July 19, behind in some polls by double digits, a sweaty Trump was pressed on his virus performance by an unlikely source. Chris Wallace of Fox News did something rare during slt-down interviews with the president. He called him out on his misinformation, such as his claim in January that the United States has COVID-19 under control.

> I'll be right eventually. I will be right eventually. You know I said, "It's going to disappear." I'll say it again.

Wallace pressed Trump on his false claims that Joe Biden was in favor of defunding the police.

> Trump pounced, believing he had caught Wallace in a mistake.
> "Chris, you've got to start studying for these."
> He called for one of his aides to give him a copy of the "charter" that lays out a platform signed by Biden and his former rival Sen. Bernie Sanders, and began paging through it, looking for the reference to defunding the police. He couldn't find it, Wallace reported in a subsequent voice-over, adding: "The White House never sent us evidence the Bernie-Biden platform calls for defunding or abolishing police—because there is none. It calls for increased funding for police departments—that meet certain standards. Biden has called for redirecting some police funding for related programs—like mental health counseling." (Christopher Wilson, Yahoo! News)

More notably, Trump refused to commit to the election results if he lost. "I have to see. Look . . . I have to see . . . No, I'm not going to just say yes. I'm not going to say no, and I didn't last time either."

I MUST BE IN THE FRONT ROW

By this point in our shelter-in-place experience, we were starved for some normalcy. And for me, nothing could be more normal than hearing the smooth stylings of San Francisco Giants TV commentators Mike Krukow and Duane Kuiper, who were celebrating their thirtieth year as a broadcasting team. I'd never needed them more.

During a warm-up game against the A's, new Giants manager Gabe Kapler made it clear that there was nothing normal about the season, both because of the pandemic and the protests still taking place around the country. He became the first manager or coach in a major American sport to take a knee during the national anthem. Kapler has a tattoo that says *Never Again* with a flame and the dates of the Holocaust on his right calf. He'd given some thought to these issues.

Trump had given thought to these issues too, but his analysis was as foul as his tweet on the subject: "Looking forward to live sports, but any time I witness a player kneeling during the National Anthem, a sign of great disrespect for our Country and our Flag, the game is over for me!"

In stadiums, fans were replaced by cardboard cutouts. The players had to follow strict rules. The setting was surreal. But at least the baseball was real.

Maybe a little too real for Anthony Fauci. The Nationals invited him to throw out the first pitch, and it was a terrible throw. Historically terrible. But if he was going to be off the mark in 2020, this was the place to do it. Even if the throw was bad, the pitch worked. The limited-edition baseball trading card featuring Anthony Fauci set a new sales record with more than fifty-one thousand cards sold in the first twenty-four hours. (I was just hoping he'd end his career with a winning record versus COVID.)

Shortly after baseball got started, the NBA tipped off its season inside an isolation zone at Disney World, otherwise known as the *NBA bubble*. Twenty-two teams, including players, coaches, staff, and a few haircutters and DJs, played and lived within the confines of Walt Disney World. There were no fans other than the ones seen cheering from home on screens surrounding the court. The suspension of the NBA season was the moment when the pandemic got real for many Americans. Having it back was a reminder of what we'd lost and how far we hoped we'd come back. Meanwhile, seeing players, coaches, and even refs kneel during the anthems was one more reminder that the world we were returning to was different in ways unrelated to the pandemic.

Even with all the politics surrounding the return of sports, it was a simple human moment that stood out to me, because it was a funny but oddly poignant reminder that, ultimately, we were all in this together. After a single hit in Chicago's opening day matchup, first baseman Anthony Rizzo greeted Brewers shortstop Orlando Arcia at the bag with a complimentary squirt of hand sanitizer.

Who's on first? It didn't matter. Whether baseball or something else was your pastime of choice, in 2020, getting a break from politics and the pandemic, and a reminder of our commonality, was a welcome distraction.

And we needed it. Because when we were not distracted, we'd notice that by Opening Day the US had passed 4 million cases. By the end of the first week of the season, we'd hit 150,000 deaths. The distractions were good. The baseball was a relief. But when it came to the virus, America was less like the modern-day MLB and more like Mudville's "Casey at the Bat."

And somewhere men are laughing, and somewhere children shout,
But there is no joy in Mudville—mighty Casey has struck out.

News Divisions
July 2020

Maddow

OPB [1]
Federal Law Enforcement Use
Unmarked Vehicles To Grab Protesters
Off Portland Streets

The New York Times [2]
Opinion | John Lewis: Together, You
Can Redeem the Soul of Our Nation

Vanity Fair [3]
How Jared Kushner's Secret Testing
Plan "Went Poof Into Thin Air"

The Washington Post [4]
"It was like being preyed upon":
Federal officers in unmarked vans
detain Portland protesters

The New York Times [5]
Trump's Request of an Ambassador:
Get the British Open for Me

Hannity/Carlson

CNN [1]
Study finds hydroxychloroquine helped
coronavirus patients survive better

Newsweek [2]
The key to defeating COVID-19 already
exists. We need to start using it | Opinion

The Hill [3]
More willful blindness by the media
on spying by Obama administration

Gateway Pundit [4]
Young White Mother Killed By
Black Lives Matter Mob for Allegedly
Saying 'All Lives Matter,' National
Media Fully Ignores

News/Talk 1130 WISN [5]
Prominent Black Trump Supporter
Murdered in Milwaukee | News/Talk
1130 WISN | Dan O'Donnell

These are the top news links shared on Twitter
in July by followers of Rachel Maddow versus
followers of Sean Hannity or Tucker Carlson.
Source: MIT Center for Constructive Communication

8

AUGUST—
LOOP DE LOOP

UNLESS YOU'RE READING AHEAD, ALL THIS TALK OF AUTHORITARIANISM and the threat to American democracy might have you rolling your eyes like my twelve-year-old daughter. So let's switch to a topic you'll both appreciate: TikTok.

If I've said it once, I've said it 2020 times: when they come for us, they'll be performing short, comedic, lip-synched dance videos. Under a Senate bill introduced in July, TikTok would be banned on government devices, and as we rolled into August, Trump took to Twitter to threaten that he might ban TikTok altogether. It was unclear if a president could actually ban an app, and Trump was mostly building leverage to enable a US company to acquire a large piece of TikTok. But the threat was just the latest of what would be many salvos in America's cold war with the social media app owned by China's ByteDance. The battle against TikTok may have seemed frivolous, but there were several interesting layers to consider, from who can access your personal information to who will win and lose in the US social media landscape, heretofore dominated by Silicon Valley.

How viral was TikTok? According to *Vice*, users worldwide spent 2.8 billion hours on TikTok. And that was just in March. The app was huge before the pandemic lockdown, and it just kept getting bigger. Even when kids weren't using the app, you'd see them in playgrounds or carpool lines or my living room practicing TikTok dance moves, sans device.

Two friends of mine, one at the CIA, one at the Pentagon, had advised me to delete the app. So I don't want to position the concerns about TikTok as an extreme position. Having a Chinese-owned social media app embedding itself into our lives is not without risk.

But it's worth noting that the things we feared from Chinese software companies—privacy invasions, data selling, democracy disruptions—are things that American social media companies were already doing with our full cooperation. It's also worth noting that American social media companies had a particular interest in reducing competition from global players, and they had never faced this kind of a domestic business threat from a China-based company. So there were plenty of powerful corporate and government players who wanted to clean TikTok's clock.

All these factors would be topics of discussion as the year wore on and the president repeatedly threatened to ban the app. But to ban TikTok, the feds would have to take on a much more formidable foe than a Wall of Moms or a few Leaf Blower Dads: my daughter. She and her friends not only loved TikTok, they needed it. Social media has destructive qualities, but it was also providing kids with a way to reestablish some of the social interactions, from school to playdates, that had been erased by the pandemic.

Trust me, if the federal government wanted to pry TikTok from my daughter's hands, it would take a lot more than unmarked vans, camouflage-clad agents, tear gas, rubber bullets, and pepper spray. I know because I'd already tried all that.

WHAT ELON STRANGE TRIP IT'S BEEN
August 2, 2020

Even though Earth sucked in 2020, we did make some progress when it came to leaving it. NASA's Bob Behnken and Doug Hurley took the first astronaut trip into orbit that was powered by a private company. Their SpaceX capsule parachuted down to the first astronaut water landing in more than four decades. When they landed about forty miles south of Pensacola, Florida, they were surrounded by an array of uninvited pleasure vehicles, including one boat that featured a large Trump flag.

The event, while inspiring and a preview of even more important human scientific advances to come, brought up a question about the astronauts that nagged many of us in the summer of 2020.

Why'd they come back?

THIS IS US

The *Atlantic*'s Ed Yong provided invaluable reporting throughout the year. In what was still a moment when we were in the thick of a viral challenge that would get much worse, Yong summed up *How the Pandemic Defeated America*.

> Chronic underfunding of public health neutered the nation's ability to prevent the pathogen's spread. A bloated, inefficient health-care system left hospitals ill-prepared for the ensuing wave of sickness. Racist policies that have endured since the days of colonization and slavery left Indigenous and Black Americans especially vulnerable to COVID-19. The decades-long process of shredding the nation's social safety net forced millions of essential workers in low-paying jobs to risk their life for their livelihood. The same social-media platforms that sowed partisanship and misinformation during the 2014 Ebola outbreak in Africa and the 2016 U.S. election became vectors for conspiracy theories during the 2020 pandemic.

Leadership failures, a broken health system, racism, a missing safety net, internet conspiracy theories . . . throw in our prideful proclivity for getting angry at lifesaving policies, and you've got yourself a pretty good environment for success. If you're a virus.

MAIL PATTERN BOLDNESS

My baby just wrote me a letter. At least I think she did. If you lived in one of many cities where United States Postal Services had been cut by Trump appointee (and donor) Louis DeJoy, you may have been left waiting by the mailbox.

How long could you expect to wait?

According to the *Philadelphia Inquirer*, "Neighborhoods across the Philadelphia region are experiencing significant delays in receiving their mail, with some residents going upwards of three weeks without packages and letters, leaving them without medication, paychecks, and bills." This was part of an increasingly national trend as DeJoy shut down services, slashed hours, and decommissioned equipment in cities across the country. In normal times, this may have looked like just another cost-cutting measure or the latest tactic in the long quest to take the USPS private. But these weren't normal times, and the slowdown of mail was accompanied by Trump's nonstop, baseless attacks on voting by mail, a method of ballot-casting expected to be more prevalent than ever during the pandemic.

Understanding Trump and DeJoy's strategy didn't take any hard-boiled detective work. Trump repeatedly explained it: "Now they need that money in order to make the post office work so it can take all of these millions and millions of ballots . . . But if they don't get [the money] that means you can't have universal mail-in voting." (Because, you know, we wouldn't want all that voting . . .)

Trump knew he was behind in the polls. He knew that Democrats were more likely to vote by mail. Because mailed ballots are often counted after those cast on Election Day, he knew that he might be leading in swing states on Election Day, but ultimately be behind once all the votes were tallied. And by now, we had all been warned that we were unlikely to know the results of the election on November 3. It could take days or even weeks to get everything tallied during the pandemic.

So Trump did what any lifelong cheat would do. He launched a never-ending attack on the election results months before the election even took place. Early on, the attack manifested itself as an attack on voting by mail. They would be hacked. They would be fake. They shouldn't all be counted. It was all rigged and he was the victim.

Did it matter that it was all based on lies? These tactics were never about convincing everybody what was real. It was about inundating us with so much bullshit that millions of people didn't trust anything, even voting by mail, a behavior that Trump attacked nonstop while giving it a literal stamp of approval with his own vote.

Unlike your mail, you didn't have to wait around to get the message being sent by Trump. The attacks on mail and the slowdown of the mail service, unthinkable affronts to the core of American democracy, were taking place out in the open, policy by policy, speech by speech, and tweet by tweet. Trump wanted the election signed, sealed, and delivered, no matter how far he had to push democracy's envelope.

SWAN DIVE

August 3, 2020

In what could have been Trump's craziest interview while in office, Jonathan Swan found the president's kryptonite: follow-up questions.

> **Trump**: You know, there are those that say you can test too much, you do know that.
> **Jonathan Swan**: Who says that?
> **Trump**: Oh, just read the manuals. Read the books.
> **Swan**: Manuals? What manuals?
> **Trump**: Read the books. Read the books.
> **Swan**: What books?

> **Trump**: Right now, I think it's under control. I'll tell you what—
> **Jonathan Swan**: How? One thousand Americans are dying a day.
> **Trump**: They are dying. That's true. And you have—it is what it is. But that doesn't mean we aren't doing everything we can. It's under control as much as you can control it.

> **Jonathan Swan**: Oh, you're doing death as a proportion of cases. I'm talking about death as a proportion of population. That's where the U.S. is really bad. Much worse than South Korea, Germany, etc.
> **Trump**: You can't do that.
> **Swan**: Why can't I do that?

Almost every answer Trump gave in the *Axios on HBO* interview was a lie. CNN's Daniel Dale, the undisputed champion of real-time fact-checking during the Trump era, counted seventeen lies in thirty-five minutes.

Trump wouldn't say whether or not John Lewis was an impressive person, but did say, "I don't know. I don't know John Lewis. He chose not to come to my inauguration . . . I never met John Lewis, actually." He also insisted that the intelligence about Russia putting bounties on US soldiers never reached his desk. It probably had. But if it hadn't, it would be even worse. And once he knew about the intel, why didn't he bring the issue up with Vladimir Putin during a subsequent phone call? "That was a phone call to discuss other things."

It all made one wonder why this president had so rarely been pressed with simple follow-up questions.

How could this be the case? To quote the president about the now 155,000 dead Americans: "It is what it is."

EXTRA, EXTRA, MISLEAD ALL ABOUT IT

If there were some manuals, you might find that one reason many Americans graded Trump on a curve was that he had been remarkably effective at beating down opinions about those who covered him. In August, a Gallup/Knight study found the continuation of some disturbing trends among media consumers. And of course, there was a partisan divide. "Nearly 7 in 10 Republicans (67%) have a very or somewhat unfavorable opinion of the news media, versus 1 in 5 Democrats (20%)."

The big issue in the broad ecosystem we loosely called news wasn't partisan reporting or media bias; that was a false equivalence effectively pushed by Fox News. The real split was between news organizations that were reporting the news and Fox News and its ilk that operated as bizarre conspiracy-driven versions of state TV, making things up and distorting reality. There was news. And there were lies. Don't get me wrong. Reporters make mistakes. Op-ed writers can be dead wrong. And the story you get in the media is rarely the whole story. But in 2020, millions of Americans were comparing one news outlet to another when what they were really seeing was news versus *The Twilight Zone*.

BEIRUT CAUSES
August 4, 2020

A massive blast at the Port of Beirut caused damage and loss of life in the city. A long warned-about cache of ammonium nitrate stored at the port had set off explosions that flattened part of the city and left a huge 141-foot crater behind. More than 200 people were killed, 7,500 were injured, and hundreds of thousands were left homeless. The explosion that damaged homes as far as six miles from the port was felt in Turkey, Syria, and Israel, and heard as far away as Cyprus.

President Trump said that the explosion "looks like a terrible attack" and later added that US officials "seem to think it was an attack. It was a bomb of some kind."

Instead, it was an instantaneous example of what Americans had been experiencing in slow motion: government neglect, incompetence, and corruption in the face of a deadly threat they were repeatedly warned about.

Shortly after Trump shared his analysis of the monster explosion, Pentagon officials corrected it and said there was no indication that there was an attack of any kind.

Ordinarily, an American suggestion of an attack in a Middle East capital would immediately put the world's governments on alert. But that didn't happen. The president's reputation, along with America's by extension, had already been blown to bits. The world had stopped taking Trump's words seriously. Unfortunately, the same wasn't true at home.

RULES OUT FOR SUMMER

Two students from North Paulding High School in Georgia shared a first-day-of-school photo on social media that featured crowded hallways and a lot of maskless students. The students were suspended for sharing the photo. The backlash from that suspension, an incident that was now getting national attention, forced school officials to reverse their position. A couple days later, the entire school shifted to online learning after six students and three staffers tested positive for COVID-19. (And for the first time, every student in a high school knew exactly what *irony* means.)

While the two students from North Paulding High School were called out for the wrong reason (telling the truth), Trump was finally starting to get called out by social media companies for spreading overt falsehoods. On the same day, both Facebook and Twitter removed Trump campaign posts because of Trump's own words suggesting that schools should reopen because kids were "almost immune from this disease."

In fairness to the president, it sort of depends on your definition of *almost*. By this point, there were hundreds of thousands of confirmed cases reported in children.

I never saw the school debate as being open versus close. It was between those who yelled, "Open!" with no data and those who said, "Of course we want to open, but let's get some facts first." In areas where there were low case counts, schools were open throughout the year. In other areas, smaller, private schools were able to maintain social distancing, so those schools often opened much sooner (further widening the education gap). Most of us wanted to open everything as soon as we could. The point was doing so without killing anyone. I was endlessly bummed that my son would be starting high school on Zoom (and he wasn't that excited about spending his freshman year staring at my balding head rising behind this laptop). But when it came to this story, one had to look back before looking forward. My kids should've been attending school in person in the fall. So should have yours. By now, the viral curve had become a self-inflicted wound. We needed a plan. We got tweets.

The same dynamic hit college sports. Because they saw the playing of college football as a political win, especially in Big Ten swing state country, the administration pushed for the leagues to kick things off. Mike Pence tweeted: "America needs College Football! It's important for student-athletes, schools, and our Nation. These Great athletes have worked their whole lives for the opportunity [to] compete on the college gridiron and they deserve the chance to safely get back on the field!"

The athletes? Yes, they deserved the chance to play. But the issue wasn't whether *they* had worked hard enough, it's whether the administration had. In sports, all that matters is what's on the scoreboard. You can't lose yardage on every play and get the win just because you bang your chest, raise your hands toward the heavens, and dump a bucket of Gatorade on your coach. You can't come from behind on a last-second field goal when you've spent the entire game on the sidelines insisting it's a hoax. Or as my high school football coach used to say, you can't make chicken cacciatore out of chicken shit.

VROOM WITH A VIEW
August 7, 2020

Nothing was the same in 2020. Except the 80th Sturgis Motorcycle Rally. Like the 79th before it, about 250,000 bikers rolled and rumbled into Sturgis, South Dakota, for an unmasked, often indoor, weekend festival. That it happened at all was an affront. Worse was the glee with which the pandemic recommendations were mocked.

> People rode from across the country to a state that offered a reprieve from coronavirus restrictions, as South Dakota has no special limits on indoor crowds, no mask mandates and a governor who is eager to welcome visitors and the money they bring. "Screw COVID," read the design on one T-shirt being hawked. "I went to Sturgis" . . .
>
> Bikers rumbled past hundreds of tents filled with motorcycle gear, T-shirts and food. Harley Davidson motorcycles were everywhere but masks were almost nowhere to be seen . . .
>
> For Stephen Sample, who rode his Harley from Arizona, the event was a break from the routine of the last several months, when he's been mostly homebound or wearing a mask when he went to work as a surveyor.
>
> "I don't want to die, but I don't want to be cooped up all my life either."
> (Stephen Groves, AP)

From Sturgis, there were reports of packed bars, bikini wrestling, and even an indoor event in which revelers competed to see who could sneeze the farthest. The bikers who attended the rally didn't want to be cooped up. Neither did COVID-19. Over the same weekend bikers gathered in

Sturgis, the US hit five million cases. Those case numbers were nothing to sneeze at.

Donald Trump on August 7: "It's going to disappear."

CHOP SHOP
August 11, 2020

According to the *Wall Street Journal*, Amazon was in talks with Simon Property Group to convert old Sears and JCPenney stores into Amazon delivery hubs. Welcome to the new economy during a pandemic. We're gonna kill your business and then use your corpse as a distribution center.

KAMALA MODE

I remember exactly where I was when I got the iPhone notification that Kamala Harris would be Joe Biden's running mate. During the Obama administration, I had a few connections in DC that could have made for a great Washington trip with my kids, who would get the VIP treatment and, I hoped, lock in some unconscious associations between global superpowerdom and their dad. The problem was that my kids were still a little too young to really appreciate the trip. And besides. What was the rush? I'd probably have a few friends in high places during the Hillary Clinton era.

Whoops.

Cut to four years later and my daughter, her friends, and a few passersby wondering why I was running around in circles, arms raised in the air, celebrating Joe Biden's running mate selection. Since we'd supported Kamala's presidential run and she's from the Bay Area, my wife got to know her. And isn't this what politics is all about? After four years on the outside, four years of donations, four years of tweets, four years of marches, I had finally clawed my way back to the place where I belonged: I knew people who knew people.

So as big as the moment was for Biden, Harris, and history, it was even bigger for me. And it was more than just the personal connection and what I was sure would be a bucket-list trip to the nation's capital. The Harris pick set up the perfect matchup.

The former San Francisco DA and California attorney general versus the administration that demonized the city and the state. The person who actually worked in the law-and-order business versus the guys who just tweeted about law and order. The woman of color against versus a guy with a long history of sexual assault and racism. In short, the prosecutor versus the criminals. If we were going to have a vote about America and her values, then let's have it.

> **Dave Pell** ✓
> @davepell
>
> Pence: A guy who's afraid to be alone with a woman.
>
> Kamala: A woman he should be afraid of.
>
> 2:35PM · Aug 11, 2020 · 🐦 Twitter

MODE DEJOY

August 15, 2020

Voting by mail remained an obsessive topic of Trump tweets and speeches, yet there was no evidence that the service would have any real problems delivering the ballots, unless those problems were caused by the Trump administration.

The postal service delivers billions of pieces of mail during the holidays. The system could handle the election. The problem was that the people arguing that the system was broken were the ones trying to break the system. Courts around the country were hearing cases aimed at preventing a mail slowdown, and the postal service inspector general was reviewing DeJoy's policy changes and potential ethics conflicts. By this point in Trump's tenure, I'd advised my kids to both try to become inspectors general. The work never seemed to run out.

Neither snow nor rain nor heat nor gloom of night stays these couriers from the swift completion of their appointed rounds. So some decommissioned sorting machines and a few thousand tweets weren't going to prevent your ballot from being delivered. The inspector general could stop the corruption, and voting rights groups could win the legal cases. But, remember, the goal was not only to break the vote-by-mail system. It was to make people lose faith in the vote-by-mail system. And it was working. According to a mid-August NBC / *Wall Street Journal* poll: "Just 36 percent of Republicans say they have confidence that the presidential election's results overall will be counted accurately, while just 23 percent say the same of ballots sent by mail. Nearly three-quarters, 73 percent, of Republicans believe that votes cast by mail will not be counted accurately."

Margaret Sullivan, the *Washington Post*'s media columnist, argued that *Trump's Attacks on the Postal Service Deserve Sustained, Red-Alert Coverage from the Media*. Of course, she was right. That coverage would help make sure the postal service got ballots delivered. But at the same time, the extensive coverage would also fuel the conspiracy machine and make a lot of people believe everything is rigged. Trump lied about the post office and tried to slow down the mail. The media rightfully covered that story as a threat. And voters were left with the impression that the ability of the postal service to deliver the mail was in question. Trump wanted the mail to be an issue. And mail became an issue. The coverage ensured the ballots would arrive on time. Faith in the system among Trump followers would be a much harder thing to deliver.

Donald Trump on August 17: "It's going to be gone. And it's going to be gone soon."

BOLT ACTION

I'm the first to admit we're weather weaklings in the Bay Area, spoiled by the mild conditions we pay top dollar to enjoy. So I didn't complain too much about the heat wave we had been experiencing for months.

But things got weird in the still-dark morning of August 16 when wrecking ball thunder woke my family, all of whom gathered by the windows to watch something I'd never seen in my half century living in the area: a massive lightning storm over the San Francisco Bay.

It was awe-inspiring. It made for some viral photos and videos. And it provided bonus entertainment for my kids, who, by this point in the quarantine, had watched all of Netflix twice.

But like everyone else in Northern California who was watching the light show that followed another unseasonably hot, dry summer, we knew what the lightning meant: fire.

It didn't help that the lightning storm wasn't part of a wet, cooling trend. A Death Valley town called Furnace Creek soared to 130 degrees Fahrenheit, among the hottest temperatures ever recorded. (Or as our grandchildren will call it: mild.)

Human nature had ruined much of 2020. Mother Nature was about to take her shot.

UNCONVENTIONAL

In 2004, I was among a group of about thirty people who were the first bloggers to attend a national convention. On our first morning, the speaker at our Blogger Breakfast in a drab hotel breakout room was a slim senator from Chicago named Barack Obama. We were followed everywhere we went. I was interviewed by NPR and featured in a live shot on CNN. Why did a bunch of bloggers get covered by big media? Because conventions are generally boring, and we were the new, shiny objects that made this one different. At least until the guy who spoke at our Blogger Breakfast gave a keynote address that would alter the course of American history.

Because of the pandemic's impact on the usual plans, the 2020 conventions were filled with new, shiny objects, and some old, dark messaging.

The Dems went first. After months of being described by the Trump messaging machine as a dim-witted, senile, barely functional crook who was hiding in his basement, Democrats were relieved, and one imagines many Republicans were shocked, to see *Sleepy Joe Biden* give a speech like he had been shot out of the basement on a rocket ship. But it was the somber moments in the speech that made the clear distinction between him and his opponent.

On this summer night, let me take a moment to speak to those of you who have lost the most. I know how it feels to lose someone you love. I know that deep black hole that opens up in your chest. That you feel your whole being is sucked into it. I know how mean and cruel and unfair life can be sometimes.

But I've learned two things. First, your loved ones may have left this Earth but they never leave your heart. They will always be with you. And second, I found the best way through pain and loss and grief is to find purpose.

Biden, whose speeches often played for nostalgia, cued an oldie none of us had heard from the top of the government for three and a half years: empathy.

> Dave Pell ✔
> @davepell
>
> It's about empathy. Bone spurs shouldn't prevent you from walking a mile in someone else's shoes.
>
> 8:51 PM · Aug 27, 2020 · ✔ Twitter

How can I be sure the speech was good? My twelve-year-old daughter reviewed it: "I like Biden. He's cool. He's chill. He seems like someone who would be Dad's friend." That's the nicest thing she said about either one of us during quarantine.

If Joe Biden surprised with his energy, Barack Obama surprised with his tone. He delivered the saddest, scariest, and starkest speech of his career, arguing that American democracy itself was at stake. It was a point that had been made with increasing urgency in columns and on TV panels for years. But it was different to hear this warning from the usually reserved former president.

This president and those in power—those who benefit from keeping things the way they are—they are counting on your cynicism. They know they can't win you over with their policies. So they're hoping to make it as hard as possible for you to vote, and to convince you that your vote doesn't matter. That's how they win. That's how they get to keep making decisions that affect your life, and the lives of the people you love. That's how the economy will keep getting skewed to the wealthy and well-connected, how our health systems will let more people fall through the cracks. That's how a democracy withers, until it's no democracy at all. We can't let that happen. Do not let them take away your power. Don't let them take away your democracy.

Dave Pell ✔
@davepell

If the Obama speech made it seem like America itself is at stake, you got it right

If it surprised you, you haven't been paying attention.

8:26 PM · Aug 19, 2020 · 🐦 Twitter

While the speeches stood out because of empathy and urgency, the Democratic roll call stood out for its commonality. Forced to nominate Joe Biden remotely, each state selected an individual or group to nominate him from their state. In the process, we saw the unique cultures, backdrops, and quirks that make America what it is, providing a much-needed reminder that our differences don't divide us, they're what make us interesting. I'm loath to suggest a reality show after four years of a reality show president, but if anyone took the roll call idea and expanded it into a weekly show where people could share small moments of their lives from different parts of the country, I have a feeling it would do well in ratings and be good for society.

Cut to the Republican convention, the first night of which featured Don Jr. girlfriend, former Fox News broadcaster, and oddly, former Gavin Newsom wife Kimberly Guilfoyle, yelling, and I mean *yelling*:

> They want to destroy this country and everything that we have fought for and hold dear. They want to steal your liberty, your freedom, they want to control what you see and think and believe so that they can control how you live. They want to enslave you to the weak, dependent, liberal victim ideology to the point that you will not recognize this country or yourself.

Speaking on behalf of they, what they really wanted was not to be killed by a deadly virus and to keep America looking and sounding like a constitution-driven, democratic republic. But I wasn't the audience for Guilfoyle (though it was so loud, I definitely heard her). And I definitely wasn't the audience for the Trump hero worship that set the stage for the rest of the convention. A few outtakes from various speakers:

"I am so in awe of your leadership."

"There's only one person who has empathized with everyday Americans and actually been fighting for them over the past four years, and that is President Donald Trump."

"Just imagine what 2020 would have looked like, fighting for your life, without Donald Trump fighting for it too. In January, there would have been no China travel ban. Millions would have died. Millions more would have been infected. There would have been no record levels of testing . . . no fast track for a vaccine."

"We will build a future where America remains the greatest country ever to exist in the history of the world. All of that is within our grasp if we secure four more years for the defender of Western civilization."

The Democrats pitched Joe Biden as a decent, honest guy who eats ice cream with his granddaughters. The GOP pitched Trump as Zeus.

For the rest of the week, Trump used the White House as a TV set for his political convention, busting norms, breaking rules, and flouting laws. From using the White House as a backdrop, to a speech from a sitting secretary of state beamed in from Jerusalem, to an on-screen pardon, Trump took a hatchet to the Hatch Act. Even the emoluments clause looked at the Hatch Act and was like, "Bro, show a little effort out there."

We knew, going into this convention, that Trump would make use of the grounds of the White House as he made his bid for reelection. But he has actually gone further, by using the actual powers his office bestows on him to perform presidential acts as part of the convention. It's strange, because the act of pardoning a reformed prisoner or naturalizing a citizen is both uniquely presidential and, for presidents, relatively routine. But turning that kind of sober, consequential, and legal ceremony into a live show that is a bid for your reelection? That would be chilling if it weren't so decidedly Mark Burnett. But it's also just really chilling. (Dahlia Lithwick, *Slate*)

During the final night of the GOP convention, Donald Trump spewed enough B.S. to keep the White House South Lawn fertilized in perpetuity. He also made it clear how thoroughly he had mowed down his party and regrown it in his image. The South Lawn may as well have been the fairway of one of his golf courses at the conclusion of a convention that featured as speakers more Trumps than Republican senators. Attendees gathered shoulder to shoulder, ignoring social distancing rules established for a pandemic they were determined to portray as being over. As the *New Yorker*'s Susan B. Glasser explained, "The real message of the evening was that nothing, not even a deadly plague or a cratering economy, can stop Trump from being Trump. He bragged. He lied. He even ad-libbed a taunt at his critics, using the White House as his prop. 'We're here,' he said, pointing to the flood-lit mansion behind him, 'and they're not.'"

Minnesota senator Amy Klobuchar got off the line of the night:

But getting this president off our lawn, or out of the White House, would be easier said than done. Tens of millions Americans saw this two-bit yard sale and were eager to buy.

TRILL SEEKERS

I'm old enough to remember when being part of the 1 percent meant you were one of the few people who used an Apple computer. Times changed. Apple became the dominant consumer computing company. And just two years after becoming the first publicly traded company with a $1 trillion valuation, Apple became the first publicly traded company with a $2 trillion valuation.

First we had to think different. Now we had to count different too.

BOXERS OR DEBRIEFS

Alexey Navalny, a Russian anti-corruption fighter and one of Vladimir Putin's only formidable opponents, was poisoned and became ill on a plane that was forced to make an emergency landing. Navalny, who fell into a coma, was airlifted to Germany, where he was treated and narrowly escaped death.

After recovering, Navalny called out Putin and those who remained silent about the use of toxins to kill and terrorize political opponents: "I think it's extremely important—that everyone, of course, including and maybe the first of all, President of United States, to be very against using chemical weapons in the 21st Century."

As was the case throughout his presidency, Trump refused to call out Putin for the poisoning.

Navalny would later act as his own undercover agent when he posed as an official in Russia's Security Council and was able to debrief an operative who had been sent in to clean up evidence after the attempted murder. During the interview, the operative confirmed that an elite toxins team from Russia's security service had planted a lethal nerve agent in Navalny's underpants.

CONWAY TWITTER

Giving less than two weeks' notice, Kellyanne Conway, a senior advisor to the president and quite often the media mouthpiece of the administration, announced that she would be stepping away from her role to focus on her family. That's a familiar excuse when retiring from politics, but in this case, Conway meant it. Her husband, George T. Conway III, a well-known conservative lawyer, and an even more well-known Twitter user who strongly opposed the administration for which his wife worked, also announced that he would be relinquishing his role at the Lincoln Project, a well-funded group of anti-Trump conservatives that put out an endless array of ads aimed at irking the president. In addition to stepping away from his role at the Lincoln Project, Conway announced that he would be taking a hiatus from tweeting.

One parent went fully off the rails in a quest for fame and power at the expense of decency and democracy. The other parent tried to pull her back to the realm of reality via that intimate family communication tool known as Twitter. And both left their kids confused as to how this broken generation could have left the family and country in tatters. And as was the case in many American households, the combined stressors of insane politics and a deadly pandemic had ripped the family's social fabric to shreds.

Their daughter Claudia Conway had become internet famous on TikTok and other platforms, and her sometimes heartbreaking tweets served as a painful metaphor for the state of mind of many Americans. Maybe more of us should have followed the plan she outlined in what would be her penultimate tweet of 2020. "this is becoming way too much so i am taking a mental health break from social media. see y'all soon."

WISCONSIN CITY
August 23, 2020

In Kenosha, Wisconsin, the summer of racial unrest suffered another crisis when police officer Rusten Sheskey shot at Jacob Blake's back seven times as Blake opened the driver's-side door of his SUV. Police had arrived on the scene after getting a call about a domestic incident. Blake had been tased before going toward his car, where the police union argued he was reaching for a knife. Blake was left paralyzed from the waist down. Wisconsin governor Tony Evers called for action: "While we do not have all of the details yet, what we know for certain is that he is not the first black man or person to have been shot or injured or mercilessly killed at the hands of individuals in law enforcement in our state or our country."

The shooting led to several nights of protests in Kenosha, and the protests devolved into arson, vandalism, and looting, bringing outsiders into the community, which was now being patrolled by the national guard and civilians armed with guns.

One of those civilians was a semiautomatic-weapon-toting Kyle Rittenhouse, a seventeen-year-old from Antioch, Illinois, about fifteen miles outside of Kenosha. By the end of his first night on patrol, Rittenhouse would be taken into custody for killing two people and injuring another.

Shortly thereafter, Mark Zuckerberg acknowledged in a video post that the company made a mistake by not taking down an event listing for militia groups that encouraged armed civilians to defend the streets of Kenosha. Zuck described the failure as "largely an operational mistake." It may have been an operational mistake, but outrage on the platform was quite obviously a strategic goal.

On Fox News, Tucker Carlson defended the Kenosha murders: "Are we really surprised that looting and arson accelerated to murder? How shocked are we that 17-year-olds with rifles decided they had to maintain order when no one else would?"

The president's view wasn't much different. Trump refused to condemn Rittenhouse and explained, "We're looking at all of it. And that was an interesting situation. You saw the same tape as I saw. And he was trying to get away from them, I guess; it looks like. And he fell, and then they very violently attacked him. And it was something that we're looking at right now and it's under investigation. But I guess he was in very big trouble. He would have been—I—he probably would have been killed."

The facts, as reported by the AP: "His implication that Rittenhouse only shot the men after he tripped and they attacked him is wrong. The first fatal shooting happened before Rittenhouse ran away and fell."

HOOP D'ÉTAT

Public protests over the Blake shooting spread to many cities and sports leagues. Minutes before their scheduled first-round NBA bubble playoff game against the Orlando Magic, the Milwaukee Bucks opted to remain in the locker room and boycott the game. Later the same day, all the NBA playoff teams decided to postpone the playoffs for the day. The WNBA, MLB, NHL, and Major League Soccer all ultimately postponed or canceled games to protest the shooting of Jacob Blake.

No charges were brought against Officer Rusten Sheskey.

News Divisions
August 2020

Maddow

The Washington Post 1
Democrats call for investigation of postmaster general over mail delays

The New York Times 2
G.O.P.-Led Senate Panel Releases Final Report on Russian Interference and Ties to Trump

Vice 3
The Post Office Is Deactivating Mail Sorting Machines Ahead of the Election

The New York Times 4
Justice Dept. Never Fully Examined Trump's Ties to Russia, Ex-Officials Say

The Washington Post 5
In secretly recorded audio, President Trump's sister says he has 'no principles' and 'you can't trust him'

Hannity/Carlson

Daily Mail 1
Bill Clinton receives neck massage from Jeffrey Epstein victim

Gateway Pundit 2
SHOCK REPORT: This Week CDC Quietly Updated COVID-19 Numbers - Only 9,210 Americans Died From COVID-19 Alone - Rest Had Other...

The Federalist 3
FBI Attorney Kevin Clinesmith Pleads Guilty To Falsifying Carter Page FISA Warrant

The Western Journal 4
Exclusive from Gen. Flynn: This Is My Letter to America

New York Post 5
This is why Jacob Blake had a warrant out for his arrest

These are the top news links shared on Twitter in August by followers of Rachel Maddow versus followers of Sean Hannity or Tucker Carlson.
Source: MIT Center for Constructive Communication

TED TALKS

I came of age during the *Nightline* era, when Ted Koppel remade the news landscape, covering the Iran hostage crisis for 444 days. One story. The same story. Every night. During the early days, Koppel's show was called *The Iran Crisis: America Held Hostage*. And we were, by a news story.

That show started in 1979. The next year, CNN brought us twenty-four-hour cable news. This was back before opinion panels took over, when cable news anchors spent the majority of each hour throwing it to far-flung reporters in the field, who covered a wide variety of stories.

It didn't take long for cable news execs to realize Americans liked to focus on one story at a time. It started with the Gulf War, broadcast live around the clock, from the time the first bombs dropped. That war put CNN on the map, and it put single-story coverage in the money.

And then, in 1995, a single story drove through our living rooms in a white Ford Bronco, with O. J. Simpson sitting in the passenger seat.

It's hard to describe how fully captivated we were by that news story. Well, it *was* hard to describe, until Donald Trump put his hand on a Bible and took the oath of office in front of a crowd, the size of which would grow to astronomical proportions in the mind of the president and his supporters.

After Trump completed his American Carnage inaugural address, George W. Bush leaned over to Hillary Clinton and said, "Well, that was some weird shit."

The *next four years* then leaned over to the former president and said, "W, hold my beer."

Walter Cronkite famously signed off his evening newscasts with the line, "And that's the way it is." Of course, viewers knew that what fit into the evening news only represented a tiny part of the way it is. But at least during that news era, even when we only had a handful of news choices, there were several unrelated stories squeezed into a half-hour broadcast. Cut to the modern news cycle when the internet provides us with infinite channels, yet somehow, all the channels ended up reporting the same stories about the same guy all the time.

The Donald Trump era was the equivalent of O.J.'s white Ford Bronco chase lasting four straight years.

Covering one story meant that the cable news networks could essentially broadcast a nonstop, scriptless soap opera. You were hooked, your friends were hooked. Everyone knew every character. Anthony Scaramucci was Trump's White House communications director for ten days, and he had more name recognition than anyone who'd ever held that job. An entire ecosystem of people talking about the same story was spawned overnight, and it never stopped expanding, as it added journalists, podcasters, former politicians, newsletter writers, celebrities, lawyers, and even epidemiologists.

But the model has some pretty terrible side effects. In addition to leaving you less informed, the cable channels were well into a migration from reporting news to just showing hour after hour of people talking about the news. This is cheaper to produce, and it made sense in 2020 since everyone was caught up on the story anyway. We just wanted to get together and vent. But in addition to leaving you less informed about anything that wasn't Trump related, this new model of news expanded the very definition of news. In the years leading up to 2020, reporting and opinion merged, and then opinion took over.

This broader definition of news allowed a similar-looking brand like Fox News to call itself *news*, even though, by 2020, it was operating as a de facto version of Trump's state media, spreading presidential propaganda in lieu of dispensing lifesaving facts.

Trump said he'd drain the swamp. He didn't. But he did turn the swamp into a giant watercooler around which we all could gather and discuss the latest scenes and character developments from the show that wouldn't end.

In an interview that would end his tenure, Anthony Scaramucci told the *New Yorker*'s Ryan Lizza, "I'm not Steve Bannon, I'm not trying to suck my own cock. I'm not trying to build my own brand off the fucking strength of the president. I'm here to serve the country."

A few days after being fired, he became a media personality who spent much of his time sharing his opinions about Trump. In other words, he built his own brand off the fucking strength of the president. I guess that's the next best thing to auto-fellatio.

9

SEPTEMBER— OFF THE RAILS

CAN SOMETHING GO OFF THE RAILS WHEN IT IS ALREADY OFF THE RAILS? Ordinarily, this would read as a rhetorical question, but by September of Trump's fourth year in office, it had already been repeatedly asked and answered with a resounding *yes*. Trump's leadership was off the rails, off the charts, off the chain, off course, off-putting, and off its rocker. As much as this style of office-holding can be a turnoff, keeping voters off track and off guard seemed to be a strategic goal of this offbeat presidency. But at some point, a switch went off.

A willingness to say anything, no matter how outlandish, no matter how insanely conspiratorial, in order to deflect reality, maintain control of the narrative thread, and keep the limelight fixed in his direction was nothing new for this president. It was his personal brand and lifelong passion. But there's a difference in spreading lies for personal gain and spreading conspiracies because you actually believe them.

I'm not a professional when it comes to psychoanalytic diagnosis regarding various stages of malignant narcissism with pronounced perverse, sadistic, paranoid, grandiose, and sociopathic features and a side order of psychopathy. But understanding it has always been a hobby of mine. And as I reflect on my nervous reading of the news, and cold, sweaty, sleepless nights worrying about the republic, it sure looks to this layperson like something snapped near a row of imaginary passengers on a phantom plane headed from an undisclosed location to Washington, DC.

During a Fox News interview with Laura Ingraham, the president explained that "people that are in the dark shadows . . . people you haven't heard of" were "controlling the streets" and also controlling and manipulating Joe Biden's reactions to some of the more frenzied protests happening across the country. Ingraham responded that parts of this claim sounded "like conspiracy theory." (And Laura Ingraham complaining that you sound too conspiratorial is like the Incredible Hulk complaining that you may have an anger management issue.)

Trump described a plot that had been intended to disrupt the Republican National Convention. "We had somebody get on a plane from a certain city this weekend, and in the plane it was almost completely loaded with thugs, wearing these dark uniforms, black uniforms, with gear and this and that . . . the matter is under investigation now."

It didn't take long to trace the *this and that* of the wild claim to its conspiratorial source.

The claim about the flight matches a viral Facebook post from June 1 that falsely claimed, "At least a dozen males got off the plane in Boise from Seattle, dressed head to toe in black." The post, by an Emmett, Idaho, man, warned residents to "Be ready for attacks downtown and residential areas," and claimed one passenger had "a tattoo that said Antifa America on his arm."

That post was shared over 3,000 times on Facebook, and other pages from Idaho quickly added their own spin to it, like the Idaho branch of the far-right militia group 3 Percenters.

One post claimed that "Antifa has sent a plane load of their people" and that the Payette County Sheriff's Office confirmed it. Within days, that version of the rumor picked up enough steam in Idaho Facebook groups that the Payette County Sheriff's Office had to release a statement insisting that the viral rumor was "false information." (Ben Collins, NBC News)

Dave Pell ✔
@davepell

Someone should explain to Trump that all those people on planes dressed in black are heading to Covid 19 funerals.

10:33 AM · Sep 1, 2020 · 🐦 Twitter

What was described as false information by the Payette County Sheriff's Office was described as real life in the Oval Office. Was the crazy story something Trump spread for personal gain, or did he really believe it? Was he acting crazy or going crazy?

Donald Trump on September 3–12:

"We are rounding that turn, and vaccines are coming along great."

"We're rounding the curve."

"We're rounding the bend, I feel that very strongly."

"We're hopefully rounding the final turn in the pandemic."

"We're rounding the turn on the pandemic."

"We're really rounding the corner. And this is actually without anything further than we already have . . . you can't use the word cure yet, but pretty close to a cure."

We were rounding the turn on the pandemic. It's just that around that turn, there was more pandemic.

KENOSHA NA NA

During a tour of Kenosha, parts of which had suffered damage during the Jacob Blake shooting, President Trump stopped for a video op with the owner of a local camera shop that was burned down. John Rode III thanked the president: "I just appreciate President Trump coming today, everybody here does. We're so thankful we got the federal troops here. Once they got here things did calm down quite a bit."

The violence and arson that ruined local businesses was of course wrong, and the president had every right to chat with an affected shop owner. But here's the thing. The president didn't send any troops to Kenosha; the governor of Wisconsin called in the National Guard. And John Rode III was no longer the owner of the shop that got ruined, and he hadn't been for nearly a decade. The actual store owner, Tom Gram, had declined the invitation to chat with the president, and told WTMJ-TV, "I think everything he does turns into a circus and I just didn't want to be involved in it."

In some ways, the Kenosha crisis wasn't that complicated. It's clearly wrong for a police officer to shoot a suspect in the back several times. It's also wrong to respond to that misdeed by burning down local businesses. It's also really wrong to get a semiautomatic weapon, head to Kenosha, and kill two people. But for Trump, three wrongs didn't make a right. They just offered more realities to distort. Kenosha needed a fire extinguisher. It got a pyromaniac.

THE CYCLE OF LIFELESSNESS

A few weeks had passed since the Sturgis motorcycle rally in South Dakota, and we had our first known COVID-19 death connected to the gathering. By September 2, we learned that a Minnesota biker in his sixties died after returning home from the event. He was the first, but he wouldn't be the last. A survey of health departments by the *Washington Post* would find at least 260 cases in 11 states that could be directly traced back to the event. And COVID-19 was just getting its motor running.

One day you're enjoying some bikini wrestling and a maskless sneezing contest, the next day a virus is spreading wildly across the Midwest.

KINGDOM COMES AROUND

I'm concerned about the challenges people could face when voting. I'm also worried that with our nation so divided and election results potentially taking days or even weeks to be finalized, there could be an increased risk of civil unrest across the country. This election is not going to be business as usual. We all have a responsibility to protect our democracy.

That was part of Mark Zuckerberg's announcement that Facebook would be banning all new political ads during the last week before the election.

Zuck explained the decision: "It's important that campaigns can run get out the vote campaigns, and I generally believe the best antidote to bad speech is more speech, but in the final days of an election there may not be enough time to contest new claims."

I've used quotes and examples in this book to explain why more speech is not the antidote to bad speech, at least not when it comes to the kind of authoritarian-curious tactics Trump was deploying. The goal of that bad speech was to overwhelm, confuse, exhaust, and ultimately leave voters not knowing what to believe. More speech doesn't provide an antidote to this kind of bad speech any more than rain offers an antidote to flooding.

Even if the no-new-political-ads rule was well-meaning, deploying it a week before the election was like hitting a corpse with defibrillation paddles. But the bigger deal here was just how big a factor Facebook had become in our electoral process, and just how much of that process was riding on the decisions made by a sole unelected leader whose only oath was to shareholders.

VAINGLORIOUS BASTARD
September 3, 2020

In the days following the summer's Bible walk and the use of federal troops to target peaceful protests, we saw the private fraying of Trump's military relationships go public. Matters were made worse with the release of a September blockbuster story from Jeffrey Goldberg, editor of the *Atlantic*: In the story, *Trump: Americans Who Died in War Are "Losers" and "Suckers,"* Goldberg described a visit to Arlington National Cemetery by Trump and John Kelly, then the secretary of Homeland Security.

> Kelly's son Robert is buried in Section 60. A first lieutenant in the Marine Corps, Robert Kelly was killed in 2010 in Afghanistan. He was 29 . . . Trump, while standing by Robert Kelly's grave, turned directly to his father and said, "I don't get it. What was in it for them?"

And then there was the canceled visit to the Aisne-Marne American Cemetery near Paris in 2018:

Trump rejected the idea of the visit because he feared his hair would become disheveled in the rain, and because he did not believe it important to honor American war dead . . . Trump said, "Why should I go to that cemetery? It's filled with losers." In a separate conversation on the same trip, Trump referred to the more than 1,800 marines who lost their lives at Belleau Wood as "suckers" for getting killed.

Were these stories accurate? Of course.

First, because the AP confirmed parts of the story and John Kelly never issued a denial. Second, because Trump already had a well-known history of attacking Gold Star families and blasting John McCain for being captured:

"I like people who weren't captured."
"He lost. He let us down. But, you know, he lost. So I have never
    liked him as much after that, because I don't like losers."

Third, because for this commander in chief, D-day was always Me Day.

DARKNESS VISIBLE

By this point in the year, we learned to expect the unexpected. But no one in the Bay Area expected what we saw in the middle of the day on September 9. Orange skies. After another dry summer of record heat, California was burning. For me, the ravaging fires and rolling blackouts seemed as novel as the coronavirus and provided a bleak reminder that the pandemic was merely a preview of what would be a much longer and infinitely more daunting challenge presented by the slow but consistent roll of climate change. For my kids, who had missed school for fires, floods, and a pandemic, this was all too normal. To them, warnings to stay indoors, soot in the air, a thickening layer of ash on the hoods of our cars parked fifty miles from the nearest flames, days without electricity, and the stench of smoke so thick it could wake you up in the middle of the night just meant fall was in the air.

But even for my climate-jaded kids, it was a bit unnerving to take a lunch break from Zoom school, look out the window at the dark, blood-orange skies that wrapped the Bay Area, and listen to the familiar sound of fog-horns blowing for the unfamiliar reason that it was nearly pitch black in the middle of the day

> **Dave Pell** ✓
> @davepell
>
> The SF Fog Horns are now playing "The End" by The Doors.
>
> 2:39 PM · Sep 9, 2020 · 🐦 Twitter

People experiencing the orange-and-red skies noticed immediately that the photos they took on their iPhones didn't do the colors justice, outputting a grayish, desaturated hue. There was a certain irony that we had created technological advances to remove the perception of the devastation associated with climate change from our images, but we hadn't done nearly enough to slow the progression of climate change that was currently burning a state and blocking the sun. At least my parents and I got a break from talking about our favorite topic (news) and had a chance to talk about our second-favorite topic (weather).

Australia had experienced historic fires. Now it was California's turn. By the end of August, the state was already fighting two of the biggest fires in its recorded history. Washington got hit. In Oregon, where more than 10 percent of the state's population was required to evacuate their homes, the skies looked even redder than ours. Colorado would soon face historic fires.

My godson Dylan experienced a fully 2020 start to his college experience. He quarantined for fourteen days at home in the Bay Area before traveling to Oregon, where he would be sequestered on the Lewis & Clark College

> **Dave Pell** ✓
> @davepell
>
> I smoke pot to keep from breathing Bay Area air.
>
> 6:09 PM · Sep 10, 2020 · 🐦 Twitter

campus while taking his courses over Zoom from his dorm room. After a few weeks, he was sent home because the smoke from Oregon's wildfires made the campus uninhabitable.

Like most other major news events of 2020, the fires that singed the West Coast were tinged with dangerous rumors and falsehoods. The fire hose of misinformation about the burn zones was similar to the one being used to keep COVID-19 burning brightly in America, but in the case of the West Coast fires, the lies weren't set against an invisible threat, they were rising from the embers of an inferno that people could see, smell, and feel.

> In the town of Mollala, Oregon, an hour south of Portland, some residents were so afraid of "antifa" and the "far left"—members of which they have never met, but whom they have seen and heard about on television and online—that they refused to leave their houses, even when authorities called for evacuation. "We're staying put," one resident told *The New York Times*, "and watching for people who aren't supposed to be here." He defined that category as "crowds of looters out of Portland." And there we have it: Mythical looters and mythical anarchists are now more frightening to some people than an actual forest fire. (Anne Applebaum, the *Atlantic*)

President Trump visited California to get an update on the fires, and during a public briefing with Governor Newsom's team, California Natural Resources Agency secretary Wade Crowfoot urged the president to "recognize the changing climate and what it means to our forests. If we ignore that science and sort of put our head in the sand and think it's all about vegetation management, we're not going to succeed together protecting Californians."

Trump: "It will start getting cooler, just you watch."

When pressed with the fact that science doesn't agree with that forecast, Trump responded, "I don't think science knows, actually."

More than two million acres of California had burned by the first week of September, breaking the state's all-time record that had been set just two years before. You'd think this, along with the consistently rising global temperatures, the arctic equivalent of heat waves melting glaciers with increasing speed, so many major US storms in 2020 that they ran out of human names and had to name storms after Greek letters, and warnings doled out by every sane scientist on the planet would be enough to give us pause. But then again, millions of deaths, tens of millions of cases, untold suffering, and the warnings doled out by every sane scientist wasn't enough to convince everyone about the danger presented by COVID-19.

QANON, AND ON AND ON . . .

Perhaps more troubling than what people refused to believe in 2020 were the fantastical, delusional things they *were* willing to believe. *Time*'s Charlotte Alter reported on the altered states of a disturbing number of Wisconsin voters.

> In more than seven dozen interviews conducted in Wisconsin in early September, from the suburbs around Milwaukee to the scarred streets of Kenosha in the aftermath of the Jacob Blake shooting, about 1 in 5 voters volunteered ideas that veered into the realm of conspiracy theory, ranging from QAnon to the notion that COVID-19 is a hoax. Two women in Ozaukee County calmly informed me that an evil cabal operates tunnels under the U.S. in order to rape and torture children and drink their blood. A Joe Biden supporter near a Kenosha church told me votes don't matter, because "the elites" will decide the outcome of the election anyway.

The notion that America was divided into two bubbles where people held different sets of opinions about a shared reality was always an absurd misrepresentation. That would make for a well-functioning democracy. That sure as hell wasn't what we were experiencing in the years leading up to (and one imagines, many years to follow) 2020. America was divided between those who live in reality, and those who live in a world in which they are bombarded with an endless stream of falsehoods, doctored videos, and fake news. People on both sides of the divide were victims of this relentless effort to trick Americans, because both sides suffer the ramifications when people base their opinions, actions, and votes on these lies.

During a family dinner that took place as the election neared, my twelve-year-old daughter said she wished someone other than Joe Biden was facing Donald Trump.

When I asked why, she explained, "Well, Biden is just sort of a pedophile."

A sick belief about Biden had come to my home to roost, oozing, by way of my daughter's TikTok stream, all the way to my dinner table.

ALL THE PRESIDENT'S MENDACITY

You just breathe the air and that's how it's passed. And so that's a very tricky one. That's a very delicate one. It's also more deadly than even your strenuous flu. This is deadly stuff.

That statement about COVID-19 would hardly be controversial coming from anyone else, but this was a quote from Donald Trump, a man who had spent months downplaying the risk of the virus, comparing it to the common flu, and pretending it was going to magically go away.

The first excerpts of Bob Woodward's *Rage* confirmed that Trump knew how serious the threat was in February, back when he was attacking Democrats, the media, and even his own administration's scientists who were trying to warn Americans of what was to come.

The excerpt from the Woodward book brought up an interesting debate about whether Bob Woodward should have spilled the details of his February interview with Trump the second he learned that the president was lying about a threat that would kill hundreds of thousands of Americans. It would have broken his agreement with the administration (the president understood these interviews were for a book and not for immediate publication) and could have impacted the access afforded to Woodward and future authors. So one can understand why Woodward would hold the information for the book . . . if this were an ordinary moment in history and an ordinary president. But neither was ordinary.

The other extraordinary aspect of this story was that the source of the damning leak was Trump himself. During the Nixon era, Woodward and Bernstein had to get the Watergate story from a secret source in an underground garage. During the Trump era, the president provided his own leaks. In the fullest actualization of his narcissism, Donald Trump Deep Throated himself.

SEASON OF WRECKONING

With daily testing and strict travel protocols, the NFL managed to kick off its regular schedule. When Patrick Mahomes, the Chiefs' Super Bowl champion quarterback and the NFL's top player, locked arms with his counterpart from the Texans, Deshaun Watson, in "a moment of silence dedicated to the ongoing fight for equality in our country," a significant smattering of fans booed. Moments later, as the game began, the Kansas City fans got on with their tomahawk chant. It was an inauspicious start to the NFL's season of reckoning.

There were schedule interruptions, and many players had to miss games due to either getting COVID-19 or being in close contact with someone who had. In one midseason matchup, the Denver Broncos were missing so many players that they had to play a game versus the New Orleans Saints without a quarterback.

There were some who thought the NFL should cancel more games and make more dramatic changes to its season for the safety of players and to send a vital message about the deadly seriousness of the virus. There were others who thought the games themselves were more vital than ever during a time when Americans were stuck home and generally bored and bummed.

But there was a third aspect that was less discussed. How did the NFL pull this off? By now, we'd learned that you could get COVID-19 from briefly sharing the air of an infected person. How did NFL players avoid a mass outbreak playing a sport that features heavy breathers traveling around the country to smash into each other for three straight hours?

The NFL's success was evidence that with enough testing and the right protocols, the viral curve could be flattened like a wide receiver catching a pass over the middle. The question that will haunt us is why, even months into the pandemic, the country had no truly effective testing program or behavioral protocols in place. And the question that will haunt the medical establishment is why our frontline responders didn't have access to the same level of testing as professional athletes. According to an analysis by the *Guardian* and *Kaiser Health News*, nearly three thousand American health care workers died of COVID-19 in 2020. Many of them had little access to testing. As far as I know, no one in the NFL was asked to play a game without a helmet. But even months into the crisis, many health care workers were forced to work without proper personal protective equipment.

HELL OF TROYE

Olivia Troye, who had served as Vice President Mike Pence's advisor for Homeland Security and was his top staff advisor on the White House Coronavirus Task Force, was in the room where it happened up until late July when she left her job. On September 17, she became one of the few insiders to whistleblow about the president's behavior in a video:

> By the middle of February, we knew it wasn't a matter of if Covid would become a big pandemic here in the United States, it was a matter of when. But the president didn't want to hear that because his biggest concern was that we were in an election year, and how was this going to affect what he considered to be his record of success. It was shocking to see the president saying that the virus was a hoax, saying that everything's OK, when we know that it's not. The truth is, he doesn't actually care about anyone else but himself. He made a statement once that was very striking. I never forgot it because it pretty much defined who he was. We were in a task force meeting, the president said, "Maybe this Covid thing is a good thing. I don't like shaking hands with people. I don't have to shake hands with these disgusting people." Those disgusting people are the same people he claims to care about. These are the people still going to his rallies today who have complete faith in who he is. If the president had taken this virus seriously or if he had actually made an effort to tell how serious it was, he would have slowed the virus spread. He would have saved lives.

The video Troye recorded was made into an ad in which she announced that she was a McCain Republican and a Bush Republican, but that she was voting for Joe Biden. Even in the form of a political ad, there was nothing about the video that even slightly deviated from what had been reported or from Trump's public behavior.

Donald Trump on September 15–16:

"It is going away. And it's probably going to go away now a lot faster because of the vaccines. It would go away without the vaccine . . . but it's going to go away a lot faster with it."

"I think by [the election], covid will be even lower, it's going to be very low."

FAMOUS LAST WORDS
September 18, 2020

"Did you hear?"

That's what my mom asked when she called me a few minutes after I had received an iPhone notification, one that deepened the pit the year had already hollowed out in my stomach. Ruth Bader Ginsburg was dead.

I'd never published my newsletter on a Jewish High Holiday, but I made what I hope will be the only exception the next morning for an exceptional person; one who is likely the most notable Jewish woman in American history. I was hopeful my rabbi would understand. I'm quite sure my mom and dad did. The Jewish holiday that was being celebrated that day is called Rosh Hashanah. Those words translate as "the head of the year." One hoped that this one would be a Ruth Hashanah, a year when America returned to the ideals of one of its greatest leaders in the fight for equality and justice. The biblical name for this holiday is Yom Teruah, literally "day of shouting or blasting." The shouting began almost immediately.

It was upsetting that the death of RBG immediately became as political as it was emotional. But Ginsburg knew her role and that, in a year of unthinkable carnage, hers would be the death that had the broadest impact on near-future America.

Legend has it that Dylan Thomas's last words at White Horse Tavern were: "I've had eighteen straight whiskies—I think that's the record." Elvis Presley said, "I'm going to the bathroom to read." James Joyce wondered, "Does nobody understand?" Groucho Marx explained, "This is no way to live!" Christopher Hitchens said, "Capitalism . . . downfall." From "Et tu, Brute?" to Steve Jobs's "Oh wow. Oh wow. Oh wow," there have been many famous last words. Ruth Bader Ginsburg placed herself toward the top of the pantheon as she dictated to her granddaughter: "My most fervent wish is that I will not be replaced until a new president is installed."

I didn't have anything helpful to say to my mom when she called that night since I hadn't had time to process the news. But I immediately knew the answer to her question about whether or not Mitch McConnell would move to confirm a replacement before the election. Of course he would. In terms of policy, McConnell was the puppet master of the Trump era; a shadow president who cared as much or more about winning as the one who occupied the Oval Office. And for McConnell, wins were measured in judges.

McConnell had blocked Obama's selection of Merrick Garland to fill a Supreme Court vacancy, explaining that it was made during the final year of the president's tenure and "the American people should have a say in the court's direction. Therefore, this vacancy should not be filled until we have a new president." McConnell would later explain, "One of my proudest moments was when I looked Barack Obama in the eye and I said, 'Mr. President, you will not fill the Supreme Court vacancy.'"

Cut to 2020 when a seat became vacant upon the death of Ruth Bader Ginsburg just weeks before a highly charged election. This time, McConnell had a different opinion when it came to the timing of court appointments. About an hour after the Supreme Court had issued a statement telling Americans that RBG had died, McConnell issued a statement of his own: "President Trump's nominee will receive a vote on the floor of the United States Senate." We'd later learn that at just about the time my mom was calling me, McConnell was calling the president to tell him that he should pick Amy Coney Barrett. Hypocritical? Yes. Unprecedented? Sure. Egregious? Of course. But those adjectives weren't even part of the game McConnell was playing. This was a game of power, and using it was the whole point of having it.

The move was predictable. The pick was predictable. And although there would be some breathless coverage surrounding it, the acquiescence of McConnell's fellow GOP senators was, by now, entirely predictable as well. It made no difference that in 2016 many of them, including Cory Gardner,

John Cornyn, Ted Cruz, Marco Rubio, Jim Inhofe, Chuck Grassley, Joni Ernst, Thom Tillis, David Perdue, Tim Scott, Ron Johnson, Pat Toomey, Richard Burr, Roy Blunt, John Hoeven, and Rob Portman had argued against the notion of confirming a justice in the final year of a presidency. And it sure made no difference that Lindsey Graham held that position in 2016 and doubled down on it in 2018: "If an opening comes in the last year of President Trump's term, and the primary process has started, we'll wait to the next election." When his interviewer Jeffrey Goldberg reminded him he's on the record, Graham responded: "Hold the tape."

We held the tape. The Senate GOP held the cards. And Lindsey Graham proved again that he was a political suppository; he'll do anything to insert himself in the annals of power.

In Barack Obama's statement on Ruth Bader Ginsburg's passing, he wrote:

> Over a long career on both sides of the bench—as a relentless litigator and an incisive jurist—Justice Ginsburg helped us see that discrimination on the basis of sex isn't about an abstract ideal of equality; that it doesn't only harm women; that it has real consequences for all of us. It's about who we are—and who we can be . . . Ruth Bader Ginsburg fought to the end, through her cancer, with unwavering faith in our democracy and its ideals. That's how we remember her. But she also left instructions for how she wanted her legacy to be honored.

Unfortunately, those to whom she left them weren't the type who follow instructions. They either ignored them, like McConnell did, or lied about them, like Trump did. On a call with *Fox & Friends*, Trump dismissed RBG's final words and claimed that RBG's granddaughter may have been part of a Democratic plot: "I don't know if she said that, or was that written out by Adam Schiff or Schumer and Pelosi. I would be more inclined to the second. That came out of the wind, it sounds so beautiful, but that sounds like a Schumer deal or maybe Pelosi or shifty Schiff. That came out of the wind."

A Reuters poll taken following Ginsburg's death "found that 62% of American adults agreed the vacancy should be filled by the winner of the

Nov. 3 matchup between Trump and Democratic former Vice President Joe Biden, while 23% disagreed and the rest said they were not sure."

After Ginsburg died, Nina Totenberg tweeted: "A Jewish teaching says those who die just before the Jewish new year are the ones God has held back until the last moment because they were needed most and were the most righteous." It's considered a big deal if a person dies on Shabbat, and an even bigger deal when it happens on Shabbat and Rosh Hashanah. Ginsburg died as the sun set into both. In Jewish tradition, this would make her a Tzadik (RBGT), a person of great righteousness. It was a shame to lose another one of those when America needed them the most.

CDC CLEARLY NOW

On September 18, the CDC reversed its earlier guidance and issued a warning that the virus was airborne and spreads via "aerosols, produced when an infected person coughs, sneezes, sings, talks, or breathes." This was common knowledge, but it wasn't part of the Trump reelection messaging. So a few days later, the CDC pulled the warning off its site, saying that the warning was only a draft and was posted in error.

In February, Trump told Bob Woodward that the virus was spread through the air. Seven months and two hundred thousand deaths later, the administration was determined to keep that information away from the American public.

Donald Trump on September 19–21:

> "Rounding the corner—when I say 'rounding the corner' they go crazy."
> "We're rounding the corner in any event, but we're going to have a vaccine very soon."
> "It affects virtually nobody. It's an amazing thing."

NOT GOING ANYWHERE FOR A WHILE?

My dad was suffering from one of the many bouts of walking pneumonia that seem to come in one's nineties. When I came by his house to hang out on the back deck, he was wearing a robe, slippers, and his mask. Even outside, I could hear Wolf Blitzer's voice on CNN blaring in the background (another symptom associated with nonagenarians is a television volume level that matches their age). I convinced him to go back inside and turn off CNN for a bit. When he came back outside, we shifted from Wolf Blitzer's views on current events to our own.

I mentioned that the numbers looked pretty good for Biden and Trump was starting to lose his grip (political and mental). My dad said, "Yeah, but he'll never accept the results."

THE CABLE GUY

It was the week my friend Mordy became a hero. We were part of a cohort of adolescent kids who were experiencing the joys of a first-generation cable box. By today's standards, the entertainment options were still laughably limited, but there was one channel that always grabbed, held, and even occasionally rubbed our attention. We'd spend hours watching a heavily scrambled feed of what was, at least to our knowledge, television's first adult channel. This was the age of *Pong* and *Space Invaders*, when choosing between Ginger or Mary Ann was about as much smoldering heat as we could handle. So it didn't matter that the channel was barely visible through the squiggled lines that distorted the nonsubscriber broadcast. It was all we needed.

Then one day, Mordy brought the news that would forever change life for every boy within fifty blocks. I still don't know where he got his information, but Mordy explained that if one simultaneously pressed down on four specific buttons on the cable set-top box, the adult channel would be descrambled.

The four-finger method worked for seven days. And during that unforgettable week, my neighborhood shut down. Nerf footballs sat untouched on driveway blacktops, tumbleweeds rolled across emptied bike paths, dust gathered on Intellivision gaming consoles, zero progress was made on Bar Mitzvah Haftorah portions. It was like a rehearsal for 2020's shelter-in-place experience.

We didn't know it at the time, but we were participants in a transition that would ultimately lead to a more divided nation, political polarization, and possibly threaten America's role as a superpower. (Don't get me wrong, it was still a great fucking week.) Our commonality of content changed with cable. It really changed with the introduction of premium cable channels. And it was obliterated by the internet. Consider the 2020 Emmy Award winners. Most of the top awards for shows, acting, and writing were split among *Schitt's Creek*, *Succession*, *Watchmen*, *Euphoria*, *I Know This Much Is True*, *Ozark*, *The Morning Show*, *Mrs. America*, and *Bad Education*. These were the shows that were watched, discussed, and read about in my social group. But they weren't necessarily the shows being watched by most of America. The one thing that all the winning shows had in common is that you had to pay to watch them. Similar to our news experience, we were living in different bubbles, and piercing from one to the other required some not insignificant discretionary cash. It was just one more example of something that we used to have in common that now separated us. If Americans can't agree to sit on the couch and watch the same show, what can we agree on?

My favorite of the 2020 Emmy winners was *Watchmen*. First, because my friend Damon Lindelof created an amazing show and helped bring awareness of the 1921 Tulsa race massacre to a broader audience as we entered a year when people would pour into the streets demanding racial justice. And second, because I was able to share a very important review with him.

My brother-in-law Douglass Fitch happened to see some *Watchmen* fan art I had purchased for my son and said, "Oh, I love that show." He told me that during one of his monthly meetings with a group of fellow Black pastors, the group's organizer advised all the attendees to go home, get HBO, and start watching *Watchmen* because it was one of the first shows that told the story of Tulsa and really got race right. Doug was especially interested because his mother survived the massacre as a child and had shared stories with him over the years.

I knew how much pressure Damon felt to get the racial aspects of the program right. As he explained to me, the only reason he pulled it off was by partnering with Black writers and artists. The next time I saw him, I told him about the rave reviews he received from Doug and the other pastors. I could tell from the expression on his face and the moisture in his eyes that this was one of his most important reviews, especially considering all the identity issues around a white guy creating a show about a Black experience. Doug and Damon were connected by something more powerful than age or race. They're both driven by the values of truth and equality.

When the pandemic hit, Damon sent Doug one of the yellow gaiters worn by some of the *Watchmen* characters, and Doug wore it as his viral protection throughout the year.

PROPERTY SETTLEMENT

"This is a tragedy. And sometimes, the criminal law is not adequate to respond to a tragedy." Attorney General Daniel Cameron announced a Kentucky grand jury brought no charges against officers for shooting and killing Breonna Taylor in her own apartment. The only charges brought in the case were against fired officer Brett Hankison, who was hit with three counts of wanton endangerment for firing his weapon into a neighboring apartment.

CRYSTAL BRAWL

Barton Gellman in the *Atlantic*:

> Let us not hedge about one thing. Donald Trump may win or lose, but he will never concede. Not under any circumstance. Not during the Interregnum and not afterward. If compelled in the end to vacate his office, Trump will insist from exile, as long as he draws breath, that the contest was rigged . . .
>
> If the vote is close, Donald Trump could easily throw the election into chaos and subvert the result. Who will stop him?

If that had been a multiple-choice question, the answer would have been *none of the above*.

Gellman's pre-election analysis, like my dad's predictions, would prove accurate. It wasn't that either had a crystal ball. They just watched Trump's

behavior and listened to what he said. On September 3, Trump again declined to commit to a peaceful transfer of power: "We're going to have to see
what happens."

> **Dave Pell** ✓
> @davepell
>
> An American president announced his refusal to agree to
> leave office should he lose the election, and it's not the top
> story on most news sites tonight.
>
> 8:56 PM · Sep 23, 2020 · 🐦 Twitter

THE FALSE PROFIT

"In addition to the 11 years in which he paid no taxes during the 18 years
examined by *The Times*, he paid only $750 in each of the two most recent
years—2016 and 2017." After years of curiosity, Americans finally got their
first glimpse into Trump's tax returns courtesy of a massive *New York Times*
exposé. What they saw was as red as a *Make America Great Again* hat.

The details from Trump's tax returns hardly represented a shocking plot
twist. I mean, you didn't think Donald Trump was hiding his taxes because
he was *more* successful than we thought. Give Trump credit for this (and by
credit, I mean the public acknowledgment kind, definitely not the financial
instrument kind): no one has ever done a better job playing the part of a successful businessman. Ironically, that's the one thing he's made a lot of money
doing. *The Apprentice* was what made him money, and by positioning him as
a strong, smart businessman, it helped propel him to the Oval Office.

As the kid of a non-leveraged, real-life real estate developer, I'd been
hearing about Trump's shenanigans for decades. At this point, the only real
mystery about Trump's finances was addressed by the *New Yorker*'s David
Remnick: *Donald Trump Barely Pays Any Taxes: Will Anyone Care?*

In his pre-politician days, Trump used to call *Forbes* magazine every year
to try to boost his rating in the Forbes 400. It was so laughably pathetic that
members of the staff would gather around a speakerphone to listen to him
plead his case. During that era, he was the only person ever to call the magazine about their ranking (other than a handful of people who requested to

be removed from the list). The façade was Trump's everything story, the one he worked on for years, and maintaining it was vital. The *New York Times* tax story was a lifelong fraud beginning to unravel.

Would anyone care? Yes. Donald Trump.

GUESS WHO'S BACK?

At least one trend united Americans across regional and party lines: economic challenges exacerbated by the pandemic were forcing young adults to move back home to live with their parents. According to a Pew Research Center analysis of the census numbers, "52% of young adults resided with one or both of their parents." And throughout the pandemic, that number grew across all major races and regions.

This was a stark difference from my generation's experience and my own. Five minutes after I moved out of my parents' house, they started remodeling my room into a gaming den. If I wanted to move back, I'd have to be willing to sleep on a mah-jongg table.

ZOOM KIPPUR

When people ask me if I'm a practicing Jew, I usually respond, "No, I just show up on game days." This year, like everything else, religious game days were a completely different ball game. Ahead of Yom Kippur, I asked my parents the ultimate 2020 question. If you're participating in temple over Zoom and the rabbi says, "Please rise," do you actually have to rise?

My mom: "I don't really think so."

My dad: "Absolutely not."

With that pregame absolution, I enjoyed temple via Zoom on my couch so much, I actually attended services at two different temples.

There were several public disputes, and a few court cases, about whether places of worship had the right to open during the pandemic. But the less contentious aspects of pandemic worship may have a greater long-term impact. Like many things that changed during 2020, Zoom temple and church will undoubtedly remain, not as a replacement for the real thing but as an additional option. My parents were both in their nineties for Yom Kippur 2020 (in other words, about the average age of temple attendees). Why shouldn't they have the option of participating remotely? Zoom means never having to say you're sorry for being unable to attend.

PONTIFIGATE

Richard Nixon famously looked pale and sweaty during the first televised presidential debate with John F. Kennedy. Ronald Reagan got off this zinger versus Jimmy Carter: "There you go again." During his next election, Reagan, whose age had become a big topic of discussion, said, "I will not make age an issue of this campaign. I am not going to exploit, for political purposes, my opponent's youth and inexperience." In a three-way debate with Ross Perot and Bill Clinton, George Bush was heavily criticized for looking at his watch during the proceedings.

Before the Trump era, these moments were about as shocking as presidential debates got. Like everything else, that changed. We got a preview of Trump's debating style during the first GOP presidential primary debate in 2015.

Moderator Megyn Kelly: "One of the things people love about you is you speak your mind and you don't use a politician's filter. However, that is not without its downsides, in particular, when it comes to women. You've called women you don't like fat pigs, dogs, slobs, and disgusting animals . . . "

Trump: "Only Rosie O'Donnell."

Trump won that election, so by 2020, the question of whether this brutish style of discourse would be a hit with a few tens of millions of voters had been asked and answered. But that night in 2015, and what felt like the few million that followed, hardly prepared us for Trump's performance in his first debate with Joe Biden.

Moderator Chris Wallace kicked off the debate and thus began a tantric tantrum that dragged America to a place many thought didn't exist: lower. Throughout the debate, Trump falsely attacked the key pillar of democracy (with a blizzard of lies about voting) and showed no sign of being willing to leave office if he lost.

Trump refused to stop interrupting Biden, and when pressed on that by Wallace, he interrupted him too.

Wallace: "The country would be better served if we allowed both people to speak with fewer interruptions. I'm appealing to you, sir, to do it—"

> **Dave Pell** ✓
> @davepell
>
> Debate drinking game:
>
> Every time Trump is still president, drink.
>
> 5:28 PM · Sep 29, 2020 · 🐦 Twitter

Trump: "And him too?"

If we learned anything, it's that kindergarten teachers should be paid more than debate moderators.

It was a joke, a mess, a disaster. A "shit show," a "dumpster fire," a national humiliation. No matter how bad you thought the debate would be, it was worse. Way worse. Trump shouted, he bullied, he hectored, he lied, and he interrupted, over and over again. (Susan B. Glasser, *New Yorker*)

What Susan Glasser described is what happened. One guy was a bully. One guy turned the debate into a debacle. But you'd hardly have gotten that picture if you read the post-debate headlines posted on major media sites.

I grabbed screenshots of many of them because it was clear that the media still hadn't fully adjusted to the Trump era, and instead continued a never-ending pattern of false equivalence and both sides–ism. Consider these headlines from the hours just after the conclusion of the broadcast:

New York Times: *Sharp Personal Attacks and Name Calling in Chaotic First Debate*

Washington Post: *Personal Attacks, Sharp Exchanges Mark Turbulent First Debate*

CNN: *Pure Chaos at First Debate*

Boston Globe: *First Debate Between Trump, Biden Marked by Chaos, Rancor as Candidates Made It Personal*

LA Times: *Trump and Biden Trade Bitter Personal Attacks in First Debate*

Bloomberg: *Trump-Biden Debate Descends into Bickering and Chaos*

Yeah, it was just a couple of guys who were both losing their cool, and there are some very fine debaters on both sides. Please. The debate did not "descend" into bickering and chaos. It was dragged there by the same guy who had dragged America to this maddeningly dangerous precipice. I could see that. America could see that. And Rosie O'Donnell sure as hell could see that. By morning, many of these headlines had been updated to more accurately depict what we all saw and heard. But the knee-jerk response was toward the false equivalence that had propped up Trump for years.

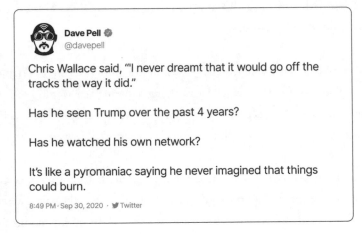

Dave Pell ✓
@davepell

Chris Wallace said, "'I never dreamt that it would go off the tracks the way it did."

Has he seen Trump over the past 4 years?

Has he watched his own network?

It's like a pyromaniac saying he never imagined that things could burn.

8:49 PM · Sep 30, 2020 · 🐦 Twitter

As offensive as Trump's demeanor was during that first debate, his performance will be etched in history not for the bombast or bluster but for a single directive.

When asked whether he would condemn "white supremacists and militia groups," Trump chose to direct part of his answer to the far right, self-described Western chauvinist group called the Proud Boys:

"Proud Boys, stand back and stand by." Most of the country didn't take those four words seriously enough. But the Proud Boys did.

The first debate's norm departures were not entirely monopolized by Trump. Joe Biden did lose his cool at one point. After being interrupted countless times, he asked Trump: "Will you shut up, man?"

That question had been asked and answered too.

News Divisions
September 2020

Maddow

> **The Atlantic** 1
> Trump: Americans Who Died in War Are 'Losers' and 'Suckers'

> **The New York Times** 2
> Trump's Taxes Show Chronic Losses and Years of Income Tax Avoidance

> **The Washington Post** 3
> Louis DeJoy's rise as GOP fundraiser was powered by contributions from company workers who were later reimbursed, former employees say

> **CNN** 4
> 'Play it down': Trump admits to concealing the true threat of coronavirus in new Woodward book

> **Politico** 5
> Trump officials interfered with CDC reports on Covid-19

Hannity/Carlson

> **Fox News** 1
> Pelosi used shuttered San Francisco hair salon for blow-out, owner calls it 'slap in the face'

> **The Federalist** 2
> 'Trump Was Right': FBI Texts Detail Furor Over 'Crossfire Hurricane'

> **New York Post** 3
> Gov. Cuomo: Trump had 'better have an army' to protect him if he comes to NYC.

> **New York Post** 4
> Project Veritas uncovers 'ballot harvesting fraud' in Minnesota.

> **New York Post** 5
> Hunter Biden received $3.5M wire transfer from Russian billionaire: Senate report

These are the top news links shared on Twitter in September by followers of Rachel Maddow versus followers of Sean Hannity or Tucker Carlson. Source: MIT Center for Constructive Communication

10

OCTOBER— A TURN OF THE CORKSCREW

By October, more than 207,000 Americans had died, and the pandemic scourge was accelerating. America was not a failed state. But it was in a vegetative state, largely because we were being overwhelmed by a constant drumbeat of misinformation. This attack on democratic norms touched everything as the election approached. Consider this example from *Politico*: "The Agriculture Department last week began mandating that millions of boxes of surplus food for needy families include a letter from President Donald Trump claiming credit for the program." (Trump-branded vegetables. I've seen it all.) Hopefully the boxes contained plenty of fiber, because it's going to take that and more to push four years of this waste out of our system. Magamucil is the new Metamucil.

Where was all the misinformation coming from? The top. Researchers at Cornell analyzed thirty-eight million articles and found that 38 percent of pandemic misinformation and conspiracies were coming from the Oval Office. "We conclude that the President of the United States was likely the largest driver of the COVID-19 misinformation 'infodemic.'" Maybe the other 62 percent of the misinformation was coming from Trump's old pseudonyms John Barron and David Dennison? While the falsehoods often seemed as ridiculous as the garbage spread by those two Trump aliases, there's no doubt that it was effective. Plenty of people were buying it. But at least one core constituent wasn't: COVID-19.

Three days after Trump ridiculed Joe Biden's mask wearing during their debate, and the first family broke the mask-wearing rules in the debate hall and waved off Cleveland Clinic staff when they offered to provide them; and one day after Trump used a radio address to inform us the "end of the pandemic is in sight," the president and the First Lady both tested positive for COVID-19 (and simultaneously experienced the first case of schaden*fraud*). The moment the news broke presented the greatest disconnect between what people said publicly ("We wish the president a speedy recovery") and what people said in private chatrooms or around the dinner table ("Ha, ha, ha, ha, motherfuckin' ha").

Fox News reported Trump's diagnosis over a loop of the handful of news images that showed Trump wearing a mask. Kudos to the intern who managed to find those needles in a haystack on deadline.

The positive tests weren't particularly surprising given three preceding factors. First, we learned that White House aide Hope Hicks tested positive. It's worth noting that the White House attempted to keep Hicks's diagnosis under wraps. After they knew about it, and her contact with Trump, the president still continued to travel and hold maskless events. Second, we had seen firsthand how the Trumps flouted social distancing rules and scorned mask wearing. Third, it was a bad sign when karma started working out to the *Rocky* theme song.

Dave Pell ✓
@davepell

Imagine this week:

The world learns you're broke.

The country finds out you're a tax evader.

You humiliated yourself in a debate broadcast across the globe.

You found out you have Covid 19.

Trump didn't pivot, life did.

6:45 PM · Oct 2, 2020 · 🐦 Twitter

CRAZE ANATOMY
October 2, 2020

Shortly after his diagnosis was made public, Trump got a suite of remedies, from Regeneron to remdesivir, and was airlifted to Walter Reed Army Medical Center, where Individual One became Patient Zero—he wasn't the first person to get COVID-19, but in his mind, he was probably the first that mattered.

Trump was a patient. And as CNN's Sanjay Gupta tweeted, he may have been a spreader as well. "Despite being diagnosed on Wednesday, the President did not isolate or even regularly wear a mask—possibly becoming a source of spread of the virus. (I cannot believe I am writing this)." In retrospect, *I Cannot Believe I Am Writing This* would have been a decent title for this book. While Trump was experiencing dizziness, cold sweats, and breathlessness from the virus, the rest of us were suffering from the same symptoms just from absorbing the news. No matter how fast and how weird the Trump news cycle got, it could always get faster and weirder. In just one week, we had a massive tax return exposé, the craziest debate in American history, and Trump being airlifted to the hospital with a virus he called a hoax. The show runners at *Grey's Anatomy* could stretch that much content into about twenty seasons.

Donald and Melania were just two of many of the GOP insiders to test positive, including Hope Hicks, senior advisor to the president; Bill Stepien, Trump's campaign manager; Republican National Committee chair Ronna McDaniel; Senator Mike Lee; Senator Thom Tillis; Senator Ron Johnson; Kellyanne Conway; White House spokesperson Kayleigh McEnany (who thankfully could still lie from home); Stephen Miller; and Chris Christie, who later said that he found out about Trump's positive test via news reports. He was never notified by the administration even though he had spent the prior week with the president prepping for the first debate.

> **Dave Pell** ✓
> @davepell
>
> Stephen Miller tests positive for Covid-19, proving it can travel from bat to human and back to bat.
>
> 4:08 PM · Oct 6, 2020 · 🐦 Twitter

Many of the cases likely stemmed from the Rose Garden celebration for Amy Coney Barrett, who had been officially nominated to the Supreme Court. Following his hospitalization, Chris Christie suddenly realized that maybe COVID-19 was a thing.

> I was wrong. I was wrong not to wear a mask at the Amy Coney Barrett announcement and I was wrong not to wear a mask at my multiple debate prep sessions with the president and the rest of the team . . . I hope that my experience shows my fellow citizens that you should follow C.D.C. guidelines in public no matter where you are and wear a mask to protect yourself and others.

Thanks, Chris Christie! But we already knew how serious COVID-19 was because 220,000 of our fellow Americans died while you were enabling a sociopath who seemed determined to increase that number.

While Trump was away, the White House got a little more serious about the pandemic and issued this order:

Effective October 2, 2020, all National Security Council (NSC) staff reporting to the Executive Office of the President campus are required to wear a mask in all common areas, including security screening facilities, elevators, hallways and restrooms.

This directive was given in October. During the prior eight months, my house had stricter pandemic rules than the White House.

> **Dave Pell** ✔
> @davepell
>
> How far into the line of succession before we hit Jacinda Ardern?
>
> 11:03 PM · Oct 2, 2020 · 🐦 Twitter

On October 5, with some unfortunate Secret Service personnel along for the ride, for no apparent reason and against the wishes of his medical staff, Trump decided to bolt Walter Reed and take a joyride in the back of the presidential SUV. You somehow knew we'd get to the point where the president was running from men in white coats. The guy whose campaign warned of the rising tide of suburban danger literally endangered Americans inside a Suburban.

Meanwhile, we got immediate takes from two of America's most astute observers.

David Remnick in the *New Yorker*:

Any ailing individual ought to be able to depend on the best wishes of others—and on affordable, decent health care. Trump can depend on both, even if millions of Americans cannot . . . Because of his ineptitude and his deceit, because he has encouraged a culture of heedlessness about the wearing of masks and a lethal disrespect for scientific fact, he bears a grave responsibility for what has happened in this country. It will never be known precisely how many preventable deaths can be ascribed to his irresponsibility, but modest estimates run into the tens of thousands.

Claudia Conway on TikTok:

im furious. wear your masks. dont listen to our idiot fucking president piece of shit. protect yourselves and those around you.

IL DOUCHÉ

A few days after his hospitalization, a mending (but still pretty out of breath) Trump returned to the White House where he bounded up the stairs, still contagious, and triumphantly removed his mask for a bizarro Mussolini-esque photo op from a White House balcony. The next day, he again compared the virus to the seasonal flu.

On one hand, thanks to Obamacare, it was nice to know that even a possibly broke American who hadn't paid any taxes could still get health care. On the other hand, imagine you were in a hospital waiting room saying goodbye to a loved one via an iPad as the leader who had done nothing to slow its spread was making a mockery of coronavirus.

CNN's Don Lemon complained about Trump that "he has turned an American tragedy into a made-for-TV travesty." But Lemon's network broadcast that travesty in real time, just as they had broadcast nonstop Trump coverage for four years. That was also a travesty. As much as they were perceived as enemies, much of the media shared a common malady with the president: they were both addicted to Trump.

Dave Pell ✔
@davepell

Medical Update: The President is lying comfortably.

9:16 AM · Oct 4, 2020 · 🐦 Twitter

Donald Trump on October 6: "Flu season is coming up! Many people every year, sometimes over 100,000, and despite the Vaccine, die from the

Flu. Are we going to close down our Country? No, we have learned to live with it, just like we are learning to live with Covid, in most populations far less lethal!!!"

SPARKS FLY

The challenge going into the vice presidential debate was not particularly great for either candidate. President Trump had set an impossibly low bar the week before, and Mike Pence managed to slither over it, while oozing so much syrupy unctuousness that I had to squeegee my TV screen. Meanwhile, since she was facing the head of the Coronavirus Task Force, Kamala Harris's bar was even lower. All she had to do is not kill two hundred thousand Americans during the debate, and she'd come out ahead.

In the recent history of vice presidential debates, the one line that really stood the test of time was Lloyd Bentsen telling Dan Quayle, "Senator, I served with Jack Kennedy. I knew Jack Kennedy. Jack Kennedy was a friend of mine. Senator, you're no Jack Kennedy."

Well, Lloyd, I hate to tell you this, but you're no fly.

In the middle of the debate, a black fly landed on Mike Pence's white hair. And stayed there. For more than two minutes. It's possible they were the most productive two minutes of memes in the history of social media. I found myself a little jealous. A fly was able to become internet famous in two minutes when I'd been trying to do the same for two decades. The fly even had perfect timing; by the time it landed, we were both vomiting every few seconds. And its landing spot made total sense, as Pence's head had been up Trump's ass for four years.

MICHUGAS

October 8, 2020

One bit of actual news from the veep debate was that Pence, like his boss, refused to commit to a peaceful transfer of power. That refusal was made all the more disturbing the next day when we learned that the FBI had uncovered a plot by several Michigan men to kidnap Michigan governor Gretchen Whitmer and hold her as a hostage in an effort to overthrow the state's government.

Remember Trump's calls to LIBERATE states, including Michigan? The would-be kidnappers remembered.

Michigan attorney general Dana Nessel would later explain: "This effort to have a mass uprising nationally is something that we should be very concerned about because, again, it's not just a Michigan problem, this is an American problem."

At rallies later in the month, Trump's adulators redirected their famous chant, "Lock her up," from Hillary Clinton to Whitmer, who was understandably concerned. On *Meet the Press*, she explained: "It's incredibly disturbing that the president of the United States—ten days after a plot to kidnap, put me on trial, and execute me . . . ten days after that plot was uncovered—the president is at it again, inspiring and incentivizing and inciting this kind of domestic terrorism."

Inciting an act of domestic terrorism? He wouldn't dare . . .

DUDE SWINGS

I've struggled with the tension between standing for free expression and the harm caused by minimizing or denying the horror of the Holocaust. My own thinking has evolved as I've seen data showing an increase in anti-Semitic violence, as have our wider policies on hate speech.

So said Mark Zuckerberg as he announced that Facebook would ban content that denies or distorts the Holocaust. I welcomed the decision, but it came more than seventy-five years after the conclusion of World War II. It made it seem unlikely that we'd solve the immediate disinformation crises in time for an election a few weeks away.

UNITED NATHAN

While on the way to work at a potato warehouse, Nathan Apodaca's truck broke down on a highway in Idaho Falls. He didn't have much time to spare, so he grabbed his skateboard and a plastic jug of Ocean Spray's Cran-Raspberry juice and decided to coast the final two miles to work. He made a quick TikTok video of himself skateboarding and grooving to Fleetwood Mac's 1977 song "Dream." It was just another one of Apodaca's many Tik-Toks. Until it wasn't.

Within a few days, the video had 35 million views and nearly 150,000 tribute videos, including those from Jimmy Fallon and Mick Fleetwood. All told, the video was seen by half a billion people on TikTok alone.

In an era where we lived in two reality bubbles, two entertainment bub-bles, and were divided on almost everything, this unplanned moment from Nathan Apodaca (or 420doggface208, as he was known on TikTok), in his gray hoodie, rolling on his longboard, drinking down a little Cran-Ras, and cranking the smooth stylings of Fleetwood Mac, somehow brought us all together.

> Apodaca became a celebrity overnight, transforming from indie-vibe hero to brand sponsor in record time. When fans found an old tweet of his, from a time when Apodaca was living in a Walmart parking lot, they mobbed his PayPal with donations. In the weeks that followed, Apodaca got a free truck from Ocean Spray, proposed to his then-girlfriend, and bought a house. (Tar-pley Hitt, *Daily Beast*)

Try telling Nathan Apodaca 2020 wasn't a good year.

The year was also good for chess set manufacturers. Following the break-out Netflix hit *The Queen's Gambit*, about a chess prodigy named Beth Harmon, chess set sales went wild. People watched chess on TV and then wanted to get a chess set for themselves. Too bad Netflix didn't have a break-out hit about a mask-wearing, science-trusting character who followed all the pandemic rules and then was first in line for the vaccine.

THE BIGLY LIE

Trump wasn't only the biggest source of coronavirus misinformation. He held that title when it came to a topic much closer to his heart: the lie that only he could win a fair election. A study from Harvard's Berkman Klein Center for Internet & Society found that Trump was the key source of disinformation associated with mail-in ballots. He was aided by other GOP officials, Fox News, and other right-leaning media outlets. The goal was to fix the outcome of the election in the minds of enough voters that a Trump victory was the only result they'd believe. This Big Lie would be front and center in the weeks following the election. But the groundwork was being laid long before the first vote was cast.

ATLAS SHRUGGED

By mid-October, the nation was fixated on the presidential race. But COVID-19 was fixated on the nation as it moved determinedly across the Midwest and into more rural areas, where hospitals were more scarce and misinformation was more abundant. Several of the states being targeted by COVID were also swing states that would soon be targeted by President Trump, who threw caution, and likely a lot of virus, to the wind, as he began a heavy schedule of outdoor, crowded, often maskless rallies.

America was facing two pandemics. The virus and the misinformation. And in mid-October, the pandemic misinformation operation had a man on the inside. The views of the actual experts were being pushed to the sidelines by an unqualified quack named Scott Atlas. Atlas was brought onto the Coronavirus Task Force after the president saw his appearances on Fox News and was impressed with the falsehoods he was spreading. Atlas was a neuroradiologist by training. Do you know what a neuroradiologist is? It doesn't matter. All that matters is that a neuroradiologist is not an expert on infectious diseases.

On October 18, Scott Atlas published a tweet: "Masks work? NO." (I'd share a screenshot, but Twitter blocked the post for breaking its rules about COVID-19 disinformation.)

Thanks in part to Atlas's influence, we had less testing, more people who didn't believe in the value of masks and social distancing, a president who still seemed to believe the pandemic was over even as he traveled from hard-hit state to hard-hit state for crowded rallies, and repeated calls for the deadly stupid idea of letting herd immunity send the American body count through the roof. Meanwhile, ten states were hitting their highest daily case counts.

Donald Trump on October 14–20:

"We're rounding the turn . . . but most people—99-point-something
  percent, if you get it, you get better."

"We're rounding the turn on the pandemic."

"The light at the end of the tunnel is near."

"We're rounding the turn, it's ending without the vaccine."

"People are tired of covid. People are tired of hearing Fauci and all
  these idiots."

"They're getting tired of the pandemic—aren't they? Getting tired
  of the pandemic. You turn on CNN. That's all they cover. Covid,
  covid, pandemic. Covid, covid, covid. You know why? They're trying to talk people out of voting. People aren't buying it, CNN, you
  dumb bastards."

SAY ANYTHING

Amy Coney Barrett said basically nothing during her Supreme Court confirmation hearings even though she could have literally said anything and still
been confirmed. *Can a president pardon himself? Can you legally intimidate
voters at polls? Should a president unequivocally commit to a peaceful transfer of
power?* Even on that last one, she told Senator Cory Booker, "To the extent
that this is a political controversy right now, as a judge I want to stay out of
it, and I don't want to express a view."

In the Trump era, everything was a political controversy.

With the president still recovering from COVID-19 and America still
recovering from the first debate, the second debate was replaced by dueling
town halls. Biden's was normal. Trump's was highly unusual because his
interviewer, Savannah Guthrie, actually pushed back on some of the more
outrageous conspiracy theories he helped spread. While claiming ignorance
of QAnon, he managed to buoy one of the key tenets of the conspiracy.

Guthrie: Let me ask you about QAnon. It is this theory that Democrats are a satanic pedophile ring and that you are the savior of that.

Now, can you just once and for all state that that is completely not true and disavow QAnon in its entirety?

Trump: I know nothing about QAnon—

Guthrie: I just told you.

Trump: You told me. But what you tell me doesn't necessarily make it fact, I hate to say that. I know nothing about it. I do know they are very much against pedophilia. They fight it very hard, but I know nothing about it. If you'd like me to—

Guthrie: They believe it is a satanic cult run by the deep state.

Trump: —study the subject. I'll tell you what I do know about: I know about antifa and I know about the radical left. And I know how violent they are and how vicious they are. And I know how they're burning down cities run by Democrats, not run by Republicans.

Later, when Guthrie again pushed Trump on this topic, he avoided the opportunity to call the craziness crazy.

Trump: Let me just—let me just tell you, what I do hear about it, is they are very strongly against pedophilia. And I agree with that. I mean, I do agree with that. And I agree with it very strongly.

Guthrie: But there is not a satanic pedophile cult being run by—

Trump: I have no idea. I know nothing about it.

Guthrie: You don't know that?

Trump: No, I don't know that. And neither do you know that.

No one really knows anything. That was a key tenet of Trumpism.

In an even more absurd exchange, Trump attempted to write off a lie he was spreading himself because he had only spread it by retweet.

Guthrie: Just this week you retweeted to your 87 million followers a conspiracy theory that Joe Biden orchestrated to have SEAL Team 6 killed to cover up the fake death of bin Laden. Now, why would you send a lie like that to your followers?

Trump: That was a retweet. That was an opinion of somebody. And that was a retweet. I'll put it out there.

Guthrie: I don't get that. You're the president. You're not someone's crazy uncle who can retweet whatever.

Mary Trump, the president's niece (and by now a best-selling author of a book about Trump's upbringing and psychological makeup), responded to that exchange by tweeting: "Actually . . . "

Good thing Cory Booker didn't ask Amy Coney Barrett about imaginary pedophilia rings, conspiratorial SEAL Team 6 killer cover-ups, or crazy uncles. It turns out those things were political controversies too.

Barrett would be confirmed by the end of the month. Before the final 52–48 vote (along party lines other than Maine's Susan Collins, who voted against), Mitch McConnell explained the importance of the era between his blocking of Merrick Garland and his confirming of Amy Coney Barrett:

> A lot of what we've done over the last four years will be undone sooner or later by the next election. They won't be able to do much about this for a long time to come.

LINER NOTES

The country was already setting records for mail-in ballots. That was expected during a pandemic. But once local polling places opened up, the lines of voters started to mass. And the lines were particularly long where people of color were the ones doing the voting. According to Ari Berman, author of *Give Us the Ballot: The Modern Struggle for Voting Rights in America*, "during [the] Georgia primary voters in predominantly white areas waited 6 minutes to vote while voters in predominantly minority areas waited 51 minutes to vote."

A deluge of voters swamped the polls in the Atlanta area during the first weeks of early voting, with about 400,000 turning out in Fulton and Cobb counties in the first 10 days. Many arrived while the sky was still dark, and lines quickly began forming through parking lots and down suburban streets. Officials initially said the sheer number of voters—including many who had originally requested mail ballots—was the main cause of the backlog, which left some voters waiting as long as 11 hours. (*Washington Post*)

The *Washington Post*'s tagline is *Democracy Dies in Darkness*, yet here they were reporting on people who actually had to line up in darkness just to vote. These lines are a form of voter suppression.

I'm a white guy who has spent most of my life in the San Francisco Bay Area. If I added up the total time I've had to wait in line to vote, I doubt it would break twenty minutes.

Dave Pell @davepell

If you see black people in a long line, there's an election coming up.

If you see white people in a long line, there's a new iPhone.

10:54 PM · Oct 19, 2020 · Twitter

COCKTOBER SURPRISE

Legal analyst and political pundit Jeffrey Toobin flirted with disaster when he left his Zoom camera on in the background while he pleasured himself, resulting in the money shot heard round the world. Maybe we owe Jeffrey a debt of gratitude for Toobin in public; after all, it was nice, for a moment or three, to finally have a different dick in the news, another jerk to circle, a stump without a speech, another apprentice to fire, a tower not named Trump, an attempted rub-out not involving white supremacists, and after six months, a reason to use wipes that didn't involve a deadly virus.

Toobin dropped trou before dropping his Zoom connection, exposing his nub on the wrong hub, and there's the rub. Thus, his colleagues from WNYC and the *New Yorker* were treated to a gratis peep show as they prepped for election night—at least in this simulation, the results were not delayed.

The Toobin news was funny and weird, and for him, one assumes, personally humiliating. But did Toobin deserve to be canceled for participating in the quarantine's most common pastime? He would end up getting fired from his job at the *New Yorker* and was suspended from CNN, despite the fact that Masha Gessen, who witnessed the event, told the *New York Times* that they felt sympathy for Toobin: "I think it's tragic that a guy would get fired for really just doing something really stupid. It is the Zoom equivalent of taking an inappropriately long lunch break, having sex during it and getting stumbled upon."

This is probably a weird place to segue to my mom, but let's do it anyway. Here was our conversation when the Toobin scandal broke:

Mom: What is going on with all of you Jewish men?

Me: Well, Mom, I'm not sure you heard about this, but guys like touching their penises a lot.

Mom: I know, but all the time? Is it a Jewish thing?

Me: Not the jerking off, but the getting caught probably is.

HUNTER FOR RED OCTOBER

The Hunter Biden laptop story was the 2020 election version of the Hillary Clinton email saga, except it was more confusing, more stupid, more fake, and more likely to be part of a Russian misinformation effort; so it's probably a little redundant to say it was promoted by Rudy Giuliani. There is no point in wasting your time, or my fingertips, typing up a summary of the ridiculousness that first appeared in the *New York Post*, before ultimately being dropped even by those who pretended it was a big story until it being one was no longer of any use to them. Suffice it to say, there was a laptop that ended up in a Delaware repair shop with contents that were purported to prove some evil connections between the Bidens and business leaders in the Ukraine. Even the Murdoch-owned *Wall Street Journal* rebuffed the idea that the Murdoch-owned *New York Post* story had uncovered any wrongdoing by Joe Biden. In 2021, Hunter Biden wrote a book in which he addressed the controversy around his laptop. I ignored his take on the matter as well. When it comes to Hunter Biden's laptop, my disinterest is unbiased and nonpartisan.

Dave Pell ✔
@davepell

I just got a tip on a story but I'm not sure if it's true.

Who's the source?

Rudy Giuliani.

Are you ебаный kidding me?

2:26 PM · Oct 17, 2020 · 🐦 Twitter

What was important about this nonstory was the absolutely endless coverage it was getting on Fox News and in the right-wing-media echo chamber. The laptop article was the most shared news story among right-leaning Facebook and Twitter users during the month of October. It wasn't just the misinformation that was worrisome, it was also the absence of real information. Every minute spent watching, hearing, and sharing false news was a minute spent not watching, hearing, and sharing the real news.

LOST AND CONFOUND
October 21, 2020

Courtesy of judge-appointed lawyers tasked with identifying family members separated by the Trump administration, we learned that nearly three years after the initial pilot program to separate kids at the border from their parents, hundreds of those parents couldn't be found.

In addition to being a reminder of past policies that had been buried beneath the deluge of 2020 news, it was also a reminder that the current headlines shared an underpinning with the older ones.

Ineptitude, indifference, and cruelty were a bad combination.

DON TRUMPED THE SHARK

The final and calmest presidential debate, one that included a mute button for the host, provided a valuable teachable moment for would-be narcissistic authoritarians: the less time you spend interrupting, the more time you have for bullshit. And from COVID-19 to the fever dreams about Hunter Biden's laptop, there was plenty of that. *The virus response is not my fault, the stimulus failures are Pelosi's fault, I'm the least racist person in the room, I've done more for Black people than any president since Abraham Lincoln.* All the greatest hits were played along with a lack of empathy for kids separated from parents, the tax returns that were *still* supposedly about to be released, and the health plan that was right around the corner. The content was absurd, but it was also material we'd heard before. If nothing else, the third debate gave Americans something that for four long years they had been yearning for: boredom.

While so much of the coverage surrounding these debates was about tone and bluster, many Americans were watching them with a more personal interest. According to Google Trends, the most searched-for term during the final debate was *wages*. That was true in every state other than the six where the top term was *unemployment*. As the debate wore on, *when does debate end* was spiking +3,050 percent.

Heading into the third and final debate, President Trump made news by storming off the set of a *60 Minutes* interview with Lesley Stahl, after complaining that she was treating him unfairly. In reality, the interview wasn't particularly contentious, but it did provide a reminder of an earlier exchange that Stahl had with Trump just after he won the 2016 election in which he explained to her why he constantly hammers the press: "You know why I do it? I do it to discredit you all and demean you all so that when you write negative stories about me no one will believe you."

Donald Trump on October 23:

> "We'll have 100 million vaccine doses before the end of the year, and maybe substantially before, and that will help. It's going away anyway."

"On Nov. 4, you won't hear anything about it [the pandemic], because we are rounding that turn."

THE RALLY OF THE SHADOW OF DEATH

Donald Trump traveled from swing state to shining swing state, gathering large, boisterous crowds, and acting as a modern-day Typhoid Mary. No one expected Trump to rise to the moment and effectively fight the pandemic. But few expected him to be an active super-spreader. Not satisfied with diffusing the virus around the Rose Garden, the administration took the show on the road. Watergate, meet Propa-gate. If you wanted to predict where COVID-19 hotspots would pop up in the weeks approaching the election, you could have just followed the path of Err Force One.

The president has participated in nearly three dozen rallies since mid-August . . . A *USA Today* analysis shows COVID-19 cases grew at a faster rate than before after at least five of those rallies. (Erin Mansfield, Josh Salman, and Dinah Voyles Pulver, *USA Today*)

Donald Trump on October 25–29:

"We're rounding the turn. Even without the vaccines, we're rounding the turn, it's going to be over."

"We are absolutely rounding the corner, other than the fake news wants to scare everybody."

"We're rounding the turn, you know, all they want to talk about is covid. By the way, on Nov. 4 you won't be hearing so much about it."

"ALL THE FAKE NEWS MEDIA WANTS TO TALK ABOUT IS COVID, COVID, COVID. ON NOVEMBER 4th, YOU WON'T BE HEARING SO MUCH ABOUT IT ANYMORE. WE ARE ROUNDING THE TURN!!!"

"Until November 4th., Fake News Media is going full on Covid, Covid, Covid. We are rounding the turn. 99.9%."

"Do you ever notice they don't use the word 'death,' they use the word 'cases?' Cases. Like, Barron Trump is a case. He had sniffles."

"A safe vaccine is coming very quickly. You're going to have it momentarily that eradicates the virus and we are rounding the turn regardless."

JUSTIN THE WIND

The Dodgers won the World Series, which, for this San Francisco Giants fan, was entirely on brand for an already terrible year. Aside from my chagrin, the World Series, played inside baseball's version of a bubble, concluded in the most 2020 way possible—short of one side trying to cheat, lying about the result, and then refusing to leave the field after the contest was over. Somehow, a COVID-19 test for Dodgers third baseman Justin Turner came back positive *during* the game. Hence, Turner was pulled from the lineup before the eighth inning. Not 2020 enough for you? Well, Justin Turner later returned to the field, where he celebrated with his teammates, occasionally without a mask. Hopefully, they were draft Dodgers as well, because something infectious was in the air. Put simply, Justin Turner's enthusiasm was contagious.

We never found out if Turner spread the virus, but in LA, the winning proved infectious. Shortly after the Dodgers won the World Series, LeBron's Lakers won the NBA Championship. As a NorCal resident, all I could do was sit back and say, "That's it, 2020. Just get it all out."

GIMME BACK MY BULLETS

From the muskets of the Revolutionary War to the AR-15s of modern America's mass shootings, the gun has always been at the center of the American story. And so it was in 2020. The stay-at-home orders made crowds less prevalent and gave Americans a brief respite from school and other mass shootings—making it feel almost like living pretty much anywhere else. But consumers were arming up and gun sales were going gangbusters.

> While gun sales have been climbing for decades—they often spike in election years and after high-profile crimes—Americans have been on an unusual, prolonged buying spree fueled by the coronavirus pandemic, the protests last summer and the fears they both stoked.

In March last year, federal background checks, a rough proxy for purchases, topped one million in a week for the first time since the government began tracking them in 1998. (Sabrina Tavernise, *New York Times*)

According to the same article, "New preliminary data from Northeastern University and the Harvard Injury Control Research Center show that about a fifth of all Americans who bought guns last year were first-time gun owners." Just what you want when it comes to gun ownership during an already high-stress year: newbies.

On October 29, in the most gun-crazy American move ever, Walmart announced that, while weapons would still be available for purchase upon request, they would be pulling all guns and ammunition off store shelves as a precautionary move ahead of the election.

Actually, the most gun-crazy American move ever came on October 30, when Walmart changed course and announced they would be putting guns and ammunition back onto store shelves.

News Divisions
October 2020

Maddow

NBC News 1
Lawyers: We can't find parents of 545 kids separated by Trump administration

The New York Times 2
'We Need to Take Away Children,' No Matter How Young, Justice Dept. Officials Said

The New York Times 3
Trump Records Shed New Light on Chinese Business Pursuits

The New York Times 4
Trump's Taxes Show He Engineered a Sudden Windfall in 2016

The New York Times 5
The Swamp That Trump Built

Hannity/Carlson

New York Post 1
Smoking-gun email reveals how Hunter Biden introduced Ukrainian businessman to VP dad

Fox News 2
DNI declassifies Brennan notes, CIA memo on Hillary Clinton 'stirring up' scandal between Trump, Russia

Fox News 3
Source on alleged Hunter Biden email chain verifies messages about Chinese investment firm

Breitbart 4
Exclusive — 'This is China, Inc.': Emails Reveal Hunter Biden's Associates Helped Communist-Aligned Chinese Elites Secure White House Meetings

New York Post 5
Hunter Biden emails show leveraging connections with his father to boost Burisma pay

These are the top news links shared on Twitter in October by followers of Rachel Maddow versus followers of Sean Hannity or Tucker Carlson.
Source: MIT Center for Constructive Communication

THE NEEDLE AND THE DAMAGE DONE

In 1993, at Rich Stadium in Buffalo, the Bills were facing a 35–3 third-quarter deficit to the Houston Oilers, a team that had beaten them 27–3 the week before. From that point, Bills backup quarterback Frank Reich led his team to the greatest comeback in NFL history. I still remember watching the game on television. Years earlier, I was lucky enough to be at the Cal-Stanford Big Game in 1982, when the Bears turned a five-lateral kickoff return into a last-second victory so unlikely that the Stanford band had already raced onto the field to celebrate. Kevin Moen famously ran over a trombone player on the way across the goal line.

That's why you watch sports even when things seem impossible. You never know when you're going to witness a great comeback, or even better, a comeback against Stanford.

But there are no comebacks in elections. We each get a vote, the votes are tallied, the result is announced. But since so many of the other aspects of politics are covered like sports, it's no surprise that election nights are covered like them as well.

We call them political *races*, but there's no clock ticking, even though it feels like there is as the *New York Times* fires up its election needle, CNN places John King in front of the giant touch screen map, and MSNBC starts intravenously filling Steve Kornacki with oceanic quantities of Red Bull.

King and Kornacki, two of the few people alive to have become household names in large part because they're really good at geography, need to be hopped up on caffeine and adrenaline to get us through what can often be long hours—or in 2020, long days—of election coverage. But it's not so much that they're *on* chemicals. They *are* the chemicals. I'm convinced that Kornacki doesn't wear a jacket so he'll be easier to snort.

To understand America on election night, picture Steve Kornacki as a finely ground mountain of cocaine on a desk. America is Al Pacino as Scarface, sticking his whole face in the pile, snorting as much as he can, and then leaning back into a giant executive chair in front of a wall of TVs: "You wanna fuck with me? Okay. You wanna play rough? Okay! Say hello to my little friend! . . . His name is Steve, and he's got some breaking exit poll news from Allegheny."

From the first exit polls to the last electoral vote, we watch, we stress, we can't look away. And I'm no exception. As is the case with my relationship with news and social media, I'm among the sickest percentile. I was the canary in the count mine.

I know the populations, demographics, and poll place locations in counties in Florida, Pennsylvania, and Georgia better than I know my own neighborhood. You show me a political focus group in any small-town diner in America and I can tell you how each participant takes their coffee. So when election night 2020 arrived, I watched every second of the coverage, I read every tweet from obscure pollsters in small towns in Nevada and Arizona, my friends and I set up a chat room to monitor the election results as they trickled in. Two of my friends in the group tracked the numbers closely enough that they decided to do their own math and then periodically present their findings to the group. We were locked in. Our chat room looked like a cable news ticker.

King says we're about to get another batch of mail-in ballots from
    DeKalb!

Kornacki says Trump's margins in Beaver County aren't as wide as
    they were in 2016.

From what I'm seeing, Trump's poor COVID performance coupled
    with him calling Elizabeth Warren *Pocahontas* has stirred up
    just enough Navajo Nation turnout to give Biden a narrow win
    in Arizona.

Key Race Alert!

Breaking News!

We're getting new ballots from a county you've never heard of in a
    race that's never over!

Stay tuned! Stay here! Stay up!

Don't worry, I was up. Kornacki and King took naps. I didn't. Give me, give me, I need. "Kids, Daddy can't help you with your homework right now. Uncle Andy's calculations suggest that the *New York Times* Needle may be off."

I was addicted to the action.

But there was *no* action. You can't come from behind in Georgia. You can't get over the top in Pennsylvania. You can't beat the clock in Michigan. Margins didn't expand or contract. There's no clock. There are votes. The votes are counted. The candidates with the most votes win. But that's not entertainment. And that won't keep you watching. And you're sure as hell not going to volunteer for a four-day United States geography lesson unless it comes with a few side orders of dopamine.

It's fun. It's exciting. It's absorbing. But it's not good for your mental health, and it's definitely not good for democracy. Covering vote counting like a sport only lends credence to the lies about rigged elections or absurdist calls to stop the count. You don't stop counting. Elections are not timed competitions. But the media makes them feel like they are because that's good for them. A well-informed citizenry is good for the republic. A fully obsessed population is good for the ratings.

You're not living in a simulation. It's worse. You're spending your whole life watching one.

It's obvious the media should refrain from sharing minute-by-minute counts and just announce each state after it's decided. But the show is more important than the democracy. And that's part of the reason we got Trump in the first place.

We treat politics like a sport, we cover politics like a sport, and like a sport, sometimes a matchup will go into overtime. So maybe we should have been prepared for a presidential race that seemed like it would never end.

11

NOVEMBER— SPEED HILL

I COME FROM A LONG LINE OF HYPOCHONDRIACS, FOR WHOM PSYCHOSO-matic symptoms are approaching weapons and the gut is the most common target. I was born with a stomachache, and even back then I was pretty confident it was something serious. Over the years, my stomach has been x-rayed, my intestines have been examined, and my stool has been sampled by some of the best minds in gastroenterology, almost all of whom ulti-mately threw up their rubber-gloved hands and asked, "Are you aware of the mind-body connection?" To which I always answered, "Yes, it's the neck, right?"

During one stomach crisis, I underwent the barium enema procedure in which, prior to an x-ray, a metallic liquid used to coat the colon for better imagery is fire-hosed into your rectum by way of a rubber tube that's held in place by a golf ball–size tip. The first time I was on the receiving end of this test, the medical technician may have had a bad day, because the golf ball felt more like a tennis ball: one served by Novak Djokovic. Within two seconds, I was spilling my name, rank, and serial number (but luckily, no barium). Meanwhile, the technician was angrily asking me why I was making so many grunting noises when the procedure really shouldn't be that uncomfortable.

A few years later, after my doctor suggested I get another barium enema, I was greeted by a much more empathetic and delicate medical provider. Once I was gowned with knees up and reclining on the exam table, the tube-wielding technician looked down into my eyes, placed a hand gently upon my shoulder, and said: "Hey, pal. You look a little nervous. Is there anything you're concerned about?"

Of fucking course there was something I was concerned about.

Which brings us to the precipice of the 2020 presidential election. The polls were looking positive for Joe Biden, and for weeks, we un-deplorables were being endlessly warned by journalists, pundits, and political operatives not to be too overconfident about Biden's chances of victory. It was the least necessary admonition of all time. No Democrat who lived through the un-forgettable night of Trump's 2016 victory could possibly be overconfident about anything ever again. Most of us weren't even fully over the initial shock of that win.

At the moment Trump crossed the 2016 electoral threshold, I was in my family room next to my old friend Phil Bronstein, the former editor of the *San Francisco Chronicle*, and a war reporter who had experienced life events with stress levels most of us have only imagined (and I'm talking about the war zones, not his marriage to Sharon Stone or the time his foot got bitten by a Komodo dragon). But when my then eight-year-old daughter ran downstairs gleefully in her homemade Hillary 2016 T-shirt at the exact moment the race was decided, even fearless Phil went full fetal position on my couch, where he would remain pretty motionless, moaning. We sold the house two years later. For all I know, Phil could still be there.

Overconfident heading into a presidential election? After that? Never. I had the same look on my face in early November as I have anytime any-one approaches me with a large plastic sack of barium. But at least in the opening days of November 2020, no one around me asked why I looked nervous.

THE COUNT OF MAR-A-LAGO
November 1, 2020

On the first day of November, as we turned the clocks back for daylight savings time, Americans got the last thing they needed: another hour of this endless campaign and year.

This is what I wrote in my *NextDraft* newsletter two days before the election:

> After four years of psychic hell, I'm worried the next month will be worse, both in terms of threats to our democracy and our health. To be clear, I'm less worried about the election itself than I am about what are the near certain efforts to prevent the counting of votes and challenge the reality of the election's outcome (and challenging reality has been Trump's brand forever). First, on the election: In 2016, Trump narrowly won in a few swing states and pulled off a near-impossible inside straight. Since then, he has become the worst president in American history, overseeing the worst crisis response in American history, and is concluding a poorly run campaign by traveling to the nation's hardest hit Covid-19 hotspots to tell people that Covid-19 is over. Even after four years of being unable to believe what I'm seeing, I still can't believe that the above is a recipe for reelection. Second, on the counting: We know Trump will do everything possible to challenge the will of the people. He challenged the popular vote in the 2016 election after he *won*. From the "perfect" call with the Ukraine president to the relentless efforts to slow down the postal service, Donald Trump has been going postal on our electoral process since the day he conned his way into the Oval Office. It's not a matter of whether he'll try to cheat. It's that he's going to continue cheating and bashing democratic norms until the end. No, he's not going to pivot. The question is whether America will. And right now, it looks like we could have the highest voter turnout in a century. Give Trump credit for this: The dude can draw a crowd.

Obviously, I got one aspect of my prediction very wrong. I was worried about the next month. I needed to be worried about the next three months.

I include the above excerpt for two reasons. First, because it was one hell of an accurate view of what was to come (you can always google for my bad predictions). Second, because Trump's plot to declare victory and attempt to steal the election had been going on in plain view for months. One didn't have to be a soothsayer to predict Trump's near future. He was doomsaying the quiet part out loud every single day. And behind the scenes, plans were in place to "win" the election regardless of which candidate actually had more electoral votes.

His former chief of staff Reince Priebus told a friend he was stunned when Trump called him around that time and acted out his script, including walking up to a podium and prematurely declaring victory on election night if it looked like he was ahead.

White House senior policy adviser Stephen Miller's speechwriting team had prepared three skeleton speeches for election night for all the possible scenarios: a clear victory, a clear loss, and an indeterminate result. But the speechwriters knew that if Trump was facing anything other than a resounding victory, the words would be his alone. This president would never admit defeat or urge patience. (Jonathan Swan and Zachary Basu, *Axios*)

In addition to laying the groundwork for the Big Lie that Joe Biden didn't win the election, Trump was laying out his clear acceptance of, and even admiration for, intimidation and violence.

President Donald Trump cheered his supporters who got into their trucks waving pro-Trump flags and surrounded a Biden-Harris campaign bus in Texas. "I LOVE TEXAS!" Trump wrote on Twitter. The footage that Trump posted appeared to be of the same truck caravan that the Biden campaign said "attempted to slow the bus down and run it off the road" on Friday. Biden campaign spokesperson Symone Sanders blasted the president for his tweet, characterizing it as "reckless, dangerous, and an intimidation tactic." She added that "it's not something we should come to accept from our leaders." (Daniel Politi, *Slate*)

I was pretty good on my post-Election Day predictions, but Garry Kasparov, as usual, was even better. He had lived through these tactics before, and he knew exactly what Americans were staring in the face. In a CNN op-ed, the chess grandmaster explained the Trumpian moves to come.

> We cannot know exactly what Trump will do in these final days, only that whatever it is, he will be thinking only of himself. If he declares victory on election night, regardless of the uncounted ballots, what then? What if he calls the entire election a fraud, a hoax, and demands that the counting stop? Or if armed Trump supporters heed his call to intimidate voters at the polls? What if he takes to Twitter with "LIBERATE AMERICA!" and his MAGA zealots respond?
>
> You may roll your eyes, but such things are not unimaginable, or even unrealistic. Normal people don't like to imagine terrible events, which is why autocrats consistently surprise them.

If any eyes were rolling when Kasparov issued this warning, they were about to slow their roll.

OUR TOWN

My daughter ran upstairs to show me a video one of her sixth-grade classmates had shared. A convoy of pickup trucks and cars, waving Trump flags and Keep America Great banners, had rolled loudly into town. The group had started in Santa Rosa, made a pit stop in Novato, and ended up in Marin City, California, one exit away from my house.

If these pickup truckers were looking to intimidate radical liberal snowflakes, they could have stayed on Highway 101 for another minute or two and found several of them on my couch watching MSNBC. So why did they pick Marin City? Because it is widely known as Marin County's predominantly Black neighborhood. If there was any doubt about that part of the strategy, it was erased when many of the flag-waving Trump supporters began to hurl racial epithets at residents, including kids, like my daughter's classmate, who were lining the streets.

Marin City wasn't the only scene of attempted intimidation:

Another [convoy] in Fort Worth cruised through a polling station in a predominantly Black neighborhood, provoking an altercation with residents. In Temecula, California, a caravan blocked access to a voting center. A group in New York shut down the Mario Cuomo bridge. In Louisville, Kentucky, a "Trump Train" member directed traffic with a gun at a high school. And in Texas, near Austin, trucks adorned with "Make America Great Again" flags swarmed a Joe Biden campaign bus in an incident that is now under FBI investigation . . .

At least 18 of the listed event organizers in 14 states have openly supported the far-right conspiracy theory known as QAnon on social media. (Jessica Schulberg, Nick Robins-Early, and Jesselyn Cook, *HuffPost*)

> **Dave Pell** ✔
> @davepell
>
> Imagine a Trump caravan of armed men in pickups showing up at Mar a Lago for a lunch reservation.
>
> 11:27 AM · Nov 2, 2020 · 🐦 Twitter

FOR MORE YEARS

For 231,000 of our fellow Americans who couldn't go to the polls, for those who said their final goodbyes to a loved one over an iPad while their president downplayed the threat, for the health workers sent into a deadly battle without basic protective equipment, for doctors who worked tirelessly only to hear themselves accused of pumping up virus numbers for financial gain, for experts who warned us again and again even as their expertise was diminished and ridiculed, for scientists who got up every morning in search of a vaccine even as science itself was under constant attack, for the thousands who watched their homes burn to the ground under a blood-orange sky while their president said to sweep the forests, for the whistleblowers who risked it all to share the facts when so few others in the administration had the guts to do so, for the Alexander Vindmans who spoke truth to power because "right matters," for Ahmaud Arbery, Breonna Taylor, and George

Floyd, whose final breaths were snuffed out beneath the knee of a tired social structure, for the millions who took to the street to say no more, for the
protesters targeted with tear gas and rubber bullets by their own government in the shadow of the White House, for our allies abroad who had been
abandoned as dictators and thugs were lauded, for the victims of hate who
were told there are fine people on all sides, for our soldiers who sacrificed
their lives for a cause the current commander in chief can't understand, for
the artists, writers, and performers who set their personal brands aside to
become political because everything was political, for the investigative journalists who got the stories out even while being attacked as enemies of the
people, for the kids who crossed the border and still didn't know where their
parents are, for the essential workers, especially the immigrants, who kept
our society functioning, for the meatpacking plant workers who kept food
on our tables even as their government increased the odds the work could
kill them, for the tens of thousands of ordinary citizens who stepped up to
fill the leadership vacuum, for the lawyers and nonprofit organizations that
bolstered democracy as it came under increasing attack, for the young people who had missed too much of their youth and the elderly who had been
imprisoned too long by a virus that was called a hoax, for Ruth Bader Ginsburg, for John Lewis, for the truth, for the rule of law, for the millions who
stood in long lines between them and the ballot box because you've got to
stand for something, for the many well-known Republicans who put country above party, and yes, for Trump's true believers; the still ardent followers
who were duped into risking their lives to attend rallies, for our parents, for
our kids, for a chance at turning the corner on climate change, for an end
to the relentless, insidious lies, for more years of American leadership, for
more years of the promise of democracy, for more years on this planet, for a
decent, good man just crazy enough to believe unity is still possible, for all
of it, it was time to tear down the wall that surrounded the White House,
it was time to tear down the walls between us, it was time to say enough is
enough. It was go time. It was Joe time. And with that, I voted.

And then I waited. And then early results started rolling in. And then
the nonstop cable news coverage of maps and counties and districts that I
only care about once every four years started. And then Trump took Florida

because of course Florida was being Florida in 2020. And then it became clear the race was going to be close. And then my stomach started hurting. And then I remembered my ironic relationship with presidential elections: each one takes four years off my life.

And then, after what felt like a few hundred hours of watching election results trickle in, I curled up on the floor of my man cave and moan-cried for about thirty minutes. It was a combination of things. Part of it was personal: I spent so much time thinking, writing, tweeting, and distracting myself with this all-encompassing political story that I may have been momentarily overwhelmed. Maybe I was also considering how much dough I spent, entering my credit card details to support various races around the country—I don't want to overstate how invested I was in these campaigns, but on election night when I heard an engine roar in front of my house, I was sure ActBlue had come to repossess my car.

The bigger part was less personal: Trump had been the same guy the whole time he'd been president. And knowing this, tens of millions of Americans still voted for him. On some level, we were broken. I get the national divide and I frankly agree with many of the complaints coming from rural America. I understand some of the anger, but I've never understood expressing that anger through Trump. And watching him go full authoritarian as the votes were still being counted made me especially sad for my parents who had to watch the rise of a strongman during the buildup to World War II in Poland and Germany when they were kids, and who now had to watch half of America embrace a guy who deployed such familiar political tactics. But then I stopped crying. Partly because no one owns this Lib! Partly because I realized that among the challenges my parents have faced, nothing about this election ranked in the top thousand. And partly because, regardless of the premature self-coronation, in America, no election is over until every last retweet is counted.

Because of the pandemic, the remarkably high turnout, and the deluge of mail-in ballots, it was going to take a while to get the counting completed. Even though we had been repeatedly warned that the results wouldn't be conclusive on election night, it was hard for me to be patient. It was impossible for Trump.

"We are up BIG, but they are trying to STEAL the Election. We will never let them do it. Votes cannot be cast after the Polls are closed!" That was Trump's key election night tweet, and he followed it up with a White House victory speech.

> Trump, standing in front of a phalanx of flags, claimed that the vote count had been "called off" because he won; that is not true on either count. He said that his lead in those swing states was insurmountable, which is also false, and that when "they"—he didn't really identify "they," except as "a very sad group of people"—realized that he was winning, they had swooped in to perpetrate "a fraud on the American public." In saying this, he was lying to the American public. And when he told the country that there was a conspiracy afoot to "disenfranchise" people who voted for him—adding, "We won't stand for it"—he seemed to be willfully prodding his supporters toward violence. (Susan B. Glasser, *New Yorker*)

It was a testament to how far from normal we'd been dragged that an American president declaring victory in an election he hadn't won wasn't even that big of a news story. As Dahlia Lithwick put it in *Slate*: "If one of the New York Mets persistently declared victory in the top of the fourth inning, he'd be medicated and hospitalized. That this is bottom-of-the-fold news when Trump does it is where we are now."

It was even worse. Imagine if one of the New York Mets persistently declared victory in the top of the fourth inning and half the stadium completely believed him and demanded that the game be stopped. The Mets would never do such a thing. But another guy from Queens did.

As the counting dragged on, Trump began issuing his latest tweet directive: "Stop the Count!" He even wanted to stop the count in places where he was behind, which may sound counterintuitive, until you realize it was all about him counting on a counterrevolution against reality.

Some ballot measures had been officially decided, and one of the year's big winners was drug law reform. From Arizona and Montana to New Jersey and South Dakota, voters turned out to legalize recreational marijuana. Good thing more people had access to the legal supply, because the need for it surged when the QAnon conspiracy supporting Marjorie Taylor Greene won her race for a Georgia House seat.

THE PETTYSBURG ADDRESS
November 5, 2020

He told us he was going to do it. Everyone was prepared for him to do it. And yet, even with that foreshadowing, it was still chilling to watch an American president stand in the White House briefing room and baselessly call an election into question.

> "If you count the legal votes, I easily win. If you count the illegal votes, they can try to steal the election from us."
>
> "A lot of votes came too late. I've already decisively won many critical states, including massive victories in Florida, Iowa, Indiana, Ohio, to name just a few. We won these and many other victories."
>
> "We were winning in all the key locations by a lot, actually, and then our numbers started miraculously getting whittled away in secret."
>
> "I've been talking about mail-in voting for a long time. It's really destroyed our system. It's a corrupt system and it makes people corrupt, even if they aren't by nature, but they become corrupt. It's too easy. They want to find out how many votes they need and then they seem to be able to find them."
>
> "We were up by nearly 700,000 votes in Pennsylvania. I won Pennsylvania by a lot and that gets whittled down to—I think they said now we're up by 90,000 votes—and they'll keep coming and coming and coming."
>
> "We also had margins of 300,000 in Michigan . . . and won the state and in Wisconsin, we did likewise fantastically well. And that got whittled down in every case. They got whittled down. Today, we're on track to win Arizona."

These were just some of a long litany of potentially violence-triggering lies as Trump began the scorched-earth episode of history's worst reality show.

> **Dave Pell** ✓
> @davepell
>
> The last four years in one tweet.
>
> > **Daniel Dale**
> > They have not won Pennsylvania.
> >
> > > **Eric Trump**
> > > We have won Pennsylvania!
>
> 12:33 PM · Nov 4, 2020 · 🐦 Twitter

None of it was true. All of it was predictable. Most of it would be followed by legal challenges brought to courts around the country. His crack team of crackpot lawyers would lose all but one of sixty cases during the month after the election (and that one victory was overturned). Trump's incendiary claims of election fraud were so dangerous that television networks finally cut away. I wish they had done that during his equally dangerous coronavirus press conferences.

This failure to turn Trump off, or to treat him any differently from any other president, was the media's biggest failing during his tenure. For four years, Trump was covered as if he were an ordinary president. By the time the media began to adjust by cutting away from the lies, it was way too late.

> **Dave Pell** ✓
> @davepell
>
> I wish Nixon were alive to see how not bad he was.
>
> 4:35 PM · Nov 5, 2020 · 🐦 Twitter

Instead of habitually lying about a variety of topics, Trump had narrowed his focus. Each of the tens of thousands of lies he had told during his presidency was loosely tied to the same end goal: maintaining power. As the calendar approached and passed Election Day, there was only one lie that could still achieve that objective.

It was the last Big Lie: that he had actually won the election. Once it was clear Biden had the electoral edge, this one lie became more urgent and its backers more determined.

How does the Big Lie strategy work? Let's ask an expert. Here's Joseph Goebbels: "If you tell a lie big enough and keep repeating it, people will eventually come to believe it. The lie can be maintained only for such time as the State can shield the people from the political, economic and/or military consequences of the lie. It thus becomes vitally important for the State to use all of its powers to repress dissent, for the truth is the mortal enemy of the lie, and thus by extension, the truth is the greatest enemy of the State."

BETTER LATE THAN WHATEVER

Like most of his disinformation, Trump's burn-it-all-down assault on the democratic process was catching fire on social media. Facebook executives announced changes to their platform after seeing growing signs of coordinated acts of violence. So it turned out that Facebook had methods to decrease the likelihood of viral and dangerous disinformation. I wonder why they waited until after the election to deploy them?

RASH ACT

At just around the moment it looked like Biden had the election wrapped up, I got an email from my son's high school indicating that a student in his COVID cohort had tested positive. So, during an already stressful week, my son and I packed our things (his included his PS4 and some T-shirts, mine included stress and anxiety) and headed off to shelter in place away from the rest of the family.

My son was running for freshman class vice president (in our family, we always aim medium), so I helped him with his video-recorded speech. He was pretty nervous until I informed him that if he lost, he could refuse to concede and insist that he had actually won.

One afternoon, we took a long walk on the trails of Mount Tamalpais, and aside from the fact that every group of hikers we passed was talking about the election, it was nice to get away from the drumbeat of political news.

The effects of news stress returned that evening when I felt some itchiness below my beltline. By morning, a reddish rash had spread over most of my body, and by the time it was safe for my son and me to return home, my body was covered with a DEFCON 1 rash, my oozy, itchy head had expanded to the size of a basketball, I could barely see out of my swollen eyes, and I had a grapefruit-size swelling in the region between my chin and neck. It didn't help matters that my daughter greeted me with, "You look normal to me."

A couple of days later, I got something called an ID rash. After googling, I learned that this reaction is a type of acute dermatitis that develops at skin locations distant from the initial inflammatory or infectious site. In other words, my rash gave me a fucking rash. Rash Part 2, which coincided with Rash Part 1, featured large, itchy welts on my face, hips, and buttocks.

I wasn't infected by COVID-19. I was infected by the news.

LET THERE BE LIGHT

They counted and they counted and they counted. CNN called it. The *New York Times* called it. The AP called it. NBC unplugged The Kornacki. And it was over. Out goes the birtherism president, and in comes Joe Biden and Kamala Harris, the first Black and South Asian American woman vice president. That's a hell of a pivot. Four years before this moment, I wrote: *I'm the progressive son of Holocaust-surviving, immigrant parents, and the father of a couple of brown kids, and this is without any doubt the hardest sentence I've ever had to type: Donald John Trump will be the 45th president of the United States.* For four years, I'd listened to my mom ask why there's still so much hate in the country. For four years, I'd listened to my dad ask me: "Why aren't the people out in the streets?" Well, Dad, they were finally out in the streets: cheering, dancing, and celebrating the end to a four-year detour from decency and decorum, a U-turn from Donald Trump's "I alone" to Joe Biden's "We together."

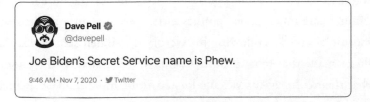

Dave Pell ✓
@davepell

Joe Biden's Secret Service name is Phew.

9:46 AM · Nov 7, 2020 · 🐦 Twitter

I was so relieved that, like, 3 percent of my rash disappeared.

Following Biden's 306–232 electoral college win, the national nightmare, the relentless news cycle, the four years of nonstop madness, and the most stressful, *Idiocracy*-inspired election was, for once and for all, over. Yes, Trump got the second-most votes of any presidential candidate with 74,222,593, but Biden earned the top spot with 81,281,502. Seven million more votes and a significant electoral win. It wasn't that close after all! Hallelujah. Let boredom ring. Let boredom ring.

This is the moment when you hear a sound effect of tires skidding as joy and relief come to a screeching halt.

Yes, in reality, the election was over. But reality was a wildly unpopular habitat for millions of Americans.

Dave Pell ✔
@davepell

Life is short.

Except the hours between now and January 20.

8:37 AM · Nov 7, 2020 · 🐦 Twitter

Regrettably, Americans wouldn't get the much-anticipated *Covffee* break. First, because Trump kept running for president after the election was over. And second, because close races in Georgia meant that two runoffs there would determine the control of the Senate. For worn-out political junkies, it was like getting dropped off for rehab on the set of C-SPAN.

EYES ON THE PFIZ

November 9, 2020

COVID-19 never cared about politics. Thankfully for the human race, scientists didn't care much about politics either, even in an era when science itself was under attack. Following his victory, Joe Biden said it was time to heal. Pfizer made that remark both serious and literal with the announcement that their coronavirus vaccine looked to be more than 90 percent effective. Both its effectiveness and the pace of its development were beyond what even the optimists had expected earlier in the year. It was the revenge of the nerds.

While Trump and Pence immediately took credit for the vaccine, it was actually the result of the very globalism they had been railing against. The vaccine was the product of a partnership between Pfizer and a German company called BioNTech, which was led by a married couple, Ugur Sahin and Özlem Türeci, both children of Turkish immigrants. They had been working on cancer drugs when they heard about a potential pandemic, and quickly shifted their focus.

The president and president-elect greeted the vaccine news in their signature styles.

Joe Biden: "We're still facing a very dark winter. The challenge before us right now is still immense and growing."

Trump: "STOCK MARKET UP BIG, VACCINE COMING SOON. REPORT 90% EFFECTIVE. SUCH GREAT NEWS!"

If ever there was a good reason to use all caps (and there's not), this would have been it. In the 1960s, scientists set the previous record, developing a vaccine for mumps in about four years. The coronavirus vaccines now had the potential to give humanity a shot in the arm in under a year. We'd later learn that another vaccine Moderna was pushing through the approval process had been created in the first couple of days after they received a sample of the virus. The breakthroughs were based on science decades in the making, but the final advances were instantaneous by scientific standards. Days after Pfizer's announcement, Moderna would announce that its mRNA vaccine appeared to be more than 94 percent effective. Toward the end of the Vietnam War, John Kerry famously asked, "How do you ask a man to be the last man to die in Vietnam? How do you ask a man to be the last man to die for a mistake?" Now the question was: How do you ask a person to die from a virus when the vaccine is in sight?

FOUR SEASONS TOTALITARIAN LANDSCAPE

While Biden won the election by a significant margin, the result was still too close for comfort, and American democracy had experienced a very real brush with death. If it had died, historians likely would have agreed that the fatal wound was dealt in the parking lot in front of Four Seasons Total Landscaping.

Rudy Giuliani, who, it was by now clear, was not the sharpest tool in the shed, was acting as the tip of the spear in Donald Trump's efforts to overthrow an American election. By most accounts, on November 7, Rudy's team was attempting to book a press conference at the Four Seasons Hotel in Philadelphia, but somehow he and his legal team had instead been booked at a landscaping store with a similar name.

I'll let the locals at the *Philadelphia Inquirer* set the scene.

What began five years ago with the made-for-TV announcement of Donald Trump's presidential ambitions from the escalator of his ritzy Manhattan high-rise ended Saturday with his aging lawyer shouting conspiracy theories and vowing lawsuits in a Northeast Philadelphia parking lot, near a sex shop and a crematorium. (Jeremy Roebuck, Maddie Hanna, and Oona Goodin-Smith)

Even though the setting was absurd, Rudy and his team went forward with the presser. They say that if you find yourself in a hole, stop digging. I guess the exception to that adage is when the shovel you're using was purchased at Four Seasons Total Landscaping.

During the bizarro press conference, Giuliani was interrupted by a reporter who told him that the networks had officially called the race for Biden.

Rudy: Who was it called by?
Mark Stone of Sky News: All the networks.
Rudy: All the, oh my goodness, all the networks. Wow! All the networks! We have to forget about the law. Judges don't count. All the networks, all the networks. All the networks thought Biden was going to win by 10%. Gee, what happened? Come on, don't be, don't be ridiculous. Networks don't get to decide elections, courts do.

Technically, neither the networks nor the courts decide elections. Voters do. Still, Team Trump appeared determined to take the will of the people and the call of the networks and the ridiculousness of the press conference venue in stride as they continued to wrestle with American democracy. Four Seasons Total Landscaping took the event in stride as well, and reacted just like any other red-blooded American business would—they started selling merch. In a Facebook post, they reflected on the unusual turn of events.

> Our team at Four Seasons would have proudly hosted any presidential candidate's campaign at our business. We strongly believe in America and in democracy. We hope that our fellow Americans can join together and support all local small businesses during this time.
>
> For those interested in purchasing shirts, our website will have a Merchandise tab uploaded by Monday Morning, just bear with us!
>
> Go Birds!

It's difficult to stand out as the weirdest moment of the weirdest year in our lifetimes. And yet, in 2020, we had an undisputed winner of this dubious honor. It was the most joked-about, meme-able moment of the year. So we laughed. We laughed hard. Who can blame us? I'm not pointing any fingers here. Humor is my defense mechanism and my *offense* mechanism. I tweeted the hell out of the press conference. I guffawed at social media posts. I ordered Four Seasons Total Landscaping T-shirts. I used a photo of Rudy's press conference setup as my Zoom background.

But while I was laughing, I kept thinking of the words of two men. My dad, who had said of Trump, "Everyone laughed at Hitler in the early days." And Steve Martin, who warned, "Comedy is not pretty."

The Four Seasons theater of the absurd was a reminder that many moments of the Trump era, in addition to being fucking depressing, fucking sad, fucking frustrating, and fucking deadly, were also undeniably fucking funny. Every Trump tweet was a challenge to see who could get off the best one-liner in response. Each of Trump's idiotic statements would be met with heaps of snark from the media. From late-night talk shows to podcasts to dinner tables, we often found ourselves just shaking our heads and laughing. They say every joke has a grain of truth. But for four long years, the primary butt of all our jokes was a man who had zero grains of it.

We laughed, but we were also being sucked into becoming participants in the Trump show. Led Zeppelin's Robert Plant wondered, "Does anyone remember laughter?" The laughter of 2020 is worth remembering, and considering. Did it aid and abet the Trumpists? Did the entertainment distract us from the threat? Were we just blowing off steam to survive an otherwise miserable year? And what about those for whom all of this, even the mad presser, was entirely serious? What if they ended up having the last laugh?

ESPER DIEM

It's an unusual and unnerving sign for a lame-duck president to remove a secretary of defense during a transition period. But Mark Esper had publicly separated himself from Trump's plank, so he was forced to walk one. Esper had disagreed with Trump on two issues: he argued that active-duty military troops should not be sent into cities to be deployed against protesters (imagine the top guy at the Pentagon not wanting to wage war on Americans), and he signed off on a plan to rename military bases that honored Confederate generals. As childish and vindictive as Trump's firing by tweet seemed, there was another more insidious angle to consider. Trump, who would continue to gut the top echelon of the Pentagon, didn't consider himself a lame-duck president. He still wanted to win the election he had just lost.

THE COUP CLUTZ CLAN

The president's refusal to concede an election that had been decided was pitiful, but entirely predictable. Slightly less predictable, and much more dangerous, was the fact that he had a growing number of allies in the GOP who were feeding into his magical thinking.

A week after the election, when asked at what point the administration's transition delays could hamper national security, Secretary of State Mike Pompeo said, "There will be a smooth transition to a second Trump administration." And then smirked. And what could be a better gag than the shameless lying that damages the country, our reputation abroad, and democracy? William Barr was equally hilarious when he wrote a memo authorizing federal prosecutors to pursue any "substantial allegations of voting and vote tabulation irregularities."

Richard Pilger, the head of the department's election crimes branch, stepped down after Barr issued his memo. But such acts of pro-democracy defiance were rare among appointed officials and even more so among elected ones. Here's a sampling of leaders who had not yet congratulated Biden on his win: Putin, Xi, Kim Jong-un, Bolsonaro, McConnell.

With his eyes on the Georgia runoff that would determine whether he held on to the Senate majority leader gig, McConnell's refusal to acknowledge Biden's win could be chalked up to political gamesmanship. But it was a game that was lost on 70 percent of Republicans, who now believed the election wasn't free and fair, despite there being no evidence of fraud.

> **Dave Pell** ✅
> @davepell
>
> It may be a pathetic coup. It may be carried out by laughable idiots in the name of a mad man.
>
> But trying to overturn accurate election results, refusing to concede, and firing everyone who tells the truth is in fact a coup.
>
> 4:17 PM · Nov 17, 2020 · 🐦 Twitter

This relationship between the GOP leadership and a vast segment of Republicans often reminded me of something Apollo Creed's trainer told him in his corner when it was clear Rocky was determined to win their first fight: "He doesn't know it's supposed to be a show! He thinks it's a damn fight!"

For many GOP insiders, the ever-popular Trump was viewed as a damn show that enabled them to amass votes and pass legislation. But for millions of voters, Trumpism was a damn fight. Trump's increasingly disconnected base was no longer a manageable, manipulatable voting bloc. It had become an uncontrollable force all its own. You can create a monster. You can't control a monster.

GRAND THEFT AUTOGOLPE

We were witnessing a self-coup and an attempt to overthrow an election by Trump, his increasingly unhinged enablers, and a large swath of Republican officeholders. But we were also witnessing the predictable behavior of a person with Trump's psychopathology, that by now manifested in such obvious and public ways that he seemed to be vying for the cover of the next edition of the *DSM*.

Trump's mental illness never got the focus it deserved, partly because diagnosing patients from afar has never garnered much enthusiasm from those in the psychological world, and partly because geopolitical events are rarely viewed through this prism in real time. The media too often treated Trump as a normal president and as a normal patient—which, given his oozing and obvious pathologies, bordered on a kind of willful blindness.

My dad always taught me to focus on the personal traits of leaders in order to better understand and predict their actions. While he understood the importance of this aspect of politics as someone who had lived through the worst humanity had to offer, my psychoanalyst friend Dr. Michael Levin understood what was going on from the other side of the couch. Levin is one of the smartest people I know, a seasoned psychoanalyst who has treated and taught about the symptoms Trump exhibited, and like I am, he's a political junkie who had spent the past four years obsessively watching the news. Levin is basically a cross between Sigmund Freud and *Network*'s Howard Beale ("I'm mad as hell, and our fifty minutes are up"), so I turned to him to help explain why Trump's behavior could continue to surprise us.

This disconnect exists because we're living in a world that is grounded and checked by reason. His is grounded only in his emotional needs and fantasies. I think this is a useful framework to understand why we all have repeatedly been shocked by his behavior for years. It's just a bridge too far for most of our psychological imaginations . . . Most of the commentary I'm seeing in the press about his narcissism seems not to get that, deep down, it's not about feeling good. It's about psychic survival. I think this is the case with most of his base too. It's not the garden-variety narcissism of someone like Elon Musk, Bill Clinton, or Dave Pell. It's much more desperate and psychotic.

We were only really applying strategic goals like winning an unwinnable election to what was a terror of shame and humiliation. Behind the bravado, losing posed a mortal threat to Trump's fragile psyche. Trump truly believed he was being cheated because the alternative was too brutal and painful to accept. The destruction of American democracy was a small price to pay for the survival of his grandiose delusions and the psychic existence upon which they depended.

When we see mental illness play out in public or celebrity spheres, we often view it as a sideshow. When we encounter it in real life, we know it's *the whole show*. Some of the politicians who cynically used Trump as a battering ram for their own ends would be able to detach from him when his usefulness declined. Some of them also shared his symptoms. It's how you end up with a pathocracy: a government made up of those with personality disorders, such as psychopaths and narcissists. Once you hear that word, it becomes clear it's what was happening under Trump.

> The attraction of gurus and demagogues is a deep-rooted impulse to return to the childhood state of worshipping parents who seem omnipotent and infallible and could take complete responsibility for our lives, and magically solve our problems. At the same time, the paranoia of pathological leaders leads them to demonize other groups and creates an intoxicating sense of group identity with a common purpose. (Steve Taylor, PhD, *Psychology Today*)

As Taylor points out, for such a leader's true believers, the relationship is less transactional and operates more like a religion. And a religious-like worship is a lot to ask someone to give up because of the small reality of a few million votes. As we'd learn from Jodi Doering, an ER nurse in South Dakota, it was even a lot to ask someone to give up even when their lives were on the line.

> I have a night off from the hospital. As I'm on my couch with my dog I can't help but think of the Covid patients the last few days. The ones that stick out are those who still don't believe the virus is real. The ones who scream at you for a magic medicine and that Joe Biden is going to ruin the USA. All while

gasping for breath on 100% Vapotherm. They tell you there must be another reason they are sick. They call you names and ask why you have to wear all that "stuff" because they don't have COVID because it's not real. Yes. This really happens. And I can't stop thinking about it. These people really think this isn't going to happen to them. And then they stop yelling at you when they get intubated. It's like a f-cking horror movie that never ends.

People who had COVID were dying in hospital rooms while denying COVID was real, and arguing it was all part of some radical Democrat plot to rig the whole world against them. For some, this delusion, a defense against the abyss of despair, humiliation, and nihilism, would live until their bodies died.

While patients were dying believing COVID was a hoax, Trump supporters who refused to accept he lost the election were marching on Washington, declaring victory, and arguing that Anthony Fauci and Bill Gates should be arrested for their roles in manufacturing the coronavirus exaggeration. Meanwhile, Scott Atlas was urging people in Michigan to "rise up" against new COVID-19 safety measures offered by their governor—who had recently faced a kidnapping and murder plot. While states were introducing new lockdowns and more stringent mask-wearing regulations, Atlas was arguing that people should visit their grandparents because "for many people this is their final Thanksgiving, believe it or not." The experts were being silenced, the president was ignoring the virus, and his favorite coronavirus "expert" was on Fox News spreading more deadly misinformation. Scott Atlas was Jeffrey Dahmer with an MD.

Bandy X. Lee is a forensic psychiatrist at the Yale School of Medicine and president of the World Mental Health Coalition. In an interview with *Scientific American*, Lee explained what attracts people to Trump, and the psychological stickiness that often defines such relationships.

The leader, hungry for adulation to compensate for an inner lack of self-worth, projects grandiose omnipotence—while the followers, rendered needy by societal stress or developmental injury, yearn for a parental figure. When such wounded individuals are given positions of power, they arouse similar pathology in the population that creates a "lock and key" relationship . . .

When a highly symptomatic individual is placed in an influential position, the person's symptoms can spread through the population through emotional bonds, heightening existing pathologies and inducing delusions, paranoia and propensity for violence—even in previously healthy individuals. The treatment is removal of exposure.

With the exposure to the Big Lie and the Bigly Liar still in full effect, the question was whether this unnerving and democracy-smashing coup-like attempt would be allowed to continue. How far would the GOP enablers take this? That was still unclear in mid-November. But it was clear that the frenzied delusions stirred up among millions of Americans couldn't be turned off with a switch.

MIRACLE STILL ON ICE

Back in stark reality, the US had recorded more than one million new coronavirus cases in the first ten days of November, and more Americans were in the hospital with COVID-19 than ever before.

After the election results were in, Ted Cruz tweeted: "Miraculous. COVID cured, the very instant the networks called the race for Biden." Cruz was insinuating that the media had stopped covering the virus now that the election was over. In actuality, it would have been the only thing they covered had it not be for the coup attempt being supported by Cruz and his cronies.

Cruz's diabolical argument that COVID-19 was overcovered before the election and stopped being a story after the election was one of the few times I wished a conspiracy theory were true. Records were being set. Cases were on the rise with the US now suffering nearly 2,000 deaths a day. By November 18, 250,000 Americans were dead. More than 900 Mayo Clinic health workers had contracted coronavirus in the previous two weeks. And unlike earlier waves that were regional in nature, this time, the pandemic was following a growth curve forged by the Big Lie. It was everywhere.

KREB NOTES

As the director of the Cybersecurity and Infrastructure Security Agency, Chris Krebs was in charge of efforts to protect the election. And ten days after America took to the polls, he wrote a memo repudiating Trump's election fraud claims.

> The November 3rd election was the most secure in American history. Right now, across the country, election officials are reviewing and double checking the entire election process prior to finalizing the result.
>
> When states have close elections, many will recount ballots. All of the states with close results in the 2020 presidential race have paper records of each vote, allowing the ability to go back and count each ballot if necessary. This is an added benefit for security and resilience. This process allows for the identification and correction of any mistakes or errors. There is no evidence that any voting system deleted or lost votes, changed votes, or was in any way compromised.

Trump responded with a tweet: "Now they are saying what a wonderful job the Trump Administration did in making 2020 the most secure election ever. Actually this is true, except for what the Democrats did. Rigged Election!"

Five days later, Chris Krebs was fired.

AIRING DIRTY FRENCH LAUNDRY
November 18, 2020

California governor Gavin Newsom was caught dining with a large group of people at Yountville's fancy French Laundry restaurant. Even if the risk was low, attending this event was a horrible decision by Newsom. It gave fuel to the restriction naysayers, and it was the opposite of leading by example. COVID presented a moment for all of us to be in one fight together. Leaders needed to act like it.

Newsom wasn't alone. Nancy Pelosi was forced to cancel an indoor dinner planned for new House members after the public got wind of the event.

> **Dave Pell** ✓
> @davepell
>
> The food at the French Laundry is to die for.
>
> 11:54 AM Dec 9, 2020 · 🐦 Twitter

And even Coronavirus Task Force member Deborah Birx was taken to task for joining several out-of-household family members at her vacation home in Fenwick Island, Delaware, over Thanksgiving weekend. The outcry over that gathering led to Birx's resignation.

When these stories rolled out, it seemed to me that there was probably an untold aspect of them. I'm guessing the attendees of the French Laundry dinner, and especially the Fenwick Island get-together, had access to COVID-19 tests that were not as readily available to most Americans. It's safe to assume that risk of spread at either of these controversial gatherings was extremely low.

But that wasn't the point. The point was that these folks knew as well as anyone that the worst of the pandemic was far from over and that the upcoming holidays would be celebrated by COVID-19 most of all. They also knew that a president, a substantial portion of his party, several TV networks, and much of the social media universe were conspiring to convince people that the virus and its associated regulations were all part of some elaborate political hoax. While feeding themselves, these leaders were also feeding the beast.

SOMEONE TO COUNT ON
November 23, 2020

Early in Trump's tenure, *the resistance* referred to those determined to use legal and legislative means to slow down the president's agenda. By now, *the resistance* referred to state officials who could count. Following a hand recount, Georgia's Republican secretary of state, Brad Raffensperger, certified that Joe Biden won the state by 12,670 votes. In exchange for sharing the accurate count, Raffensperger found himself under heavy pressure from fellow GOP members and was the recipient of death threats. Arizona officials also confirmed that Biden had won that state, regardless of Trump lawsuits and claims otherwise.

> In Michigan, where Biden won by more than a hundred and fifty thousand votes, the state Board of Canvassers is expected to certify the result on Monday. On Friday, Mike Shirkey, the Republican majority leader of the state Senate, and Lee Chatfield, the Republican speaker of Michigan's lower house, attended a hastily arranged meeting at the White House. With some of the President's allies openly calling on G.O.P.-controlled state legislatures to take the extraordinary step of appointing slates of Trump loyalists to the Electoral College, and with Trump having personally called a Republican member of the Board of Canvassers in Wayne County earlier this week, the get-together raised alarms. But, after the White House meeting, Shirkey and Chatfield issued a statement that said, "We have not yet been made aware of any information that would change the outcome of the election in Michigan and as legislative leaders, we will follow the law and follow the normal process regarding Michigan's electors." (John Cassidy, *New Yorker*)

Aside from a handful of Republicans, like Mitt Romney, who called the efforts to overturn the election "undemocratic," the results and re-results coming from state leaders was largely met with silence from GOP leaders, who still refused to acknowledge Biden's victory.

Meanwhile, Trump's legal "strike force" continued to strike out, losing cases and suffering various forms of humiliation in courtrooms and during press conferences. About thirty minutes into one Q&A session, Rudy Giuliani began to leak some black sludge from both temples. The goo dripped all the way down his cheeks, although no one on his crack legal team felt compelled to let him know about it. There was some debate whether it was hair dye or some sideburn touch-up that melted when combined with TV lights and profuse sweating. To me, it looked like snake oil.

FLYNN THROUGH THE OUT DOOR
November 25, 2020

President Trump and Bill Barr were determined to free Michael Flynn from paying any penalty for lying to FBI officials during the Mueller investigation, so it was entirely unsurprising when Trump issued Flynn a full pardon. It probably shouldn't have come as much of a surprise that the fully free Flynn would then spread his wings and spread conspiracy theories and dangerous ideas about overthrowing the election. Days after his pardon, Flynn tweeted a full-page ad purchased by a group called the We the People Convention, which urged the POTUS to "immediately declare a limited form of Martial Law, and temporarily suspend the Constitution and civilian control of these federal elections, for the sole purpose of having the military oversee a re-vote." Flynn added: "Freedom never kneels except for God."

The following month, Flynn's Twitter account was banned as part of a broader QAnon account purge. I guess freedom never kneels except for God or @Jack.

ALL OVER AGAIN

Three weeks after Election Day, Joe Biden won the presidency yet again. This time, the victory came via Emily Murphy, Trump's head of the General Services Administration, who wrote in a letter to President-Elect Joe Biden that her office was ready to begin the formal presidential transition. The letter was wildly late and only came after intense media scrutiny. If nothing else, the four years of Trumpism gave us all a very uncivilized civics lesson. Who knew we'd get a three-week lesson on the machinery and machinations of the GSA? What tipped the GSA scales? Was it the remarkably embarrassing court appearances? The sludge leaking from Rudy's temples? Or, more likely, the corporate chorus of CEOs who had seen enough and even discussed withholding campaign donations from the two Republican Senate candidates in Georgia? Whatever it was, the letter was sent, and the transition had officially started. But only officially in the *not normal* way to which we'd grown accustomed.

In the three weeks it took Emily Murphy to do her job, Donald Trump continued to diligently carry out his duties: watching cable news and tweeting. According to the *New York Times,* the president had "posted some 550 tweets—about three-quarters of which attempted to undermine the integrity of the 2020 election results."

By now, he didn't waste much time on his deadly pandemic lies, or most of the hundreds of other topics that had been part of his four-year set list. It was all about overthrowing the election. At long last, the president was focused.

HERD, HERD, HERD, HERD IS THE WORD

Ahead of Thanksgiving, Americans were warned of the dangerous viral surge that continued to grow. Here's how I was thinking about Thanksgiving 2020: you were either close to someone already lost to COVID-19, or you were thankful as hell you weren't—and you expressed that gratitude by keeping yourself and others safe. It's not like you couldn't get as bloated as you do every year and still argue with your relatives on Zoom. If it hadn't been for the success of the vaccines, the Zoom mute button would have ranked as humankind's greatest invention of 2020.

Most people followed the advice of the experts. But with COVID-19, *most* was never enough, and airports were experiencing the biggest crowds since March. This was happening despite the fact that vaccine-fueled hope was on the horizon. No one was being asked to give up Thanksgiving. They were just being asked to give up some of their traditions for *one* Thanksgiving.

Like mask-wearing, this directive didn't seem that hard to follow. While my wife was cooking a turkey, my kids and I drove to my parents' house. We spent fifteen minutes catching up in the driveway. Then we did the same at each of my sisters' houses. Including the driving, I performed all my familial Thanksgiving duties in under an hour. That's what we called sacrifice in 2020? It may have been my greatest Thanksgiving ever.

While many Americans were deciding whether or not to travel and gather for the holiday weekend, a growing number were trying to figure out how to get some food. If you're looking for a defining moment in a divided America's pandemic, consider this. On the day the Dow broke 30,000, the

Washington Post informed us that twenty-six million Americans said they didn't have enough to eat.

Not clear enough? Here are two more *WaPo* headlines that, even without the accompanying stories, explain the divide:

Stealing to Survive: More Americans Are Shoplifting Food as Aid Runs Out During the Pandemic.

Plastic Surgeons Say Business Is Up, Partly Because Clients Don't Like How They Look on Zoom.

Maybe America just doesn't like what it sees when it looks in the mirror.

As the holiday weekend drew to a close, two dictionary companies, Merriam-Webster and Dictionary.com, chose the same noun as the word of the year: *pandemic*.

Meh. The word of the year for 2020 was *2020*.

News Divisions
November 2020

Maddow

The Washington Post 1
Georgia's secretary of state says fellow Republicans are pressuring him to find ways to exclude legal ballots

The Washington Post 2
Postal worker admits fabricating allegations of ballot tampering, officials say

The Washington Post 3
A little-known Trump appointee is in charge of handing transition resources to Biden — and she isn't budging

The New York Times 4
Growing Discomfort at Law Firms Representing Trump in Election Lawsuits

The Washington Post 5
Federal court orders ballot sweep of 12 USPS districts covering 15 states

Hannity/Carlson

New York Post 1
Tax filings reveal Biden cancer charity spent millions on salaries, zero on research

Gateway Pundit 2
BREAKING EXCLUSIVE: Analysis of Election Night Data from All States Shows MILLIONS OF VOTES Either Switched from President Trump to...

The Federalist 3
5 More Ways Joe Biden Magically Outperformed Election Norms

The Philadelphia Inquirer 4
Trump set to hold 4 rallies in Pennsylvania as campaign nears the finish line

Gateway Pundit 5
BREAKING EXCLUSIVE: System 'Glitch' Also Uncovered In Wisconsin - Reversal of 19,032 Votes Removes Lead from Joe Biden

These are the top news links shared on Twitter in November by followers of Rachel Maddow versus followers of Sean Hannity or Tucker Carlson. Source: MIT Center for Constructive Communication

12

DECEMBER— REVERSE SIDEWINDER

ON THE MORNING AFTER DONALD TRUMP'S 2016 ELECTION VICTORY, I WAS in a state of near-catatonic depression. I needed some perspective. I needed to snap out of it. I needed a little cheering up.

So I called my mom.

She said something that defined my writing for the next four years. "The real message here is that we all need to become activists. Right now. Today. You know, last night I kept thinking back to my childhood. Maybe if we had organized and fought back against Hitler's rise, right from the beginning, we could have prevented what happened. Sorry, I don't think I'm doing a very good job of cheering you up."

But then she added one more thing, and it was a vital thing, given that she knew as well as anyone what was possible over the next four years: "We didn't like the way Donald Trump ran for president, but he won the election. This is America. He deserves a chance to lead."

A few days later, I was in a room filled with about fifty disappointed, highly educated liberals. As the fever rose in the room, a few people started to quote arcane election legalese and argue that there was still time, a week after the election, to convince electors not to back Trump.

I interrupted, quoted my mom's comment from our phone call earlier in the week, and argued that resistance was fine, even noble. But trying to undo the democratic process was not only completely nuts, it would do more damage to the country than the election results had already done.

The room fell silent, a cool breeze blew in my direction, and I'm pretty sure I heard Ennio Morricone's whistled theme song from *The Good, the Bad, and the Ugly*. I've never been less popular at a social gathering than I was at that one (and believe me, that's saying something).

Of course, such emotionally driven post-election notions quickly wore off from that room and hundreds of others across the country as we all got back to the business of democracy.

That transition from rage to resistance was helped by the words Hillary Clinton had shared in her concession speech.

> Our campaign was never about one person, or even one election. It was about the country we love and building an America that is hopeful, inclusive, and big-hearted. We have seen that our nation is more deeply divided than we thought. But I still believe in America, and I always will. And if you do, then we must accept this result and then look to the future. Donald Trump is going to be our president. We owe him an open mind and the chance to lead. Our constitutional democracy enshrines the peaceful transfer of power.
>
> We don't just respect that. We cherish it. It also enshrines the rule of law; the principle we are all equal in rights and dignity; freedom of worship and expression. We respect and cherish these values, too, and we must defend them.

But what if Hillary Clinton hadn't given that speech? What if she had spent the months leading up to the election arguing that Trump was working to rig it (which, given the Russian interference and the man in question, wouldn't have been much of a stretch to believe)? What if after the election, Clinton refused to concede and insisted that Trump and his cronies had cheated? And what if it didn't stop there?

What if just about every significant Democratic politician joined that chorus? What if Barack Obama and Joe Biden said Trump cheated and investigations had to happen before the election could be certified? Let's say that Nancy Pelosi, Chuck Schumer, Elijah Cummings, Elizabeth Warren, John Lewis, Kamala Harris, Bernie Sanders, Cory Booker, Dianne Feinstein, and Al Gore joined the chorus. While we're at it, let's assume that your favorite state and local leaders not only agreed that the election was rigged but were also working in legislatures and courts to overturn the results. A few weeks into the fight, maybe there were a handful of folks who finally congratulated Trump, but they were called traitors by most of the Democratic leadership. When you had inner doubts about the rigging or wondered what toll the fight was having on America's democracy or global status, you'd look to the party elders—Jimmy Carter, Michael Dukakis, Howard Dean, Madeleine Albright, Bob Kerrey, and George Mitchell—and the most they offered was silence. And filling that void would be your trusted news sources, from CNN and MSNBC to the *New York Times* and the *Washington Post*, all bombarding you with news of the steal; a din only out-volumed by the election-thieving stories your friends were sharing on social media platforms with algorithms tweaked to turn rage into revenue.

Is it possible that the people in that room with me would have been compelled to rise up? And would there be one or two from that room and one or two from another, and so on, that would find themselves on the steps of the Capitol, thinking of themselves as patriots?

This thought experiment is not intended to offer solace or sanctuary to anyone who would ultimately breach the nation's holiest house after being incited by the president, their party, and their media sources. And make no mistake, those who propagated the most dangerous falsehood of a lie-filled presidency should be shamed and shunned. But it's worth remembering that the first victims of the Big Lie were those who believed it.

WARPED

The Trump administration had dubbed its vaccine creation and distribution plan *Operation Warp Speed*. The project, led by Moncef Slaoui, was viewed as a new sort of Manhattan Project and some even considered naming it

Manhattan Project 2 (maybe they were worried about having a Manhattan Project run by a guy from Queens). Led by private companies and global partnerships, the creation and the testing of the vaccines really did achieve warp speed. The manufacturing and distributing of doses, however, were just warped. So was the behavior of many who were reckless while waiting to get the much-needed shot in the arm. Six million Americans had taken flights over the Thanksgiving weekend, which meant the vaccine race had never been more urgent. It was the best of times, it was the worst of times. But not necessarily in that order.

With the president fully fixated on the alleged election-rigging, the CDC's Robert Redfield was free to speak the truth about the nation's rising fever: "The reality is December and January and February are going to be rough times. I actually believe they are going to be the most difficult time in the public health history of this nation." The CDC also issued a directive advising that masks be worn indoors at places other than your home. This advice came more than ten months after America suffered its first case of an airborne virus. Why all the concern? The US has had topped 3,100 COVID-19 deaths in a day, more than 100,000 Americans were hospitalized, and we hadn't even seen the inevitable surge related to the Thanksgiving holiday weekend.

While much of the pandemic news was mixed, one story was wholly positive: Scott Atlas resigned his position as a special coronavirus advisor to the president. (Dr. Kevorkian had a better lifesaving track record than this guy.)

A PRO AT CONS
December 2, 2020

The people in charge of election security had told us the election was free, fair, and secure. The courts had thrown out every challenge. And by early December, even Attorney General Bill Barr signaled he wasn't interested in remaining a part of the charade as he announced, "To date, we have not seen fraud on a scale that could have effected a different outcome in the election."

What was the reaction of Trump's media sycophants when a guy who had bent and nearly broken the Justice Department in the name of protecting his corrupt boss and previously jail-bound friends told the obvious truth?

Lou Dobbs, who had become Fox News–ish even by Fox News standards, summed up the reaction: "For the attorney general of the United States to make that statement—he is either a liar or a fool or both." Dobbs also suggested that Barr had been "perhaps compromised" and had "appeared to join in with the radical Dems and the deep-state and the resistance."

Trump responded to the setback by launching into a forty-six-minute rant that he said "may be the most important speech I've ever made." And if you considered the risk of what he was putting forth, he may have been right.

I am determined to protect our election system, which is now under coordinated assault and siege. . . .

I want to explain the corrupt mail-in balloting scheme that Democrats systematically put into place that allowed voting to be altered, especially in swing states, which they had to win. They just didn't know that it was going to be that tough, because we were leading in every swing state by so much, far greater than they ever thought possible. . . .

On top of everything else, we have a company that's very suspect. Its name is Dominion, with the turn of a dial or the change of a chip, you could press a button for Trump and the vote goes to Biden. What kind of a system is this? . . .

Millions of votes were cast illegally in the swing states alone, and if that's the case, the results of the individual swing states must be overturned, and overturned immediately. . . .

It means you have to turn over the election . . . When those votes are corrupt, when they're irregular, when they get caught, they're terminated, and I very easily win. In all states, I very easily win, the swing states, just like I won them at 10 o'clock in the evening, the evening of the election. . . .

This election was rigged. Everybody knows it. I don't mind if I lose an election, but I want to lose an election fair and square. What I don't want to do is have it stolen from the American people. That's what we're fighting for. . . .

If we don't root out the fraud, the tremendous and horrible fraud that's taken place in our 2020 election, we don't have a country anymore.

It's worth noting the particular lies in this particular speech. First, Trump built upon the voting-by-mail falsehoods he had been spreading for months. Second, Trump continued his habit of using language that strongly insinuated that people should rise up and defend the country. And third, while there was a personal-gain element at work. Trump had already raised more the $200 million from donors to his *Stop the Steal* efforts. And for those who think his madness was mere words, it's worth noting that Trump was also working the phones, pressuring state leaders to overturn the election. In the week following this speech, he made two calls to the Speaker of the Pennsylvania House of Representatives for help altering that state's results.

My favorite Trump-era cartoon was published by the *New Yorker*'s Barry Blitt right around this time: Donald Trump is on a therapist's couch. In the chair next to him sits a psychologist holding his pen to a notepad. But when you scan up, you realize that the shrink's head has exploded.

Trump was conning us. He also pretty clearly believed what he was saying. That's an explosive combination.

RUDY AWAKENING
December 7, 2020

If you have grease leaking from your temples and feel detached from reality, you could have COVID-19. At least that seemed to be one of the lessons of the news that Rudy Giuliani was the latest Trumpian to take a trip to the hospital with a case of coronavirus. And before you use this news as a warning not to spend the twilight of your career spreading unhinged, seditious lies, keep in mind that doing so has its benefits. Unlike most hospitalized patients, Rudy was treated to the antiviral meds enjoyed by the president, and he was back out lying in no time.

Rudy himself acknowledged the special treatment in an interview with WABC: "If it wasn't me, I wouldn't have been put in a hospital frankly.

Sometimes when you're a celebrity, they're worried if something happens to you they're going to examine it more carefully, and do everything right."

When you're a star, they let you do it. You can do anything . . . Grab 'em by the prescription.

THE TAMING OF THE BREW
December 8, 2020

A week before her ninety-first birthday, Margaret Keenan made history becoming the first person who wasn't part of a clinical trial to receive the Pfizer/BioNTech vaccine.

The UK grandmother explained: "I feel so privileged to be the first person vaccinated against COVID-19. It's the best early birthday present I could wish for because it means I can finally look forward to spending time with my family and friends in the New Year after being on my own for most of the year."

The second person to get a first injection of the two-shot dose was an eighty-one-year-old guy from Coventry. His name: William Shakespeare.

The vaccine was here. Yes, now was the winter of our discontent. But spring was within sight. All it would take is wearing a mask and avoiding indoor dining for a few months. How poor are they that have not patience? What wound did ever heal but by degrees? It wouldn't be easy, but you have to break a few eggs to make a Hamlet. A man can die but once. But zero times is better. This above all: to thine own-self be true. And occasionally tell the truth to others as well. Uneasy *lies* the head that wears the crown— in contrast to the head that got a PhD in immunotherapy. Some are born great, others achieve greatness, and some have greatness thrust upon them by a good science teacher. And those who continue to lie about the virus, come, let's away to prison. To be or not to be? That was the question. But millions of our fellow Americans were getting the answer wrong. Lord, what fools these mortals be! But all's well that ends well, assuming your doctor is not a fan of QAnon. I could go on, anon. But, brevity is the soul of wit, and this narrator doth need another hit.

Even Shakespeare's words fail to do justice to the idea of rising death tolls when we had a vaccine at hand. Martin Kenyon, who also got the vaccine on day one, managed to share a line that even Shakespeare couldn't outdo: "Well, there's no point in dying now when I've lived this long, is there?"

INJUNCTIVITIS

The application for injunctive relief presented to Justice Alito and by him referred to the Court is denied.

That was it. With one sentence, the Supreme Court denied a Republican challenge to Joe Biden's Pennsylvania win. The Trump legal team now had a worse record than the Washington Generals. But the team, along with the tweeter in chief, was having the desired impact on public opinion. More than a month after the election was decided, according to a NPR / PBS NewsHour / Marist survey, just 24 percent of Republican respondents said they trusted the results.

Trump's election overturning gained steam with the public, in part because those in his party continued to either vocally support his efforts or silently enable them. The first exception was Mitt Romney:

This is madness. We have a process. Recounts are appropriate. Going to the court is appropriate. Pursuing every legal avenue is appropriate. But trying to get electors not to do what the people voted to do is madness.

Someone once asked me how I'd grade Romney's performance during the Trump era. That depends. If we're considering his colleagues and grading a on a curve, it was an A+.

WHERE'S THE BRIEF?

The challenge here is an unprecedented one, without factual foundation or a valid legal basis.

That's how Michigan responded to a Texas lawsuit to invalidate millions of votes that had been cast, counted, and certified in several states that *weren't* Texas.

The Texas lawsuit against the voting results in other states wasn't the solo work of a legally challenged attorney general from Texas (Ken Paxton had recently learned he was under FBI investigation for helping out a wealthy donor). His effort was joined by 17 state attorneys general, 106 Republican members of Congress who signed an amicus brief, and a sea of GOP senators and House members who tacitly supported the effort by refusing to acknowledge Biden's win. This wasn't just the last gasp of a canceled reality show host or the final rantings of a sociopathic narcissist. This was a movement to overturn an election, an international humiliation, and an American tragedy.

A REAL SHOT IN THE ARM
December 14, 2020

Sandra Lindsay, an ICU nurse at Long Island Jewish Medical Center in Queens, became the first American to get the COVID-19 vaccine. She used the public attention to target the other virus that was impacting her field: "I believe in science. As a nurse I am guided by science."

In a trend that would continue, the hopeful milestone was paired with an ominous one. On the same day Lindsay got her shot, the US passed three hundred thousand COVID-19 deaths.

LINCOLN LOGGERHEADS

Lincoln is one of dozens of historical figures who, according to a school district renaming committee, lived a life so stained with racism, oppression or human rights violations, they do not deserve to have their name on a school building.

That's the *San Francisco Chronicle*'s Jill Tucker on a San Francisco school naming committee assigned to rebrand schools named after the undeserving. And somehow, Abe Lincoln made the shit list. So did George Washington. This story was evidence that the crazy wasn't completely confined to one side of the political divide. And keep in mind that this nonsensical hogwash was being debated at a time when San Francisco public schools were nowhere close to reopening for in-person instruction. At this point, every school had the same name: Zoom school.

Reading about the school board's seven-hour meeting that resulted in a decision to change the name of some San Francisco schools for utterly ridiculous and/or historically inaccurate reasons awakened me to that fact that I had spent 100 percent of my 2020 time hating people on the other side of the political spectrum. I didn't realize how much I missed hating people on my own side.

In my hometown, there was a heated debate over the renaming of Sir Francis Drake Boulevard and Drake High School. I suggested that they just rename the school after the rapper Drake; that way, they wouldn't have to change any of the signage.

THE ATTORNEY GENERAL MOTORS

Was it really a resignation, or was he squeezed out because he wouldn't get on board with Trump's efforts to overturn the election? I'll let you do the math on that one. Maybe he had an idea of what was coming in the next few weeks. Whatever it was, we learned from a Trump tweet that William Barr was resigning and would give up the attorney general gig before Christmas. (This made up for the fact that the Trump administration didn't get me anything for Hanukkah.)

RESTING MITCH FACE
December 15, 2020

A day after the electoral college made the election results official—a customary act that we usually don't pay much attention to—and five weeks after he knew full well who won the election, Mitch McConnell finally congratulated Joe Biden and Kamala Harris, acknowledging their win.

The president wasn't happy. The base wasn't happy. But McConnell tried to soften the blow by pairing his congratulatory remarks for the election winners with some for its loser.

> The list of American accomplishments since 2016 is nearly endless. It would take far more than one speech to catalog all the major wins the Trump administration has helped deliver for the American people . . . I look forward to finishing out the next 36 days strong with President Trump.

Around the same time McConnell was signaling that the election rigging farce should end, Trump was retweeting Attorney Lin Wood, who would later have his account suspended.

President Trump @realDonaldTrump is a genuinely good man. He does not really like to fire people. I bet he dislikes putting people in jail, especially "Republicans."

He gave @BrianKempGA & @GaSecofState every chance to get it right. They refused. They will soon be going to jail.

The constant lying continued to have an impact on Trump's followers. And those followers had enough of an impact on Georgia governor Brian Kemp that he spoke out:

It has gotten ridiculous—from death threats, [claims of] bribes from China, the social media posts that my children are getting. We have the "no crying in politics rule" in the Kemp house. But this is stuff that, if I said it, I would be taken to the woodshed and would never see the light of day.

One thing Kemp still wouldn't take to the woodshed was his bootlicking of the president who had stirred up all the rage: "As far as I know, my relationship with the president is fine. I know he's frustrated, and I've disagreed on things with him before. At the end of the day, I've got to follow the laws and the Constitution and the Constitution of this state."

What a drag to have to follow the Constitution when it upsets the president. No wonder so few other enablers did it.

HACK JOB

In mid-December, we became aware of a widespread Russian hack that had infiltrated many government offices as well as private corporations. Heretofore, it had been more common for Russians to target individuals or small groups. This was a new strategy, and the scope of the breach was massive.

Those products had been installed as far back as March, meaning that the attackers had been able to observe crucial aspects of our government from the inside for as much as nine months. Government officials found out about the breach only after a private cybersecurity firm, FireEye, realized it had been hacked and alerted the FBI. (Heather Cox Richardson, *Letters from an American*)

The impact of this hack, America's response, and the need to shore up our defenses and possibly reduce federal government's reliance on private companies would all be topics for the months and years to come. For the 2020 story, what was notable was the president's silence on the hack. It was an all-too-familiar response when it came to Trump and Putin.

Mitt Romney again took the role of the conscience of his party: "In this setting, not to have the White House aggressively speaking out and protesting and taking punitive action is really quite extraordinary."

PLANES, TRAINS, AND AUTONOMY

The pre-Thanksgiving warnings came. The post-Thanksgiving surge came. The same pattern would repeat over the Christmas holidays. According to the TSA, during the first few days of the traditional Christmas break, travel was down by about 60 percent at the nation's airports. But that still left millions of travelers who were carrying on cases of COVID-19.

One traveler explained her thinking to the AP's Tamara Lush: "My mom's worth it. She needs my help,' said 34-year-old Jennifer Brownlee, a fisherman from Bayou La Batre, Alabama, who was waiting at the Tampa airport to fly to Oregon to see her mother, who just lost a leg. 'I know that God's got me. He's not going to let me get sick.'"

Maybe, with 323,000 deaths and counting, God was trying to send us a sign?

A couple of weeks after Christmas, America's cases were soaring. To put things into depressing perspective, while America was experiencing more than 200,000 cases a day, Taiwan announced that it had experienced the first case of local transmission in 255 days. Yes, Taiwan is smaller. Yes,

Taiwan is an island. But populace and geographic differences don't explain away a performance edge that dramatic.

Much like other rule-following Americans, I spent the winter holidays hunkered down with my family as we continued our pandemic tradition of gluttony, screen time, and nonstop bickering. The same routine was playing out for most families I know. During 2020, Facebook and other social media platforms were blamed for allowing the spread of fake news and false theories. But at times, it seemed the spread of fake smiles and false happiness was an even more prevalent scourge. I tried everything from buying extra presents to parting with my long-standing refusal to get a Christmas tree. In the end, all that got me was a dismantled tree, tossed into the garage now bulging with a heap of delivery boxes, torn and stomped flat, much like the mood in my household. While we were yelling and arguing through the reality of the holidays after months in quarantine home confinement, others were filling my Facebook feed with ornament hanging, cute kids doing cute things, and well-behaved pets. But I didn't buy any of it. In fact, I didn't *see* most of it because my daughter stole my iPad and wouldn't give it back.

> **Dave Pell** ✔
> @davepell
>
> In many parts of the world it's already 2021.
>
> In America, we still have 20 days to go.
>
> 8:25 AM · Dec 31, 2020 · 🐦 Twitter

As the end of December approached, I ran across a CNN headline that surfaced one of my frequent fears and managed to sum up the feeling I had during so much of 2020:

190,000 Ceiling Fans Recalled Because the Blades Detach and Fly Off.

News Divisions
December 2020

Maddow

Business Insider 1
EXCLUSIVE: Jared Kushner helped create a Trump campaign shell company that secretly paid the president's family members and spent...

Politico 2
'We want them infected': Trump appointee demanded 'herd immunity' strategy, emails reveal

The Wall Street Journal 3
Opinion | Is There a Doctor in the White House? Not if You Need an M.D.

The New York Times 4
Trump administration officials passed when Pfizer offered in late summer to sell the U.S. more vaccine doses.

TIME 5
Joe Biden and Kamala Harris Are TIME's 2020 Person of the Year

Hannity/Carlson

Breitbart 1
Texas Sues Georgia, Michigan, Pennsylvania, and Wisconsin at Supreme Court over Election Rules

Washington Examiner 2
Peter Navarro releases 36-page report alleging election fraud 'more than sufficient' to swing victory to Trump

Politico 3
Judge blocks voter purge in 2 Georgia counties

Axios 4
Exclusive: How a suspected Chinese spy gained access to California politics

Rumble 5
ELECTION NIGHT ERRORS - HOW DID THAT HAPPEN?

These are the top news links shared on Twitter in December by followers of Rachel Maddow versus followers of Sean Hannity or Tucker Carlson. Source: MIT Center for Constructive Communication

CONFESSIONS OF THE INTERNET'S MANAGING EDITOR

We're approaching the station to mark the end of a year, an era, and the ride of a lifetime. Now what? As a news addict, I planned to take a few moments to get reacquainted with my wife and kids. It turns out my son is in high school now. I rediscovered my pets (my beagles were like, "Woot!" and my cats were like, "Wait, you were gone?"). I've shared some takes about the line that separates the real-time news from our real lives. For me, that line was long ago riddled with enough holes to make it look like a repeating SOS pattern. I've probably suffered because of that. My family certainly has. I could provide endless details about talking to my kids over the top of my laptop, pulling out my iPhone at all the wrong times, or just staring off into space thinking about the last headline I saw instead of looking at what was right in front of my face. But you don't need those details. You've been there.

At the beginning of this ride, I described some of my parents' experiences during the Holocaust. For them, a news addiction made sense.

The world headlines of their youth were literally a matter of life and death. And as their child, the news fixation made sense for me too. It was a point of connection. They were into it. So, I got into it.

Considering my past and my passion, it was predictable that I'd get drowned by the flood of news. When you cover all the news, there's never *not* a story to think about. But when you're thinking about all those stories all the time, other things are lost.

CONWAYS AND MEANINGS

When I was working at my dad's office during a summer away from college, I used to convince everyone in the office to come with me to my favorite lunch spot: the Sizzler salad bar.

This was during the early days of cell phones when they resembled a brick, both in size and weight. During one of our lunches, we saw a guy who had hoisted one of these new-fangled devices to his head, and was carrying on a too-loud work conversation.

My dad gestured in the direction of the guy: "Don't ever let that happen to you," he warned. "Can you imagine having a job so terrible that you can't even get away from your boss long enough to eat your lunch? They make him carry around that contraption." Everyone at the table nodded in agreement.

I didn't listen. Neither did my family. Neither did the Conway family. For Kellyanne and George, the familial tribulations associated with kids and social media got so extreme in 2020 that they realized they had to take a break from their fast-paced, always-on lifestyle. Kellyanne stepped down from her high-powered role as White House advisor. George stepped away from his role at the anti-Trump political machine known as the Lincoln Project. And Claudia, who had begun to overshare the family's conflicts on TikTok and other social platforms, decided she needed a mental health break. They all announced a break from social media.

It lasted about as long as the break from social media the members of my family announced in January, and February, and March, and so on. Within weeks, the Conways were back. Claudia shared unappealing home videos when she and her mom both suffered from COVID-19.

The ugly political divisions that were tearing the country apart were having a similar effect in the Conway living room. In January 2021, police showed up after someone reported that Claudia shared a video of her mom screaming at her, calling her names, and telling her she had a social media addiction and should be taken away in an ambulance. There was also an incident where Kellyanne, accidentally or otherwise, may have momentarily shared a naked photo of Claudia.

Screen rage. Oversharing. A blurred line between work and home. The seeping of political views into family conversations. Screaming at each other over social media use. I don't know how that sounds to you, but to me, it sounds familiar.

Forget the Trumps or the Bidens, the Conways were America's real first family. They knew social media was ruining their lives, and they still couldn't stop. How much more 2020 America can you get than that?

IT'S NOT ME, IT'S YOU

I'm not worried about me. I'm worried about you. During the rise of the internet age, I've seen more and more of you acting like me. When I first started writing a newsletter covering the day's most fascinating news, I intended it to be your shelter from the news storm. I'd wade out into the cesspool to find the most interesting stories so you wouldn't have to. Every afternoon I'd offer up myself for news captivity to free tens of thousands of other potential hostages. Now when I wade out into that cesspool, I see millions of you out there with me. Friends who never had the slightest interest in the news are now texting me about something they saw on Maddow. And friends who once had a passing interest in current events are collecting and sharing stories like they're working the national desk at the *New York Times*.

During the dog days of the pandemic, I had a weekly Zoom video call with four of my childhood friends. For decades, we had never run out of personal topics to discuss. But during this moment in time, our conversations were all about the news. One of the members of our group went through a mid-pandemic divorce and found himself living in the same house with his soon-to-be ex-wife. The rest of us felt sympathy for the situation, but we were probably a little thankful for an engrossing topic other than Trump news. That's how desperate we were for a break from the same grinding topic. But we almost never took one. Just when we thought we were out, the story pulled us back in.

Don't get me wrong. The news obsession made some sense for us. And, at least during the Trump era, it made sense for you too. The events taking place were both global and personal. America was exposed, stripped to its flaws for the world to see. Our perception of the country was repeatedly hit in the face by a two-by-four. From your health, to your job, to your savings, to your kids' school schedule, everything was touched by the news.

In other words, you'd be forgiven for keeping a close track of the headlines during 2020; and it made sense for us to become more news-fixated as the topic narrowed to a germ that could literally enter our bodies, and when every other form of distraction—from sports to live music to sitting in someone else's house having a chat—was taken off the table. You followed the news like your life depended on it because some days it did.

But too often that news distracted us and hardened us to the experiences of those around us, and even to the human experiences of our fellow citizens during the pandemic.

ONE SINGULAR SENSATION

Trump news was so addictive that even Trump spent much of his day watching Trump news. And the show made household names out of even short-term administration officials and created hundreds of new media stars.

New York Times editor Dean Baquet knows you were fixated on Trump news. That's why he said, "Trump is the best thing to happen to the Times' subscription strategy. Every time he tweets it drives up subscriptions." The *New York Times*'s Jonathan Mahler saw the change in your behavior and wrote, "CNN had a problem, Donald Trump solved it."

Indeed, there were plenty of people and organizations that got tired of all the winning during the Trump era. News consumers just got tired.

I'VE GOT NEWS FOR YOU

Ask yourself this question about news: Why do you continue to buy a product that makes you feel terrible?

And let's not delude ourselves, it's a product. The first and most essential job of any news organization is to convince consumers of the inherent value of the news. But is news actually inherently valuable?

Sure, democracy depends on an informed electorate. But did the thousands of hours of compulsive news absorption and analysis actually change a single one of your votes? Probably not. Imagine having limited your news time to five minutes a day to catch up on headlines. Would that change have made a difference in your voting or other behaviors? I doubt it. Did consuming news make you feel better? I'm guessing no. What if you had spent all of 2020 living off the grid, unreachable by headlines or tweets? Would your year have been better or worse?

Forget living off the grid. Let's try baby steps. What if you just turned off news notifications?

Here's some breaking news: you're not in the news business. It's nice that you want to be well informed, but does a protest in Belarus really need to drag your attention away from your kid's soccer game? Empathy is a good thing, but do you really need to be distracted from a quiet, introspective moment to be made aware of a mudslide, flood, or other natural disaster a world away? You're not a first responder. The only thing you're responding to is the bait being dangled by news organizations trying to convince you that you need to know something now when you probably don't need to know it at all.

Breaking news? The only thing that's breaking is you. El Chapo wished he had a customer base this addicted.

The notion that you need to know about world events right when they happen is a marketing creation of media brands. And yet, those news stories mingle in the same lock screen with the personal reminders and calls from your mom. The stuff that has something to do with you is now almost impossible to distinguish from the stuff that doesn't.

Trust me, that news alert can wait until later. Like most things on the internet, it can wait until never.

You're not Batman. You're not going to do anything about the news alerts, so they can wait. As a general rule, you don't need to be immediately notified of any breaking news that's happening more than about eighteen feet from where you are right now. At most, your alerts should only cover your locality. Even Bruce Wayne only covers Gotham.

THE OPIOID CRISIS OF THE MASSES

News is the opioid crisis of the attention economy. The prescribed amount can provide a benefit, but it's dangerously easy to overdose. You consume more than you need, and that's just what the dealers want. They're not just, as Noam Chomsky argued, manufacturing consent. They're manufacturing attention. Donald Trump knew that as well as anyone. He fed the machine, and we kept eating the output. He was manipulating us; we knew it, we felt it, and yet we continued to allow ourselves to be manipulated. All he wanted was our undivided attention, and that's exactly what we gave him. Being obsessed with Donald Trump was the only thing that united a divided nation.

I'm not arguing that you ignore the news. Like it was for my parents in the war years, 2020 news was a matter of life and death when it came to the pandemic, and a matter of grave concern when it came to the rise of inequality and the move toward fascism. But that doesn't mean you can't wait until later in the day to catch up on the day's events. America beat fascism once without news alerts vibrating in our pockets. We can do it again.

Don't allow news to take so much of your attention that you end up ignoring your own life. The news is a powerful tool. I've used it to block out a lot of my feelings. My parents used it to block out the darkness of their lives. But when you block the darkness, you also block the light.

In 2020, you were told to please scream inside your heart. Hopefully this book helped you let it out and make room for something else. During a year that included a pandemic, historically large crowds marching in the street to fight for justice, and the most important election in a generation, it makes sense that our interest in the news would reach a feverish peak. This was not a roller coaster we boarded voluntarily. But as the ride comes to an end, it's time to get off and visit some of the other attractions in the amusement park of life.

I don't know about you, but I'm starting with the house of mirrors. I suggest the rest of America do the same.

But first, sadly, there's just a little more news to cover. . . .

13

JANUARY 2021— REACHING ESCAPE VELOCITY

Bubbly was poured. Glasses clinked. Resolutions made. The Times Square ball dropped. A muffled version of "Auld Lang Syne" could be heard through face masks. People counted down the last few seconds of a year that had become universally symbolized by an image of flames lapping over the edges of a dumpster. Someone with a taste for tradition cued up Barry Manilow's "It's Just Another New Year's Eve." But alas, it was just another night like all the rest.

We still had twenty more days of antidemocratic acts from a president and his enablers who were determined to pour kerosene on December's embers. These days would not be without a certain value. They clarified some things for historians who will review this era. This was never all about Trump. Every mob boss needs a mob family, and Trump's made men were looking to unmake an American election. Capos Ted Cruz and Josh Hawley welcomed the new year by leading a group of seditious senators who planned a contemptuous objection to the usually pro forma certification of the election results. Truth-assassinating soldiers like jacket-less Jim Jordan and devilish Devin Nunes would be honored with the Presidential Medal of Freedom. (Freedom from what? Ethics?) And hundreds of elected GOP associates joined in the effort to further stir up the rabidity of an increasingly dangerous and deluded base.

It wasn't just opinion editors or the so-called liberal media ringing alarm bells about the threat facing the nation in the waning days of a president who continued to wax dictatorial. At the urging of Dick Cheney, all the living former US defense secretaries (including the two who had served under Trump) issued an unprecedented warning in a *Washington Post* op-ed:

> The time for questioning the results has passed; the time for the formal counting of the electoral college votes, as prescribed in the Constitution and statute, has arrived.
>
> As senior Defense Department leaders have noted, "there's no role for the U.S. military in determining the outcome of a U.S. election." Efforts to involve the U.S. armed forces in resolving election disputes would take us into dangerous, unlawful and unconstitutional territory. Civilian and military officials who direct or carry out such measures would be accountable, including potentially facing criminal penalties, for the grave consequences of their actions on our republic.
>
> Transitions, which all of us have experienced, are a crucial part of the successful transfer of power. They often occur at times of international uncertainty about U.S. national security policy and posture. They can be a moment when the nation is vulnerable to actions by adversaries seeking to take advantage of the situation.

When the people charged with running the world's most powerful military join together to state their worries, it's time to worry.

Mitt Romney was again one of the few leading GOP senators to denounce the pathetic election-overturning efforts from his colleagues: "I could never have imagined seeing these things in the greatest democracy in the world. Has ambition so eclipsed principle?"

(Has Mitt been paying attention?)

A CRANK CALLS

Trump had described his phone conversation asking the Ukraine president for dirt on the Bidens as a "perfect call." So for the one he made to Georgia's Republican secretary of state, Brad Raffensperger, we'd need to dig up some Latin: *plus quam perfectum*, or "more than perfect." Given Trump's record for paying bills, I wouldn't be surprised if he called collectum.

The *Washington Post* obtained a recording of the call in which Trump cajoled and pressured Raffensperger and his legal counsel to change the official election numbers enough to swing the Peach State in his direction.

Dave Pell ✔
@davepell

Let's not feign shock. The whole Trump era has been a slow motion act of treason, sedition, and constant damage to America. Why would this phone call be any different?

9:02 AM · Jan 4, 2021 · 🐦 Twitter

Raffensperger explained that the debunked conspiracy theories were not, alas, just cause to overturn an election: "Mr. President, the challenge that you have is, the data you have is wrong."

Trump, with Chief of Staff Mark Meadows by his side, unsurprisingly persisted:

> "So look. All I want to do is this. I just want to find 11,780 votes, which is one more than we have. Because we won the state."
> "So what are we going to do here, folks? I only need 11,000 votes. Fellas, I need 11,000 votes. Give me a break."

Throughout the call, Trump repeated the phrase "There's no way I lost Georgia" and added, "We won by hundreds of thousands of votes."

At this point, there was little reason to doubt that Trump was convinced of what he was saying and had become a believer of the kinds of conspiracy theories he once peddled to confuse others. This was not a drill. The president of the United States was actively trying to overturn the election.

During the same week Trump was trying to turn Georgia in his favor, behind the scenes, he was plotting to replace the new acting attorney general, Jeffrey Rosen, with Jeffrey Clark, a low-ranking justice department lawyer who was more enthusiastic about Trump's seditious plans.

The Justice Department's top leaders listened in stunned silence this month: One of their peers, they were told, had devised a plan with President Donald J. Trump to oust Jeffrey A. Rosen as acting attorney general and wield the department's power to force Georgia state lawmakers to overturn its presidential election results.

The unassuming lawyer who worked on the plan, Jeffrey Clark, had been devising ways to cast doubt on the election results and to bolster Mr. Trump's continuing legal battles and the pressure on Georgia politicians. Because Mr. Rosen had refused the president's entreaties to carry out those plans, Mr. Trump was about to decide whether to fire Mr. Rosen and replace him with Mr. Clark.

The department officials, convened on a conference call, then asked each other: What will you do if Mr. Rosen is dismissed?

The answer was unanimous. They would resign.

Their informal pact ultimately helped persuade Mr. Trump to keep Mr. Rosen in place, calculating that a furor over mass resignations at the top of the Justice Department would eclipse any attention on his baseless accusations of voter fraud. Mr. Trump's decision came only after Mr. Rosen and Mr. Clark made their competing cases to him in a bizarre White House meeting that two officials compared with an episode of Mr. Trump's reality show "The Apprentice," albeit one that could prompt a constitutional crisis. (Katie Benner, *New York Times*)

VEEP CREEP

In the annals of history, there was perhaps no purer example of servile, submissive enabling than that delivered to Donald Trump by Mike Pence. It's not as if Pence got nothing in return. He got more pro-life judges, more support for religious groups, less support for the LGBTQ community, and every politician's favorite gift: power. Pence went about as far as any sub could for any dom. But in the end, he made the unforgivable choice of yelling out the couple's safe word: *Constitution*.

To this point, Pence had supported the president's lies about election rigging, both tacitly and verbally. In Georgia, the day before the Senate runoffs, Pence was met with chants of, "Stop the steal!" He responded: "I know we all have got our doubts about the last election. I want to assure you that I share the concerns of millions of Americans about voting irregularities. I promise you, come this Wednesday, we will have our day in Congress."

But hours after Trump tweeted, "The Vice President has the power to reject fraudulently chosen electors," Pence informed the president during their weekly lunch that he held no such power and would be unable to stop the electoral college certification. Trump was furious. He banned Pence's chief of staff, Marc Short, from entering the West Wing and he continued to point to Pence as being the one guy who could save the election, if only he would "do the right thing."

Sooner or later, Trump throws everyone under the bus. Pence probably wasn't surprised by that. But he was probably pretty shocked when the metaphorical bus became real busloads of people, some of whom were calling for his head. Literally.

THE PEACH PIT

From Fulton, Gwinnett, Cobb, and DeKalb, to Clay, Webster, Quitman, and Taliaferro, every political junkie had spent weeks going full Kornacki on Georgia geography in preparation for the runoffs that would decide the Senate. Political donations had been pouring in from across the country (I sent so much money there that my wife was convinced I had a second family in Atlanta). In the end, a massive turnout and a segment of voters turned off by Trump's attacks on the election gave Democratic challengers Jon Ossoff and Raphael Warnock narrow wins over the incumbents, David Perdue and Kelly Loeffler. And with that, the Senate was evenly split fifty-fifty. With Vice President Kamala Harris holding the tie-breaking vote, the power shifted left, and Chuck Schumer would become majority leader, while Mitch McConnell would now hold the Senate minority leader title.

> **Dave Pell** ✔
> @davepell
>
> A Jewish guy and a Black man walk into the Senate.
>
> And the joke's on Mitch McConnell.
>
> 11:02 PM · Jan 5, 2021 · 🐦 Twitter

On any normal Wednesday in January, the shift of power in the Senate would have led the news. On any abnormal Wednesday in January, the fact that twelve senators led by Josh Hawley and Ted Cruz planned to object to the certification of the electoral vote would have topped the news. Wednesday, January 6, went beyond normal and abnormal, and straight to abysmal.

HEARD MENTALITY

During his first year in office, Donald Trump responded to the white supremacist–incited, deadly violence in Charlottesville, Virginia, by saying that there were "very fine people, on both sides." Joe Biden would later refer to that as the moment he decided to run for president: "With those words, the president of the United States assigned a moral equivalence between those spreading hate and those with the courage to stand against it."

For those who would do violence in the name of false patriotism, it was just one of many times when Trump indicated support for their efforts. The calls to act became almost deafening in the weeks leading up to and following the presidential election, and they didn't fall on deaf ears. They were heard when the presidential call to LIBERATE MICHIGAN was followed by an armed militia storming the state capitol building in Lansing; some of them entered, holding weapons, and demanded access to the House chambers where lawmakers were meeting. They were heard when those violent protests were followed by a tweet from the president that suggested "the Governor of Michigan should give a little, and put out the fire. These are very good people, but they are angry. They want their lives back again, safely! See them, talk to them, make a deal." They were heard when the Trump campaign sent out an email "For Patriots Only," in which recipients were invited to join the Trump Army and become the "first line of defense when it comes to fighting off the Liberal MOB." They were heard when Trump refused to denounce the killings committed by Kyle Rittenhouse in Kenosha. They were heard when, in a presidential debate viewed by tens of millions, Trump told the Proud Boys, "Stand back and stand by." They were heard when Trump refused to denounce QAnon and repeated their absurdist nonsense about pedophilia. They were heard when Trump criticized Michigan governor Gretchen Whitmer for not being grateful enough that the FBI arrested those who planned to kidnap her. "It was our people—my people, our people that helped her out. And then she blamed me for it. She blamed me and it was our people that helped her. I don't get it. How did you put her there?" They were heard when Trump expressed enthusiasm for supporters who tried to force a Biden campaign bus off the road. "Those patriots did nothing wrong." They were heard when he supported the violent protests in DC on December 12. "Wow! Thousands of people forming in Washington (D.C.) for Stop the Steal. Didn't know about this, but I'll be seeing them! #MAGA." They were heard over and over with baseless attacks on the vote-by-mail system. They were most definitely heard when Trump paired his election conspiracy theories with a call to action:

> "Statistically impossible to have lost the 2020 Election . . . Big protest
>   in DC on January 6th. Be there, will be wild!"
> "The BIG Protest Rally in Washington, D.C. will take place at 11:00
>   A.M. on January 6th. Locational details to follow. StopTheSteal!"

Would-be rioters heard Ted Cruz when he said, "We will not go quietly into the night. We will defend liberty. And we are going to win." They heard the president's son Don Jr. when he addressed rally attendees the night before the Georgia election: "They're not taking this White House. We're going to fight like hell." They heard when the president blamed Mike Pence on January 5. "The Vice President has the power to reject fraudulently chosen electors." They heard him that night at a rally in Georgia when he explained: "I hope Mike Pence comes through for us, I have to tell you. I hope that our great Vice President, our great Vice President, comes through for us. He's a great guy. Of course if he doesn't come through I won't like him quite as much." They heard on January 6 when the president tweeted, "The States want to redo their votes. They found out they voted on a FRAUD. Legislatures never approved. Let them do it. BE STRONG!" They heard when militia-loving, lie-spreading, newly elected Colorado congresswoman Lauren Boebert (who proudly shared a video of herself carrying a gun into Congress) tweeted, "Today is 1776." They heard when fellow freshman, QAnon aficionado, and conspiracy theorist Representative Marjorie Taylor Greene of Georgia tweeted, "FIGHT. FOR. TRUMP."

They heard every time Trump alleged that the election was rigged and refused to commit to a peaceful transfer of power.

Throughout his term in office, Trump displayed his love of Putin's Russia. With his election lie, he even borrowed a strategy from a Russian story. "Ivan Ilyich has died." With that line, Leo Tolstoy began his famous novella *The Death of Ivan Ilyich* at the chronological end of the story. We knew in advance how the story ended. And so it was with the saga of Donald Trump.

Trump's novella was written in tweets, and his attack on American democracy began, oddly, after he *won* the presidency. Weeks after his unlikely electoral victory, Trump argued that he would have won the popular vote as well, had the election not been rigged.

Here's his tweet from November 27, 2016:

In addition to winning the Electoral College in a landslide, I won the popular vote if you deduct the millions of people who voted illegally.

When thousands of Stop the Stealers gathered in front of the White House on January 6 as Mike Pence was leading the election certification inside the Senate chamber, it was a chapter of a story Trump had foreshadowed before he had even taken office.

The end of the story was clear at the beginning. That's why it wasn't all that shocking when Trump supporters heard Don Jr. admonish Republican lawmakers not willing to commit sedition for his dad, "If you're gonna be the zero and not the hero, we're coming for you." They heard Rudy Giuliani say, "If we're right, a lot of them will go to jail. So let's have trial by combat . . .

I'll be darned if they're going to take our free and fair vote . . . We're going to fight to the very end to make sure that doesn't happen."

And then the President of the United States of America stood before the increasingly charged crowd:

> "We're going to walk down to the Capitol, and we're going to cheer on our brave senators and congressmen and women and we're probably not going to be cheering so much for some of them."
>
> "You'll never take back our country with weakness. You have to show strength, and you have to be strong."
>
> "Something is wrong here, something is really wrong, can't have happened and we fight, we fight like hell, and if you don't fight like hell, you're not going to have a country anymore."
>
> "So we are going to—we are going to walk down Pennsylvania Avenue, I love Pennsylvania Avenue, and we are going to the Capitol, and we are going to try and give—the Democrats are hopeless, they are never voting for anything, not even one vote but we are going to try—give our Republicans, the weak ones because the strong ones don't need any of our help, we're try—going to try and give them the kind of pride and boldness that they need to take back our country. So let's walk down Pennsylvania Avenue."

The mob listened. They marched to the Capitol. Earlier, they had seen Senator Josh Hawley enthusiastically raise his left fist as he entered the Capitol. They followed in his footsteps toward the Capitol, climbed to its balconies, and eventually overpowered the vastly outnumbered Capitol Police, who were, unexplainably, totally unprepared.

The breach of the Capitol was both shocking and unsurprising; unthinkable and fated. The nation and the world watched as law enforcement was overwhelmed and the Capitol was stormed by those who called themselves patriots and insisted they were saving the republic from dark forces out to steal the election. Members of Congress were hurried to secure locations. So was Vice President Pence.

After Mike Pence was urgently whisked away by the Secret Service, Trump tweeted, "Mike Pence didn't have the courage to do what should have been done to protect our Country and our Constitution, giving States a chance to certify a corrected set of facts." Right around that time, some in the mob began chanting, "Hang Mike Pence." Later we'd see photographs of a noose dangling outside the Capitol.

You can choose your adjective to describe the horrendous, suffocating, sick, sad, and pathetic stench of Trumpism that blanketed and breached America's Capitol building on January 6, 2021. My word? *Inevitable.* We'd been seeing authoritarianism in the White House for years. And now, we were seeing it in the streets.

Americans watched as insurrectionists wreaked havoc inside the Capitol. The indelible images included officers being beaten, a former member of the armed services carrying zip ties through the chamber, one rioter marching a Confederate flag through the hall, and another who wore a sweatshirt that read CAMP AUSCHWITZ. Shots were fired. Tear gas forced members of Congress to grab for masks. Rioters were taking selfies inside vandalized offices, including Nancy Pelosi's. One of them made it all the way to the dais in the Senate chamber and started yelling, "Trump won the election!" He was basically doing what Trump had told Pence to do.

Some of the rioters were easily identifiable, like the bare-chested, red, white, and blue face-painted Jake Angeli, who wore the same fur hat with horns he had donned at Donald Trump rallies. Adam Johnson, a father of five from Florida, waved toward a camera and smiled as he carried Nancy Pelosi's podium out of the Capitol. Richard Barnett of Arkansas posed for a photo with his foot up on Nancy Pelosi's desk.

It was a riot made for Instagram, intended to go viral, and at times, like so many Trumpian moments, it was almost so outrageous as to be farcical.

But it was also damaging and deadly. One rioter was shot and killed. A police officer named Brian D. Sicknick was injured trying to protect those in the Capitol and died at home the following day after suffering two strokes. A total of five people died during or after the insurrection that placed a large portion of the nation's line of succession in mortal danger. According to prosecutors, at least 139 police officers were assaulted.

After years of Trump figuratively defecating on the Constitution and American norms, his most ardent followers, incited by his words, entered the Capitol and literally urinated and defecated on its marble floors. This was, plain and simple, Trumpism manifested.

For hours, the current president did nothing to stop the mob. Meanwhile, the president-elect went in front of the cameras and called for a stop to the madness.

At this hour, our democracy's under unprecedented assault. Unlike anything we've seen in modern times. An assault on the citadel of liberty, the Capitol itself. An assault on the people's representatives and the Capitol Hill police, sworn to protect them. And the public servants who work at the heart of our Republic . . . Let me be very clear. The scenes of chaos at the Capitol do not reflect a true America. Do not represent who we are. What we're seeing are a small number of extremists dedicated to lawlessness. This is not dissent. It's disorder. It's chaos. It borders on sedition. And it must end now.

What was Trump doing? Watching TV.

As senators and House members trapped inside the U.S. Capitol on Wednesday begged for immediate help during the siege, they struggled to get through to the president, who—safely ensconced in the West Wing—was too busy watching fiery TV images of the crisis unfolding around them to act or even bother to hear their pleas . . .

The president himself was busy enjoying the spectacle. Trump watched with interest, buoyed to see that his supporters were fighting so hard on his behalf, one close adviser said. (Ashley Parker, Josh Dawsey, and Philip Rucker, *Washington Post*)

After receiving many requests from inside the Capitol and inside his own administration (including some reported threats of resignations), Trump finally released a recorded statement shortly after 4:00 p.m.

"You have to go home now, we have to have peace . . . We love you,
    you're very special."
"I know your pain. I know you're hurt. We had an election that was
    stolen from us."

In a tweet she later deleted, Ivanka Trump referred to the insurrectionists
as "American Patriots."

And why shouldn't they have seen themselves like that? A president and
a huge segment of an American political party had been constantly duping
them into believing this was their role.

The absence of protection around the Capitol on a day that experts saw
coming was notable both because of the stakes and because of its stark contrast with the massive show of force during the Black Lives Matter protests
earlier in the year; those peaceful protesters walked into what looked like
a military zone, where they were hit with tear gas and hounded by Black
Hawk helicopters.

Along with the broken glass of the Capitol, any illusions about Trumpism
were shattered on January 6 as Confederate flags, anti-Semitic messaging,
and violent white supremacists breached the Capitol, yelling racial epithets
at Black officers. Was it all about race? Is every Trump supporter a racist?
No, but to ignore this core aspect of Trump's messaging and appeal is to be
in as much denial as the conspiracy theorists.

Birtherism was about racism. Very fine people on both sides was about
racism. The Muslim ban was about racism. The Wall was about racism.
"When the looting starts, the shooting starts" was about racism. Lafayette
Park was about racism. The Capitol breach was, at least in part, about
racism.

The *New Yorker*'s Luke Mogelson was embedded among the rioters and
described the common theme that underpinned the breach:

There was an unmistakable subtext as the mob, almost entirely white,
shouted, "Whose house? Our house!" One man carried a Confederate flag
through the building. A Black member of the Capitol Police later told Buzz-
Feed News that, during the assault, he was called a racial slur fifteen times.

If anything positive came out of the Capitol insurrection, it's that many Americans finally woke up to the threat of Trumpism and the rising threat of violent white supremacist groups. Our House had been pierced, but so had the façade that this was just another presidency. The people who had been warning you about Trumpism and these trends for several years were not hysterical, they were not liberal snowflakes, they were not rabid partisans. They were people like my parents who had seen this play out before and tried to tell us what we were looking at. If anything, those who raised the alarm were too reserved in their assessment of the risks. Trump tried to overturn the election. Trump incited a mob that breached the Capitol, some of whom were hell-bent on murdering American officials, including his own vice president. After four miserable years of Trump being covered like he was an actual, normal president, at long last the country could see that Trump being Trump was Trump being an authoritarian madman. Those who covered what Trumpism really was weren't politically biased, they were biased in favor of the truth. The media was never too hard on Trump. They were too easy on him.

Hours after the mob first approached the Capitol, with the approval of Mike Pence (notably, not the president of the United States), the National Guard was brought in, the rioters were removed, and the perimeter of the Capitol was secured.

Later, Trump tweeted: "These are the things and events that happen when a sacred landslide election victory is so unceremoniously & viciously stripped away from great patriots who have been badly & unfairly treated for so long. Go home with love & in peace. Remember this day forever!"

We will.

AT THE BREAK OF DON
January 7, 2021

The breach of the Capitol was one of the saddest moments in American history, but it was only the second saddest of its news cycle. When the lobbies, halls, and chambers of the Capitol were cleared and order was reestablished, members of Congress returned to go about what should have been the routine business of certifying the election.

First, the good news: after a dark day for democracy, Congress affirmed the Biden victory in the early hours of January 7. Trump released a middle-of-the-night statement acknowledging that the vote "represents the end of the greatest first term in presidential history" and "even though I totally disagree with the outcome of the election, and the facts bear me out, nevertheless there will be an orderly transition on January 20th."

Of course, nothing would be orderly. I turned again to my friend Dr. Michael Levin to help me understand what was happening from an analyst's perspective. Trump's behavior during his last days in office was entirely predictable given his obvious psychopathology. Trump's entire life had been devoted to earning the regard of a monstrously tyrannical, sadistic, sociopathic father for whom the world was divided into predators and prey, "killers" and suckers, winners and losers. We should imagine that, from his childhood perspective, sons that "win" or "kill" are accepted and valued; those that lose deserve what the psychoanalyst Leonard Shengold called *soul murder*.

Trump had lost before, and suffered numerous bankruptcies and failures, but what he feared here was the perception of failure. The election-rigging story had to survive so he could. As the walls of reality closed in, he saw himself becoming the most famous loser in the world. He was facing the fact that he'd failed at the only task that has ever mattered to him (being perceived as a winner), and he was about to be murdered, psychically, by his internal father. Trump was literally scared out of his mind—that is, he was now delirious or psychotic. We got several descriptions that fit this profile from insiders who leaked their concerns to the media. He would do anything to restore his feeling of victory and save his own psychic life. And he still had access to the world's largest megaphone, a cult of hypnotized followers, and the nuclear codes as external tools to pursue his internal objective.

None of Trump's behaviors in the final weeks would surprise a decent psychoanalyst. Even a layperson like my dad, who had experienced the gamut of human behavior in his lifetime, predicted, over and over, that there was no way Trump would leave peacefully.

And while they may have used less diagnostic terms than psychoanalysts, or less stark terms than my dad, by January of 2021, Trump's actions and words couldn't have surprised any of his enablers. That's what made their seditious behavior all the more deflating. After seeing the damage and death caused by their support of the Big Lie, 8 GOP senators (including ringleaders Josh Hawley and Ted Cruz), and 139 GOP House members *still* voted to overturn some of the election results. These so-called leaders, armed with nothing but rebuffed conspiracy theories, voted to overturn an American election in the hours *after* the Capitol was terrorized, in the name of maintaining the good graces of a guy who belonged in a straitjacket. Just as the Capitol insurrection will line the pages of American history books, so too should the names of those who plotted against democracy be etched into our national memory.

Josh Hawley's name was etched into the first rough draft of history by the editorial board of his home-state paper the *Kansas City Star*.

No one other than President Donald Trump himself is more responsible for Wednesday's coup attempt at the U.S. Capitol than one Joshua David Hawley, the 41-year-old junior senator from Missouri, who put out a fundraising appeal while the siege was underway . . .

And no longer can it be asked, as George Will did recently of Hawley, "Has there ever been such a high ratio of ambition to accomplishment?" Hawley's actions in the last week had such impact that he deserves an impressive share of the blame for the blood that's been shed . . .

No doubt plenty of Americans will see even this free-for-all in the temple of democracy as defensible. And those of you who have excused all of the brazen lawlessness of this administration can take a little bit of credit for these events, too. They couldn't have done it without you.

Ted Cruz received a similar first rough draft of history etching from the editorial board of his home-state paper the *Houston Chronicle*.

A brilliant and frequent advocate before the U.S. Supreme Court and a former Texas solicitor general, Cruz knew exactly what he was doing, what he was risking and who he was inciting as he stood on the Senate floor Wednesday and passionately fed the farce of election fraud even as a seething crowd of believers was being whipped up by President Donald Trump a short distance away.

Cruz, it should also be noted, knew exactly whose presidency he was defending. That of a man he called in 2016 a "narcissist," a "pathological liar" and "utterly amoral." . . .

The consequences of Cruz's cynical gamble soon became clear and so did his true motivations. In the moments when enraged hordes of Trump supporters began storming the Capitol to stop a steal that never happened, desecrating the building, causing the evacuation of Congress and injuring dozens of police officers, including one who died, a fundraising message went out to Cruz supporters:

"Ted Cruz here," it read. "I'm leading the fight to reject electors from key states unless there is an emergency audit of the election results. Will you stand with me?"

Cruz claims the message was automated. Even if that's true, it's revolting.

Cruz and Hawley didn't resign in the wake of the insurrection. So at this point in US history, Jeff Toobin had been fired for exciting himself, while Josh Hawley and Ted Cruz still had their jobs after inciting an insurrection.

During the overnight Senate certification session, Senator Ben Sasse explained: "Our kids need to know that this isn't what America is."

This is exactly wrong. Our kids need to be warned that this is what any country can become if its citizens and leaders cower and lies are allowed to spread unimpeded. Our kids need to learn the lesson too many of their parents forgot: democracy is not a gift. It's a job.

While we were trying to hit the brakes on the January 6 riot, COVID-19 just kept pushing on the gas. The day of the insurrection was also the pandemic's deadliest day so far, with 3,964 deaths.

ANYONE FOR SECONDS?

Senate majority leader Chuck Schumer and Speaker Nancy Pelosi called for Trump's immediate removal from office for "insurrection." The *Washington Post* editorial board agreed: "Trump caused the assault on the Capitol. He must be removed." So did the *New York Times* editorial board: "The president needs to be held accountable—through impeachment proceedings or criminal prosecution—and the same goes for his supporters who carried out the violence." Even the *Wall Street Journal* editorial board joined the chorus: "If Mr. Trump wants to avoid a second impeachment, his best path would be to take personal responsibility and resign."

After Mike Pence refused Democrat entreaties to invoke the Twenty-Fifth Amendment, the House moved to impeach Trump for the second time in just over a year.

PLATFORM OVER FUNCTION

It made sense when Facebook and Twitter banned Donald Trump from their platforms for repeatedly inciting violence. In a perfect world, you'd ban someone for incitement *before* the violence actually occurred, but at this point, anything was better than nothing. Trump tweets and posts would be blocked by the social media giants for the duration of his presidency and longer, giving the administration a parting policy win: Melania had promised to focus on ending cyberbullying, and with two weeks to go, the biggest bully of them all was, at long last, silenced. Financial columnist Andrew Ross Sorkin summed up the moment in a tweet: "So Trump has access to the nuclear codes but he can't tweet or post to Facebook." Most of the other social media platforms followed the leaders, and Trump was pretty effectively removed from the social internet. In a final irony, TikTok banned Trump before he banned them.

Trump's supporters in Congress argued that the move by the socials was an attack on free speech. One assumes they knew how absurd the claim was since freedom of speech does not apply to platforms owned by private companies that are perfectly within their rights to remove any user for breaking the rules.

But this wasn't just any user, and the banning of the president of the United States, however justified (and however late), pushed the issue of social media regulation and moderation to the top of our minds. And not a second too soon.

I always figured Donald Trump would eventually be told, "You have the right to remain silent," but I didn't expect him to have silence as his only option. As always, the bigger tech issue was that too few companies had way too much power over our democracy. We meant to build a distributed network where everyone would have a voice, and we ended up building centralized mega-platforms with CEOs who have the power of God.

THE CHIEFS AND THE PATRIOT
January 12, 2021

While the president gave lip service opposing violence and promised an orderly transition, the one thing he didn't say was the only thing that really mattered: that the election was free, fair, and accurate.

With the Big Lie still intact, concerns about the security at the Capitol and statehouses grew, DC filled with armed National Guard members, and the Joint Chiefs of Staff felt compelled to issue a public memo to its forces and the country.

> The violent riot in Washington, D.C. on January 6, 2021 was a direct assault on the U.S. Congress, the Capitol building, and our Constitutional process. We mourn the deaths of the two Capitol policemen and others connected to these unprecedented events. We witnessed actions inside the Capitol building that were inconsistent with the rule of law. The rights of freedom of speech and assembly do not give anyone the right to resort to violence, sedition, and insurrection. As Service Members, we must embody the values and ideals of the Nation. We support and defend the Constitution. Any act to disrupt the Constitutional process is not only against our traditions, values, and oath; it is against the law.

Meanwhile, corporations started distancing themselves from the president. The PGA pulled a tournament from Trump's Bedminster course, and Marriott, Blue Cross, and Hallmark began cutting ties with Trump and others who challenged the electoral results.

New England Patriots' coach Bill Belichick was scheduled to receive the Medal of Freedom from Trump, but opted out following the violence on

January 6: "Recently, I was offered the opportunity to receive the Presidential Medal of Freedom, which I was flattered by out of respect for what the honor represents and admiration for prior recipients . . . Subsequently, the tragic events of last week occurred and the decision has been made not to move forward with the award. Above all, I am an American citizen with great reverence for our nation's values, freedom and democracy."

An NFL football coach felt compelled to declare his reverence for democracy. Thankfully, that was still the Patriot way.

ET TWO, BRUTE?
January 13, 2021

No, you weren't seeing double. The man who always considered himself number one made history with number two. Donald Trump became the first president to be impeached twice.

The second impeachment of Trump had only a single article for "incitement of insurrection" for his actions leading to the Capitol breach, and cited his efforts to pressure Georgia officials into overturning the state's presidential election results.

All the House Democrats were joined in the impeachment vote by 10 of their Republican colleagues. Ten was the largest number of opposing party members ever to vote for a president's impeachment, and these folks should be lauded for their decision. But 197 others is a whole lot of folks voting against impeachment after what Republican Liz Cheney accurately called the greatest "betrayal by a president of the United States of his office and his oath to the Constitution." People died. The members themselves were targeted. All the incitement was fully out in the open. And that gets you 10.

Some GOP House members indicated to reporters that they would have voted for impeachment but they feared for their lives. This, alas, is the very definition of living in an autocracy: fear of violence bends elected officials away from the people they represent, or the law, in favor of the autocrat's will. It's how the Mafia runs. It's how bullies rule the schoolyard. It's not how America is supposed to work. It was also pretty gutless, as Colorado representative Jason Crow explained: "Some of my Republican colleagues are afraid of the consequences of an impeachment vote. This congress sends our young men and women to war. [I'm] not asking my colleagues to storm the beaches of Normandy, only to show a fraction of the courage we ask of our troops. It's time to lead."

Dan Newhouse of Washington was one of the ten GOP House members to vote to impeach Trump, and to his credit, he was perhaps the only one to truly own the moment: "We are all responsible. My colleagues are responsible for not condemning rioters this past year. Others, including myself, are responsible for not speaking out sooner before the president misinformed and inflamed a violent mob who tore down the American flag and brutally beat Capitol Police officers."

Before the vote, House minority leader Representative Kevin McCarthy said: "The President bears responsibility for Wednesday's attack on Congress by mob rioters. He should have immediately denounced the mob when he saw what was unfolding. These facts require immediate action of President Trump." But then, like many of his GOP colleagues, he argued that impeachment would divide the country.

Within a few weeks, the GOP would unify around Donald Trump. Liz Cheney was being attacked by many in her party and at rallies in her home district. Eventually, Cheney would be removed from her leadership position in the Republican caucus.

Kevin McCarthy's short-lived flirtation with standing up to Donald Trump would be erased as he made a visit to Mar-a-Lago to kiss the ring and get a photo op with his favorite insurrectionist.

Jim Jordan, election denier, Trump dead-ender, and, sickeningly, Medal of Freedom recipient, blamed cancel culture for the attacks on the president: "It won't just be the president of the United States. The cancel culture will come for us all." Luckily, just before he made this comment, I canceled my subscription to absolute nonsense.

Georgia representative Marjorie Taylor Greene, who had suggested that the 2017 Las Vegas mass shooting was a setup by anti-gun activists, called the Parkland school shooting a "false flag" event, hinted that the Sandy Hook school massacre was a staged event, and intimated that California's wildfires may have been caused by space lasers controlled by Jews, wore a face mask with the word *censored* on it as she freely addressed the nation and the world. Greene was living proof that the madness had breached Congress before the rioters did. (At least when you get hit by a Jewish laser, it's a dry heat.)

Throughout Trump's final year in office, there were endless debates about whether he was the cause of the rot that had infected the GOP or whether he merely grew from that rot like an uncontrollable weed. The answer was both. By the time the party of Trump galvanized around the idea that the incitement of insurrection was acceptable, you could no more separate Trump from the GOP than you separate manure from fertilized soil.

It was also impossible to separate COVID-19 from our communal experience. On the day Trump was impeached for a second time, the US reached a new record with 4,300 pandemic deaths. While Trump was being impeached for one offense, the virus reminded us of his deadlier misdeeds.

AND THE SOURCE YOU RODE IN ON

We weren't imagining it. The internet had become a better and more honest place in the few days since Trump had been de-platformed from social media. With the Source in Chief behind tens of thousands of often deadly lies silenced, misinformation levels plummeted:

> Online misinformation about election fraud plunged 73 percent after several social media sites suspended President Trump and key allies last week, research firm Zignal Labs has found, underscoring the power of tech companies to limit the falsehoods poisoning public debate when they act aggressively. (Elizabeth Dwoskin and Craig Timberg, *Washington Post*)

THE BRAID BUNCH

When we got started on this ride, I mentioned that when you're in the thick of the news cycle, stories seem like thousands of strands of hair shooting off in a million different directions. But when you pull back, you realize you're looking at a braid.

The attack of January 6 was that braid. It was the coming together of all the stories of the year. The misinformation, the lies, the violence, the rage, the racism, the anti-Semitism, the attacks on democracy, the treachery, and even the virus. At least three members of Congress tested positive for coronavirus after the insurrection. This included Pramila Jayapal of Washington, who explained the layers of danger she faced on January 6: "Only hours after Trump incited a deadly assault on our Capitol, many Republicans still refused to take the bare minimum COVID-19 precaution and simply wear a damn mask in a crowded room during a pandemic—creating a superspreader event ON TOP of a domestic terrorist attack."

The insurrection and its aftermath also provided a clear example of the different way law enforcement treats people depending on their race. Just about all the insurrectionists departed the federal building they had breached without being arrested on the spot. Richard Barnett, who put his foot up on Nancy Pelosi's desk with a stun gun in his pocket and bragged about his exploits, was allowed to turn himself in two days after the crime. Several of those arrested for the Capitol riot were released pending trial. One of those people was twenty-two-year-old Riley Williams, who stood accused of stealing Nancy Pelosi's laptop. The charges against her included theft, trespassing, and disorderly conduct on Capitol grounds. Days after her arrest, she was released, with travel restrictions, into her mother's custody.

Here's a thought experiment. Imagine if the Capitol insurrection had been carried out by a large mob of Black people. Think any of them would have been preparing for their trials at home with their moms? Let's take it a step further. Imagine that the mob of Black insurrectionists was incited by a Black president. Think he'd be spending the next weekend playing golf on one of his courses like Trump was?

HORATIO OUT THERE MYTH

It's hard to truly understand 2020 without understanding the My Pillow Guy. But it's hard to understand the My Pillow Guy without wanting to smother yourself with one of his products.

Mike Lindell was a former crack addict and alcoholic turned wealthy businessman, conspiracy theorist, and evangelical Christian with an honorary degree from Liberty University. With that résumé, it goes without saying that he was also a personal advisor to the president.

Lindell had spoken at Trump rallies, supported the president in many ways after becoming enamored during the 2016 campaign, and often referred to Trump as "the greatest president in history" and "chosen by God." Lindell helped pay the bail for Kenosha shooter Kyle Rittenhouse and promoted a plant extract called oleandrin as a miracle cure for COVID-19. Unsurprisingly, Lindell had a financial stake in a company that sold the extract. Equally unsurprisingly, oleandrin can be poisonous at relatively low doses. For weeks, Lindell had been supporting Trump's claims about election rigging.

All of this made it fitting that the My Pillow Guy was the last dead-ender to advise the president to go to the mattresses. On January 15, Lindell was photographed outside the Oval Office with a piece of paper that referred to martial law and the Insurrection Act.

It was a moment that had all the earmarks of the Trump era. A lunatic had made it past the lunatic fringe and into the highest hall of power. Lindell represented the Christian extremism whose adherents had made peace with the idea that their movement could be violent and its leader a wanton sinner. And Lindell, like so many other characters in this sad saga, was both ridiculously funny enough to be parodied on *Saturday Night Live* and deadly serious enough to get an audience with the world's most powerful person as he thrashed through his final days in the Oval Office.

SEE YOU LATER, AGITATOR

With his Senate impeachment trial on the horizon, Donald Trump used his last hours in office to issue a series of pardons, including one to Steve Bannon, who had served with such distinction as America's secretary of flooding the zone with shit. After the pardons were issued and the bags packed for Mar-a-Lago, Trump took one last opportunity to soil American democracy as he boarded Air Force One, shamefully avoiding the inauguration and the peaceful transfer of power.

Trump had dominated the attention economy. Every time you tried to look away, the show got more crazy, more frustrating, or more dangerous, and drew you back in. What if Trump told us that his only true mandate was to give the audience the show of its life? In that, he surely succeeded.

But in the end, like so many crime series, the finale fell flat. It would have been more fitting if he and Melania had left in a white Ford Bronco.

Before boarding the aircraft, Trump said, "So just a goodbye. We love you. We will be back in some form." (Hopefully in an orange jumpsuit.) He then added: "Have a good life." For once, his words matched the moment, as millions of Americans felt like that directive was suddenly possible.

FIGHT CLUB

Before we close out the already extended year, we need to skip forward and tie up some loose ends, beginning with the liberation of the top infectious disease expert. Trump's removal from social media gave a little more breathing room to reality. His removal from the White House would make room in America for the truth. Nowhere was that clearer than in the words spoken by Anthony Fauci, who was now working under new management. That was clear in his first Biden-era press conference.

> I don't want to be going back, you know, over history, but it is very clear that there were things that were said, be it regarding things like hydroxychloroquine and other things like that, that really was uncomfortable because they were not based on scientific fact. I can tell you, I take no pleasure at all in being in a situation of contradicting the president, so it was really something that you didn't feel that you can actually say something and there wouldn't be any repercussions about it. The idea that you can get up here and talk about what you know, what the evidence—what the science is and know that's it, let the science speak, it is somewhat of a liberating feeling.

Shortly thereafter, Fauci made his first appearance on MSNBC's *Rachel Maddow Show*. He described the change in his marching orders under Biden.

> I mean, he said, let science speak. Let science be the thing that drives us. Let's just be open and honest and transparent. We're not going to get everything right. There will be some mistakes, there will be some missteps. The response to that is to fix it and not to point blame and point fingers.

It was just—just an amazingly refreshing experience and conversation that we had, and he wasn't doing it for show. This was, like, behind closed doors in the White House where he was just telling the team how he wanted this to go looking forward.

In an interview with CNN, Fauci described the obstacles once again: "There's no secret. We've had a lot of divisiveness, we've had facts that were very, very clear, that were questioned. People were not trusting what health officials were saying." When asked if the lack of candor over the last year cost lives, Fauci responded, "You know, it very likely did."

More than four hundred thousand Americans had died of COVID-19 by the time Trump left office, some of whom perished questioning how they could have been so misled. How many of those deaths would have been prevented if scientists were free to speak the truth? How many of those deaths would have been avoided if Trump had warned Americans of the threat as soon as he himself said he was aware of it? How many of those four hundred thousand Americans would have lived if Trump wore a mask, and urged people to take minimal precautionary measures? How many fewer deaths would we have had if almost any American other than Donald Trump had been in the Oval Office during the pandemic year? Two hundred thousand? One hundred thousand? Fifty thousand? One thousand? One hundred? How many deaths should it have taken for a president's enablers to say, "Enough"?

The un-caging of Anthony Fauci and the nation's scientific institutions was a refreshing and promising sign. But his new candor brought up deeper questions about how government officials should respond when faced with an authoritarian-minded leader. Should they resign as many did? Those resignations didn't seem to work. Should they speak out and suffer the consequences like many did? That didn't seem to work either. Should they figure out a way to adjust to the authoritarian in enough ways so they could keep their jobs and try to help Americans from the inside? This is what Fauci did. Would more lives have been saved had Anthony Fauci resigned and done a press tour explaining that the president's lies were killing people? I really don't know. And I really don't know the best way to turn back an authoritarian leader like Trump when you can't trust seventy-five million voters to see his flaws; and when those you trust to be democracy's gatekeepers instead play the role of gate smashers.

As the Trump era ended and gradually grew smaller in our rearview mirror, we were left with the fundamental question about liberal democracy: How do we keep it?

Toward the end of the interview Fauci was finally allowed to do with Maddow, he discussed the often-forgotten COVID-19 victims, the ones who had survived the virus, but who still had a variety of serious symptoms months later.

> They are virologically okay. The virus is no longer identified in them, but they have persistence of symptoms that can be debilitating—extreme fatigue, muscle aches, temperature dis-regulation.
>
> Some of them even have situations with what they call brain fog, where it's very difficult for them to focus or to concentrate. It can be really quite disturbing.

When you consider how close we came to losing our democracy, it almost sounded like Fauci was describing America after Trump. The virus was gone. The symptoms remained.

And like the long haulers still suffering serious, debilitating effects from having COVID, America was still at the beginning of what would be a long haul to rein in misinformation and get democracy back to a healthy state. For both types of patients, the long haulers and America itself, it was still too soon to say if there'd ever be a return to full strength.

Alexey Navalny returned to Russia, where he was immediately arrested and sentenced to nearly three years in prison, leading to mass protests in Russia. As Garry Kasparov explained, Navalny was thrown in prison "for the crime of failing to die when they tried to assassinate him." Derek Chauvin was found guilty of murdering George Floyd and was sentenced to twenty-two-and-a-half years. The forty-three-year-old Tom Brady won his seventh Super Bowl, this time with a new team, the Tampa Bay Bucs. After Super Bowls, the MVP usually says, "I'm going to Disneyland." Brady couldn't do that since

Disneyland's *Toy Story* parking lot was being used as a mass vaccination site. (Don't worry, Brady's been to Disneyland enough as it is, and he got to go to Gisele instead.) Harry and Meghan appeared in an interview with Oprah Winfrey that earned huge viewer numbers and got Trump-like coverage around the world. Claudia Conway appeared as a contestant on *American Idol*; both of her parents appeared on her first episode. And what about us and our news obsession? It dropped dramatically in the first six months of 2021. This was especially true at the partisan outlets, but they weren't alone in their loneliness. According to *Axios*, "Mainstream publishers including the *New York Times, Wall Street Journal, USA Today,* and Reuters dropped 18%."

And then there was the second Senate trial of Donald Trump.

The character Tyler Durden explained, "The first rule of Fight Club is: You do not talk about Fight Club. The second rule of Fight Club is: You do not talk about Fight Club."

Donald Trump broke both those rules nonstop in the months leading up to the Capitol insurrection. He talked about Fight Club before it happened. He talked about it after it happened. And he talked about it while it was happening, sending out tweets attacking Mike Pence, even as Secret Service agents hustled the vice president away from a mob of rioters, some of whom had made it clear they were there to assassinate him.

Led by Congressman Jamie Raskin of Maryland, who had lost his son, Tommy, to suicide just a week before the insurrection, the House managers did a solid job laying out the timeline of Trump's inciting comments, his insistence that the election was stolen, and repeated calls to action in the months, days, and minutes leading up to the Capitol breach.

House impeachment manager Joe Neguse summed up the case: "When he saw firsthand the violence that his conduct was creating, he didn't stop it. He didn't condemn the violence. He incited it further. And he got more specific. He didn't just tell them to 'fight like hell.' He told them how, where and when. He made sure they had advance notice—18 days advance notice. He sent his save the date for Jan. 6. He told them to march to the Capitol and 'fight like hell.'"

And when they fought like hell, the president took no action to defend the Capitol.

The facts of the case were not so much presented by the House managers as confirmed by them. After all, we heard the lies and incitement with our own ears, and we saw the violence with our own eyes. We then saw and heard Trump's response to the violence; and no one even disputed that he never called in the National Guard or condemned the attacks that left 139 law enforcement officials injured and led to 5 deaths. According to most accounts, he delighted in the violence and he was thrilled by the loyalty his patriots showed him.

Trump's defense was manned by a collection of last-minute hires, none of whom were remotely qualified to argue a constitutional case on the floor of the Senate. Michael T. van der Veen made his bones as a personal injury lawyer in Philadelphia. His last-minute addition to the team actually made some sense since Trump's enablers had been defending his ego from personal injury for more than four years.

In short, Trump couldn't find one decent lawyer to defend his actions. Yet he found plenty of senators who would.

Ultimately, the case was less about the defendant and the quality of the lawyering, and more about the jury. The senators who would have the final verdict included a few, like Josh Hawley and Ted Cruz, who could have just as easily appeared as codefendants, and many more who acted as coconspirators by promoting the Big Lie. Having accessories to the crime sit in judgment of the crime gave new meaning to getting a jury of one's peers. Not satisfied with avoiding the defendant's seat, Senators Lindsey Graham, Mike Lee, and Ted Cruz were seen at one point huddling with Trump's defense lawyers, sharing advice about how best to deliver their closing arguments.

Like the first impeachment trial, this second one had a foregone conclusion when it came to the legal result. But in the eyes of history, the judgment may weigh more heavily on the jurors than the person they acquitted.

The remorseless, crushing power of the House managers' evidence, all backed by horrifying real-time audio and video recordings, shuttered any good-faith defense of Trump on the merits of the case . . . There is no defense. There is only complicity, whether motivated by weakness and fear or by shared guilt. (David Frum, *The Atlantic*)

During the first impeachment trial, when Mitt Romney stood and said, "I'm Spartacus," he stood alone. During impeachment trial two, a handful of other GOP senators stood with him. Richard Burr, Bill Cassidy, Susan Collins, Lisa Murkowski, Ben Sasse, and Pat Toomey joined Romney in voting to convict Trump. It was the most bipartisan impeachment vote ever, but not bipartisan enough, falling ten votes shorts of the two-thirds majority needed for a conviction.

Dave Pell ✔
@davepell

Trump's enablers have developed herd immunity to the truth.

12:58 PM · Feb 11, 2021 · 🐦 Twitter

In one last act of Trump-era hypocrisy, Mitch McConnell, who had pushed for the trial to be held after Trump left office and then used the fact that it had been held after Trump left office as his reason for voting to acquit, suggested that the buck could still stop. It just had to stop somewhere else. "We have a criminal justice system in this country; we have civil litigation. And former presidents are not immune from being accountable by either one . . . This body is not invited to act as the nation's overarching moral tribunal."

That's not quite right. The body *was* invited to be the nation's moral tribunal. It just RSVP'd *no*.

During the trial, Jamie Raskin described a conversation he had with his daughter Tabitha. Raskin had invited Tabitha and her husband, Hank, to join him at the Capitol on January 6 to witness what should have been a peaceful transfer of power. Instead, like so many others, Tabitha and Hank found themselves cowering under a desk, behind a locked door, sending out what they worried might be their final text messages.

Raskin promised his daughter this would never happen during any of her subsequent visits to the Capitol. She responded, "Dad, I don't want to come back to the Capitol." Raskin explained, "Of all the terrible, brutal things I saw and heard on the day and since then, that one hit me the hardest."

Just after the Senate trial, a Morning Consult / *Politico* poll found the share of Republicans who said Trump is very or somewhat responsible for the Capitol insurrection had fallen to 27 percent, while the share of GOP voters who blamed President Joe Biden for the riot had increased to 46 percent. Yes, you're reading that right. More Republicans blamed Joe Biden for the riot than blamed Donald Trump.

My friend Congressman Jim Himes of Connecticut, who was a steadfast defender of the truth during both impeachment cases, put the second trial into perspective in a Facebook post:

> Anyone with eyes, ears, and the ability to discern fact from fiction could clearly see Donald Trump incited a seditious riot—an act of domestic terrorism—to break the American tradition of the peaceful transition of power on January 6. The lies Donald Trump told leading up to this riot, and continued telling even as insurrectionists breached the Capitol, left many dead, hundreds injured, and countless traumatized. Today, despite the failure of a two-thirds majority of the Senate to ratify these facts and convict Donald Trump, I am heartened by the courage of 57 patriots who upheld their oaths and stood on the right side of history. History will be the ultimate judge of the actions of Donald Trump. And history now looks upon us to do the work of the American people, and turn the page from this dark chapter.

Forty-three senators forsook their roles as gatekeepers of our democracy with the widespread support of their party, so turning that page could take a long time in America. But Himes's words do provide a welcome segue for us to turn the page on this dark chapter of this book.

SOUL PROPRIETOR

January 20, 2021

For months, I had been schmoozing my friends in high places so I could score an inauguration ticket and deliver this final missive on the year that wouldn't end from the scene of its turning point: the steps of the Capitol, as Joe Biden and Kamala Harris were sworn in. But just like everything else in 2020, things didn't go according to plan for any of us.

The usually joyous and crowded inauguration festivities were dramatically pared down because of the ongoing viral risk, and because the Capitol insurrection had created a need for significantly upped security levels. More than twenty thousand armed National Guard members blocked off streets, and barricaded buildings, and endless coils of barbed wire had turned Washington, DC, into a warlike green zone.

When Biden clinched the election, there were scenes of people dancing in the streets in several cities. But after two months of rising COVID-19 cases and assaults on democracy, Americans were less in the mood to dance and more in the mood to find some relief, and to finally disembark from the roller coaster. With a sparse and socially distanced crowd, even on Capitol steps, Kamala Harris made history as she took the oath of office. Joe Biden rose to the moment, giving one of the better inauguration speeches in memory. Because of the events that preceded it, including a mass pandemic and a wanton attack on democracy, it was also one of the strangest.

Biden noted how close the country had teetered toward ruin:

This is democracy's day. A day of history and hope of renewal and resolve through a crucible for the ages. America has been tested anew and America has risen to the challenge. Today, we celebrate the triumph not of a candidate, but of a cause, the cause of democracy. The people, the will of the people, has been heard and the will of the people has been heeded.

We've learned again that democracy is precious. Democracy is fragile. At this hour, my friends, democracy has prevailed.

After an era of lies, Biden gave Americans a reality check about the challenges ahead:

Few people in our nation's history have been more challenged or found a time more challenging or difficult than the time we're in now. A once-in-a-century virus that silently stalks the country. It's taken as many lives in one year as America lost in all of World War II. Millions of jobs have been lost. Hundreds of thousands of businesses closed. A cry for racial justice some four hundred years in the making moves us. The dream of justice for all will be deferred no longer.

The cry for survival comes from the planet itself, a cry that can't be any more desperate or any more clear. And now a rise of political extremism, white supremacy, domestic terrorism that we must confront and we will defeat.

To overcome these challenges, to restore the soul and secure the future of America requires so much more than words. It requires the most elusive of all things in a democracy: unity, unity.

In another January, on New Year's Day in 1863, Abraham Lincoln signed the Emancipation Proclamation. When he put pen to paper, the president said, and I quote, "if my name ever goes down into history, it'll be for this act. And my whole soul is in it."

My whole soul is in it today. On this January day, my whole soul is in this: Bringing America together, uniting our people, uniting our nation. And I ask every American to join me in this cause.

And most important, Biden addressed the key challenge the country would face moving forward. It wasn't about left and right, or Republicans and Democrats; it was about something core to our future, and so damn absent, from our unforgettable year. The truth.

What are the common objects we as Americans love, that define us as Americans? I think we know. Opportunity, security, liberty, dignity, respect, honor and, yes, the truth.

Recent weeks and months have taught us a painful lesson. There is truth and there are lies, lies told for power and for profit. And each of us has a duty and responsibility, as citizens, as Americans, and especially as leaders, leaders who have pledged to honor our Constitution and protect our nation, to defend the truth and defeat the lies.

And, as he almost always does, Joe Biden mentioned the influence of his parents. It's a trait, as you've undoubtedly noticed, that we have in common.

Look, I understand that many of my fellow Americans view the future with fear and trepidation. I understand they worry about their jobs. I understand, like my dad, they lay in bed at night, staring at the ceiling, wondering, can I keep my health care? Can I pay my mortgage? Thinking about their families, about what comes next. I promise you, I get it. . . .

If we show a little tolerance and humility, and if we're willing to stand in the other person's shoes, as my mom would say, just for a moment, stand in their shoes. Because here's the thing about life. There's no accounting for what fate will deal you. Some days, when you need a hand. There are other days when we're called to lend a hand. That's how it has to be. That's what we do for one another. And if we are this way, our country will be stronger, more prosperous, more ready for the future.

As memorable as Biden's long-awaited moment was, the experience many Americans will remember from his inauguration was falling in love with a twenty-two-year-old youth poet laureate named Amanda Gorman, who entered the body politic like an emotional vaccine. In her poem, Gorman didn't shy away from the events of the preceding weeks. Like any good teller of a true story, she didn't shy away from anything.

> We've seen a force that would shatter our nation
> rather than share it
> Would destroy our country if it meant delaying democracy
> And this effort very nearly succeeded
> But while democracy can be periodically delayed
> it can never be permanently defeated
> In this truth
> in this faith we trust
> For while we have our eyes on the future
> history has its eyes on us

After a year of breathing in the air that made up the news universe, infected by a deadly virus, polluted by smoke from fires, permeated with the vitriol of hate, and saturated by an endless barrage of lies, it was such a relief

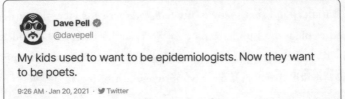

Dave Pell ✓
@davepell

My kids used to want to be epidemiologists. Now they want
to be poets.

9:26 AM · Jan 20, 2021 · 🐦 Twitter

not only to exhale but to inhale the humanity, decency, and plain, simple, and endangered truths spoken by the new president and his unstoppable poet.

But for me, the air began to clear the night before Biden was sworn in. He and Kamala Harris stood before the Lincoln Memorial Reflecting Pool after a year when America's reflection was so sad and so stark and at long last mourned the now more than four hundred thousand COVID dead. I got the sense he was mourning our loss of innocence as well. There, on the precipice of his presidency and in the shadow of a lifetime of personal loss, Joe Biden honored the dead and explained, "To heal we must remember."

GOING TO EXTREMES

A few years ago I accompanied my parents on a trip to Washington, DC. We had traveled across the country because my mom had a question.

On the first day of the trip, we went to the Holocaust Memorial Museum. My ninetysomething dad got checked, rechecked, and metal detected on the way into the museum. He joked, "I guess once you're on the list, you're on the list."

I took a photo of my parents under their names on the donor wall. The museum had arranged for a docent to give us a private tour of the museum, but my parents politely declined. They didn't need another tour. They knew the story. And we weren't there for a tour, we were there because my mom wanted to meet with the heads of the museum and ask them a question that had been bothering her for a long time.

Nearly eight decades after a friend told her in her backyard that they couldn't be friends anymore because my mom was Jewish, after years in an ever-threatened children's home, after years of donating money to museums like this one, and to universities, scholars, and schools, after endless semesters working with professors to develop courses on the Holocaust and the Spanish Inquisition and anything else that could provide a clue to the answer she sought, she still had a question.

She pulled out a few newspaper articles she had folded in her purse; each one with a story about a hate crime or a hate movement.

"Why is it still happening? We're supposed to be such smart people. So why can't we stop anti-Semitism?"

My mom's an autodidact. Reads everything. Never forgets. Saw it all firsthand and has been studying it ever since.

"We're doing a lot. But are we doing the right thing? What more could we be doing to stop this?"

They didn't have much. You wouldn't expect them to. It was an impossible question, but when a museum benefactor and survivor who lost much of her family wants you to meet with her, you take the meeting.

And when they ask why the hate isn't gone yet, what are you going to say?

What are you going to say when a woman who's been confounded by the same question all her life asks you if you have the answer to this?

"Why would anyone want to kill my parents? They were such wonderful people."

I didn't have the answer either. But the exchange reminded me of a question I'd had all my life. How can you experience the worst of humanity but still have faith in the goodness of people? How the hell can you go on, start a new life, raise a family, still believe in anything?

What I do know is that we have to keep asking the question. I also know that much of the hate between people is manufactured by others who derive power from division. Politics is often about selling division. Media thrives on extremism. *If it bleeds, it leads*.

News is about telling stories and good stories are about conflict. Politics is about driving enthusiasm, and rage is a hell of a motivator.

Because extremes sell in news and politics, we're unlikely to find a path toward unity in either. And unity is what we need. You can't beat divisions with divisiveness. You can't beat hate with more hate. You can't overcome what you're convinced is the terrible reality about your fellow Americans by furiously screaming about them from a distance.

As the godson of David Duke and the son of the publisher of the first major white nationalist website, Derek Black was considered the bright future of white supremacy. Even at a young age, he was beloved at conferences, understood the power of effective messaging to move the political needle, and was being groomed to be a leader in the movement.

All that changed when he attended a liberal arts college. But it didn't change overnight. And it didn't change because the people Black had been trained to hate turned around and hated him back.

Donald Trump shocked people like Derek Black by speaking their language of hate on the presidential campaign trail and later from the Oval Office. Shortly after Trump's 2016 election, Black reflected on his experiences leaving hate behind, a move that would cost him fame and family.

> Several years ago, I began attending a liberal college where my presence prompted huge controversy. Through many talks with devoted and diverse people there—people who chose to invite me into their dorms and conversations rather than ostracize me—I began to realize the damage I had done. Ever since, I have been trying to make up for it . . .
>
> For a while after I left the white nationalist movement, I thought my upbringing made me exaggerate the likelihood of a larger political reaction to demographic change. Then Mr. Trump gave his Mexican "rapists" speech and I spent the rest of the election wondering how much my movement had set the stage for his. Now I see the anger I was raised with rocking the nation.
>
> People have approached me looking for a way to change the minds of Trump voters, but I can't offer any magic technique. That kind of persuasion happens in person-to-person interactions and it requires a lot of honest listening on both sides. For me, the conversations that led me to change my views started because I couldn't understand why anyone would fear me. I thought I was only doing what was right and defending those I loved. (*New York Times*)

I thought I was only doing what was right and defending those I loved. Let's start there. That's a value we all share. Some of us may be defending them from an imaginary enemy. Others may be alienated and stirred to violence under false pretenses. But we all want what's best for those we love, and most of us want to do what's right.

Following the January 6 Capitol insurrection, Arnold Schwarzenegger shared some memories from his childhood.

I grew up in the ruins of a country that suffered the loss of its democracy. I was born in 1947, two years after the Second World War. Growing up, I was surrounded by broken men drinking away the guilt over their participation in the most evil regime in history. Not all of them were rabid anti-Semites or Nazis, many just went along, step-by-step, down the road. They were the people next door. Now, I've never shared this so publicly because it is a painful memory, but my father would come home drunk once or twice a week, and he would scream and hit us and scare my mother. I didn't hold him totally responsible because our neighbor was doing the same thing to his family, and so was the next neighbor over. I heard it with my own ears and saw it with my own eyes. They were in physical pain from the shrapnel in their bodies and in emotional pain from what they saw or did. It all started with lies, and lies, and lies, and intolerance.

The levels are not equal, but when it comes to hatred, both the hated and the hater are victims. So it's worth asking yourself who's benefiting from all the hate. Perhaps it's a president or a leader of a party. Perhaps it's someone who runs a media outlet that makes more money when viewers are angry. Maybe it's someone who knows you'll be more likely to buy into the culture wars than the economic policies they're passing.

In *The Art of War*, Niccolò Machiavelli explains that "a Captain should endeavor with every art to divide the forces of the enemy."

Let's rework that a little. If a captain is endeavoring with every art to divide your forces, then that captain must see *you* as the enemy.

There's a reason the phrase *divide and conquer* has been around so long. It works. But what's good for the divider isn't so good for the divided.

Machiavelli also said, "Men are driven by two principal impulses, either by love or by fear."

In 2020, we had enough fear to nearly topple a democracy. Maybe it's time to try the other impulse.

EPILOGUE:
THE END OF THE RIDE

I have to tell you this: this whole thing is
not about heroism. It's about decency.

—Albert Camus, *The Plague*

IN 1993, A FEW YEARS AFTER THE BERLIN WALL CAME DOWN, MY SISTER
and I joined my parents and a busload of other Jews on an educational trip
through Poland. It was less a vacation than a sightseeing trip through the
many sites of genocidal anti-Semitic acts.

One morning, we broke away from our travel companions and hired a
taxi to take the four of us from our Warsaw hotel to Biała Podlaska, the town
where my dad had grown up before the Holocaust changed everything. It
would be the first time my dad had returned to his hometown since just after
the war. He didn't remember that much Polish anymore, but he remembered
how he used to bribe his way around postwar Europe. So when we got into
the taxi, my dad had two cases of Marlboros that he had brought from the
Bay Area, and a thick wad of Polish zlotys for payoffs.

Luckily, we didn't need anything other than cab fare for the two-hour
ride. Biała Podlaska was still the small town my dad grew up in, and in
1993, the only Americans who would possibly be dropped off near the town's
central square were Jews like us, visiting someone's prewar home. The second we got out of the car, two families ran from their houses, as one of the

matriarchs insisted over and over that the Germans had made them move into the houses and that they didn't steal them from the Jews. By now, my dad was a successful businessman from America. The last thing he wanted was to move back into his old house, where the current occupants were still pumping water from the same well he remembered from his childhood.

Before this trip, my dad only spoke sporadically about his past, and he had little interest in returning to Poland. I think in the back of his mind he always worried the onslaught of painful memories would break him. Instead, that day in Biała Podlaska freed him from the fear of those memories and opened him in dramatic ways.

The day also changed my perspective of my dad. Up until that point, I had filled the vacuum of his silence with visions of a Jewish superhero who had a bravery I couldn't comprehend and a strength I couldn't imagine. But in Biała Podlaska, I saw something else. My dad excitedly jogged from place to place to show my mom, my sister, and me where he swam, where his family's butcher shop used to be, and where he got in trouble for breaking the rules (there were a lot of those landmarks). As he did, I saw a guy who was just a kid, a teenager faced with unimaginable challenges and ferocious losses who did what he had to do.

He reminded me of his humanness years later when, during a particularly rough period of my life, I told him and my mom that I was feeling overwhelmed with shame and felt that I had failed to live up to my potential.

After I unloaded, my dad paused and said, "You know something, David. I feel the exact same vay."

This was coming from a guy who crawled, family-less, into a Polish forest during the darkest days of World War II and came out the other side as an embodiment of the American dream. When he was a kid, he'd travel to the weekly market in rural Poland, where his older brother Simcha taught him to negotiate for animals to stock their family's kosher butcher shop. When a deal was struck, the participants would slap hands, and my dad and his big brother would begin the long walk back to the village, where their family of seven shared a one-bedroom apartment, with no electricity or plumbing.

Aside from my dad, everyone else in his family was killed, some after possibly being shipped off to concentration camps, others certainly shot in the back while standing on the edge of massive open graves.

After arriving in America and seeing a poster of the Golden Gate Bridge at a bus station, he moved to the Bay Area, where he went from working in an ice cream store, to owning an ice cream store, to building a four-unit apartment building where he lived in one apartment with my mom and rented out the other three, to becoming one of Northern California's most successful real estate developers and philanthropists. With the help of a Jewish historian named Fred Rosenbaum, he eventually published a book about his life, in the forest and in America, that would be taught in university courses.

In that book, called *Taking Risks*, he wrote about the night he escaped from near certain death, knowing full well he'd never see a member of his family again.

Afraid of being seen on the streets, even at that hour, we went through backyards, fields, and narrow alleys on all fours, crawling in the dark over dirt and animal shit. We arose to climb over walls and fences, but it's fair to say the way we got to the woods was on our hands and knees. Not until we entered the forest did we stand upright.

We ran deeper and deeper into the black woods. When we were out of breath, we walked almost the rest of the night. A little before dawn we collapsed on the ground. With nothing more than the light summer clothing I'd been wearing, I was utterly unprepared for the rigors of the forest.

But I kept alive, joined a band of partisans, and fought back.

Many times in my life I've been in danger and somehow survived, even thrived. Usually it wasn't the result of long, deep philosophizing, but, rather, quick thinking and then action. And I needed a lot of luck along the way, too.

My life has been one of extremes. I've known luxury but also have had to scrounge for potatoes to keep from starving. Much happiness has come my way and yet nothing can make up for what I lost. And for all my daring and independence, I'm actually quite shy. I have even been of two minds about telling this story; most of the time, I've wanted to keep it locked inside me.

How could this guy who rose from his hands and knees to live an undeniably amazing life feel the same shame as I did? He explained that he always regretted not being a bigger success.

I argued that the business part of his life would always feel less than fully satisfying because the people he wanted to impress the most didn't survive long enough to see his success. His facial expression suggested that maybe my theory made sense, and he responded, "Maybe you should be my therapist."

The truth was that this wasn't the first time my dad seemed insecure or even ashamed. He ruminated on decisions more than the average person, he regretted many of the ones he made (even though almost all of them paid off), he lamented missed opportunities. I don't remember him ever getting a truly good night of sleep. In short, he was a normal human with the same fears and insecurities as the rest of us. My dad was not born a hero. No one is. He was considered the little shit of his family, and his father regularly expressed the view that he'd never amount to anything. So what turned him into what others, especially those in the Jewish community, would call a hero?

When the darkest forces of history pushed, he pushed back. When the moment demanded it, an ordinary person became extraordinary. I never really liked it when people referred to my dad as a survivor. He was a fighter.

Throughout a year when a pandemic tore through our communities and an administration and its enablers tore through the fabric of democracy, we rightfully focused on lies, malfeasance, deadly incompetence, and lethal indifference. But that wasn't the whole story. Thousands of people treated the sick and fed the hungry. Journalists wrote and spoke the truth regardless of risk. Whistleblowers leaked reality, insiders quietly defended the Constitution, and truth-tellers stepped forward regardless of what it meant to their careers, and despite the inevitable slings and arrows they'd suffer at the hand of the thin-skinned president and his most rabid fans.

In 2020, we got a new definition of who was essential. We received lessons in bravery from doctors and nurses who risked everything to heal the afflicted in their communities and then, after flattening the curve, packed up their paltry personal protective equipment and moved on to other cities where the virus was at its worst. Local leaders protected their neighbors, providing accurate information even while being attacked for doing so. Health officials broadcast the reality of our challenge, over and over, even after realizing they'd need their own security details because of the dangers associated with embracing the truth. Peaceful protesters waved off tear gas and returned to protest again, even in places where their friends and neighbors had a less generous version of what justice and equality should look like. Little kids had bake sales to support frontline workers, families sewed masks to make up for the PPE shortage, lawyers and nonprofits worked nonstop to defend America against the attack from within. There were countless acts of empathy and leadership that filled the administration's void.

Joe Biden made this point during his final address of 2020: "My mother used to have an expression, she said bravery resides in every heart and someday it'd be summoned."

Early in the pandemic, I began publishing a daily selection of positive stories from around the country, and I never came up short of material. Ordinary people, with the same fears, anxieties, and insecurities as the rest of us were pushed by a dark moment in American history, and they pushed back. They were summoned, and they answered. The story of this year is theirs too.

In the waning days of the year, 2020 came for my family too. On December 28, my phone rang, and I saw that it was my mom calling. When you have parents of a certain age, you wonder if every incoming call from a family member is *that* call. This one was. My dad, after suffering through a terrible night with a sepsis infection, had to be rushed to the hospital. Like hundreds of thousands of families, the pandemic prevented mine from being at our loved one's side. On December 29, we got the call from the doctors that we'd better come to the hospital. After parking my car, I waited in front of Marin General Hospital for my mom and sisters to arrive. As I stood there, I heard the bells clang at the church across the street. By the time we worked our way through the hospital COVID protocols and made it upstairs, we were a few minutes too late. In the shadow of hundreds of apartments he had built decades earlier, and in a hospital with an entrance that bore his name, my dad died.

We were allowed to sit at my dad's bedside in groups of two. For several minutes, I sat by Mom in silence. Finally, I said, "Maybe now Dad can finally see his other family." My mom responded, "That's a nice thought, David. But you don't really believe that, do you?" I probably didn't, but I'd been preparing that line for my dad's eventual memorial service for years. Of course, in 2020, there would be no memorial service, just a small gathering of masked family members and a quiet goodbye.

I could say that my dad and I were too focused on news and that his obsession about the threat of Trumpism ultimately amounted to wasted time that could have been spent on less external issues. If this were a novel, now would definitely be the point where I'd deliver just that lesson. But we had enough fiction in 2020. Every person in my family mentioned that they were relieved my dad lived long enough to see America vote Trump out of office.

While we had long talks, many of them about the news and world events, my dad was a man of few words. When I was a kid, he was almost silent. Once, a high school friend who had known my family his whole life asked me if my dad spoke English. Because he was so quiet, the words he spoke stood out, and were forever lodged in my otherwise porous memory.

In fourth grade, I showed him a report card with several As and an A-. He looked at it for a few seconds and said: "Vhy the minus?" That was quite literally the only conversation we ever had about academics. On our one American-ish father-son fishing trip on Oregon's McKenzie River, we both noticed a very full-figured woman in a ribbed T-shirt casting a line from her perch on a large boulder. My dad whispered into my ear, "Vow, dey really grow 'em good up here." I didn't realize it at the time, but that was my dad's version of the birds-and-bees talk. The *whole* version. We never really talked about sex, love, or relationships aside from that exchange.

But we did talk about his past and how it related to the world that was unfolding. When my dad asked me, "Vhat's cooking?" he meant it in the geopolitical sense. He taught me to read between the lines when it came to news stories, to think analytically about what world leaders were trying to achieve, and above all else, to apply a common-sense filter to the world around me.

When I was an adult hanging out with him, he'd often sit on his chair with the news on in the background and predict how world events would unfold. The day the United States shocked and awed its way into the Iraq War, he said, "You vatch, they vill let the Americans go straight to Baghdad and then the real war vill start and it will be with insurgents." He knew, in part because he was a tactical savant and in part because he once was an insurgent. Every once in a while, I'd share my dad's latest takes and predictions with a friend who works in high places in the Pentagon, and my friend would joke, "Considering how often he gets it exactly right, we should really hire your dad."

My dad was street-smart about world affairs. He lived through the consequences of authoritarianism and fascism, and he fought tooth and nail to defeat them. He recognized political dark forces and could feel dangerous trends as sure as he could feel the mud and shit through which he crawled to survival. Those who so deeply offended America's better angels could never write off my dad as a liberal snowflake. He wasn't a "radical Democrat"; in fact, for most of his years, I doubt he was even a Democrat at all. He wasn't weak, passive, or touchy-feely. Without a gun, he never would've survived. Without becoming violent, he would have died as a teen, I'd have never been born, and you'd be nearing the end of a much less entertaining review of America's year turned dumpster fire. Trump couldn't call my dad a sucker or loser in battle (he lived, he was never captured). And while Trump the braggart squandered a real estate empire and turned fortune into debt, my dad humbly built a real estate empire out of less than nothing and died without a single loan out on a single property (he'd want me to mention that).

My dad was one of the last in a generation who had stared World War II–era evil in the face, so he knew what it was 2020 America was staring at. He knew what authoritarianism sounded like, and he understood the sad, terrible depths of human nature. He knew what, under the right circumstances, his neighbors were capable of.

So much of Trumpism was summed up by Trump's comment: "Just remember, what you are seeing and what you are reading is not what's happening."

My dad's message is the opposite. What it looks like is exactly what it is.

When Trump was campaigning, my dad said, "You know, this guy sounds a lot like Hitler to me. Everyone laughed at him too." He didn't mean we were heading toward a Holocaust. I grew up with almost no relatives. I don't need to be reminded that Trump isn't Hitler and his enablers aren't the Nazi Party. But when it comes to messaging, these guys were basically the Fourth Reich.

During the run-up to the 2016 campaign, my dad said, over and over, "CNN is showing this guy twenty-four hours a day. They're going to get him elected."

When Trump began putting the norms of democracy into a wood chipper, my dad lamented, "Vhy aren't the people in the streets?"

Even as he lost his energy and was, at ninety-six, essentially under COVID-19 house arrest, he argued that Trump would never accept the results in the election and would never voluntarily leave the White House. "He's out to hurt this country."

From the earliest days of Trump's presidency, my dad warned me to keep an eye on the way Trump would always kowtow to Putin and would make decisions that seemed intended to harm American democracy.

He explained that Americans had never experienced a criminal like Trump in the White House, so we didn't have the guardrails in place to stop him from doing so much damage. "Ve need fewer norms, and more laws."

Vas he wrong? Nope. What you thought you were seeing in 2020 was really happening. Trump tore through the myth of American exceptionalism as the country's place in the world was deeply harmed, hundreds of thousands of your fellow Americans died, and democracy teetered on a razor's edge.

When the Trump era began, and especially during 2020, I realized I had a small role to play in my dad's larger-than-life story. My job was to put into words what he often couldn't. He wasn't the type to stand up in front of crowds or issue broad warnings about the state of the world. Most of my dad's geopolitical takes were reserved for our family or a couple of his closest friends.

One day during the pandemic, as we sat outside, masked, talking about what was cooking, my dad told me he was a little worried about my daily news coverage in which I never shied away from the truth. "Maybe it's a little too risky?"

It was almost comical that a guy who lived his history and named his own memoir *Taking Risks* was worried about my safety when all I was doing was sending out a daily newsletter. The only thing I'd ever been unwilling to risk as a writer was my parents being disappointed in me. But maybe this man of action and few words saw something threatening about speaking out. Luckily, his son is a man of little action but a hell of a lot of words.

But they're not all my words. They never have been. They're his words too. This book is for him. But it's also from him.

During our last time going out to lunch before the pandemic, my dad and I were walking toward a restaurant, and he expressed his dismay that Americans weren't taking the threat to our country seriously enough. I suggested that while most Americans were concerned, they didn't see the Trump era as being that ominous because they assumed the kinds of things that happened in his life could never happen here.

My dad stopped walking, looked at me, and asked, "You think when I vas a kid any of us thought it could happen *there*?"

Some of our greatest leaders, from Martin Luther King Jr. to Barack Obama, have liked to paraphrase an old quote from abolitionist minister Theodore Parker: "The arc of the moral universe is long, but it bends toward justice."

I never liked that quote much. The arc of the moral universe is indeed long, but it doesn't bend. It needs to be bent. And if it's bending in the wrong direction, don't look away. Do what my dad did. Stare it in the eye and push back.

Yes, this is a personal way to end a book about the national news and a global pandemic. But this was a year when the news was highly personal.

After my dad died, I spent a lot of time with my mom in my childhood home. We missed my dad. I wish he could have experienced part of the new year, gotten vaccinated, and been able to hang out with his kids and grandkids. And yes, I also wish he'd been around to see decency return to the White House, because I know how much that meant to him. And, man, would we have had an epic news conversation on January 20.

Now that it was just my mom and me, the conversations often steered to more personal subjects like relationships, parenthood, and the history of anti-Semitism. One Saturday night, we were contemplating those topics and, as is often the case in homes occupied by those of a certain age, the family room temperature was dialed in at a solid 87 degrees Fahrenheit. At one point, over the blaring TV, my mom asked, "Have you ever thought about seeing a doctor about your sweating problem?"

On Sunday morning, we toaster-ovened and buttered a couple of bagels that were probably frozen during the first Bush era. After breakfast, my mom turned on the TV. It was already tuned to CNN. She sat in her chair and I sat in my dad's, and together we watched Fareed Zakaria's show.

ACKNOWLEDGMENTS

As a newbie in the print world, I was fortunate to have the guidance and support of Vendela Vida and Dave Eggers. Vendela spent hours listening to my whining, and gently guided and supported me through the publishing process. Dave thankfully explained why my initial book proposal was all wrong, and then read, edited, and provided excellent advice about an early draft of the book. Dave even presented me with a type-written note on the proper usage of the semicolon. (It turns out they're not just commas, but funnier.)

Thanks to my literary agent, Jackie Ashton, and the team at Lucinda Literary. Jackie immediately got the idea and added valuable early structure to the book. She also had to welcome this solo, ornery newsletter writer to the collaborative world of book publishing. At the beginning of the process, Jackie and I lived in the same community and our kids went to the same school. By the time the book was completed, Jackie had pulled her kids from the school and moved clear across the country. In other words, she reacted to working with me a lot better than most predicted. I couldn't have gotten this done without her.

In addition to being an excellent writer, Sarah Stewart Taylor is an amazing editor. The speed with which she got me critical cuts and edits was remarkable.

Shout out to the team at Hachette, including Alison Dalafave, Fred Francis, Michael Barrs, Quinn Fariel, Sarah Falter, Zach Polendo, Amy Quinn, Lindsay Ricketts, LeeAnn Falciani, and of course my editor and fellow baseball fanatic, Dan Ambrosio. Dan believed in the idea and the need for a time capsule of 2020, and thankfully cut about a billion words from my first draft (I'm rounding up, but not by much). Thanks also to copyeditors Sara and Chris Ensey. They certainly had their work cut out for them.

The team at the MIT Center for Constructive Communication couldn't have been more helpful and accommodating in turning their news data into monthly lists of the top stories shared in the opposing news universes. The data gave this book a bit of gravitas that sure wasn't going to come from its author. Thanks to my friend Deb Roy and his team, including Wes Chow, Spencer Yen, Perris Richter, and Andrew Heyward. Andrew also got stuck reading a remarkably long version of the book and, as the former President of CBS News, gave me great feedback on my takes about the media.

Joel Stein is not just one of America's funniest writers, he also sparked this book project with the line "Have you ever written a book? I think you should." Having started this madness, he was sucked into becoming one of my guides through the publishing world. Phil Bronstein is my longtime friend, advisor, and podcast cohost, and, as a person a few years my senior, responds to every one of my physical or mental ailments with the line "It gets worse." That, it turns out, is excellent advice for the book-writing process. But Phil made the process better. Arthur Phillips is an upsettingly attractive and troublingly intelligent author. He is also a fellow beagle owner and gave me tips on getting a book published.

For early reads and valuable time, thanks to Norman and Lyn Lear, Laurie Segall, Soledad O'Brien, Maria Konnikova, Steve Bodow, Jeff Jarvis, and Dahlia Lithwick.

Other readers, editors, advisors, and supporters include super-connector and Pell BFF Zem Joaquin—who is the conduit to so many important connections and supports everything we do—two-time Pulitzer-winning editor Anne Kornblut, my frequent email pen-pal Harry Shearer, Damon Lindelof, Congressman Jim Himes, Senator Cory Booker, Jonathan Hoefler, Mark Tauber, Ashley Bernardi, Blaine Heck, Caroline Pruett, Tom Goldstone, Ram Ramgopal, Yuto Yamada, Tiffany Shlain, Peter Coyote, Sean Martell, and designer extraordinaire Tamir Karta.

Thanks to the many journalists who summoned the energy and courage to cover an uncoverable year. They say the enemy of my enemy is my friend. Thanks, friends.

We all needed our pandemic crews during 2020, and I was lucky that mine included my childhood friends Mark "Mordy" Sedway, Andy Lefferts, Dave Mandelbrot, and Dr. Michael Levin, who edited and fine-tuned key parts of the book and provided endlessly valuable insights on the psychology driving those who drove the news.

Without *NextDraft*, there would be no book. I could have called it *Next-NextDraft*, but *Please Scream Inside Your Heart* had a better ring to it. The hardest part about being an indie creator on the internet is the real-life loneliness of working alone. I'm fortunate that one of my best childhood friends was my virtual officemate during the Trump era. Rob "RD" Dunn proofs just about every blurb I publish, and he did the same for every page of this book. But it's not about the typos. I have a few tens of thousands of readers more than willing to point those out. It's about the friendship, support, and inspiration. When we were kids, RD once responded to my request to hang out over the weekend with the line "See you Monday." Apparently, he wasn't as busy as he thought, because Monday has been pretty much every day for the past few decades.

Thanks also to my *NextDraft* crew that keeps the newsletter, blog, app, and website running: Chris Morris, Andrew Norcross, and especially my design partner, Bryan Bell. He's a Dodgers fan who made me a custom SF Giants mask during the pandemic. The fabric was itchy. (I assume he didn't want to lose too much credibility among Dodgers' fans.)

Fred Rosenbaum had the unique qualities required to get my dad's story out of him and then out to the world in their book, *Taking Risks*. The book enriched my life and influences most everything I write.

Thanks to my sisters, Debra, Karen, and Becky, for their love and support during what turned out to be a difficult year for our family, and to my mom, Eda, for her intelligence, knowledge, and humor, and for signing off on the final draft of the book with the note "I think it makes us sound a little eccentric, but I suppose it's fine if that's how you see us." And of course, to my dad for sharing the wisdom and experiences that made this book possible. I could go on, of course, but this whole book is basically one long acknowledgment of and for my parents.

Thanks to my kids, Herschel and Octavia, for sharing their Wi-Fi with me during quarantine and for handling the crazy year with maturity, humor, and patience, and for understanding why I had to tell them to take a break from their devices even when I wouldn't take one from mine. (Kids, I'm a professional.)

Over the past couple decades, I've repeatedly approached my wife, Gina, and said, "OK, I think I have an idea for a book." Each time, she shook her head and explained why the idea wasn't quite right. Early in our pandemic year, after falling asleep on the couch, I woke up at three in the morning, ran upstairs, and said, "I've finally got it." I described the idea for this book. She nodded. "Yes, that's it!" The very next morning, she began making calls. She found me an agent, encouraged the writing, edited the book, and like most other things in our family, she made things happen, all while suffering my insecurities, naysaying, and cynicism. Luckily, by now she knows that's my brand. Like me, Gina is an online publisher. We're basically the Beyoncé and Jay-Z of the internet. (Though, after a year locked in family quarantine, we were more like the Mr. and Mrs. Smith of newsletter writers.)

Finally, thanks to my *NextDraft* subscribers, many of whom joined me on this journey several years ago and provided much-needed feedback and support when the news became overwhelming. On the internet, there are a lot of things that compete for your attention, and I'm grateful each time anyone chooses to read my latest daily edition, just as I am to all who read this book.